90 0785788 4

D1757384

Review of Adult Learning and Literacy

VOLUME 6

*Connecting Research, Policy,
and Practice*

WITHDRAWN
FROM
UNIVERSITY OF PLYMOUTH
LIBRARY SERVICES

Review of Adult Learning and Literacy, Volume 6, is an important part of the Dissemination Initiative of the National Center for the Study of Adult Learning and Literacy (NCSALL). NCSALL is a collaborative effort of the Harvard Graduate School of Education; World Education, a nonprofit organization based in Boston; the Center for Literacy Studies at the University of Tennessee; Rutgers University in New Jersey; and Portland State University in Oregon. NCSALL is funded by the Educational Research and Development Centers Program, Award Number R309B60002, as administered by the U.S. Department of Education's Institute of Education Sciences.

NCSALL is pursuing a program of basic and applied research that is meant to improve programs that provide educational services for adults who have low literacy skills, who speak limited English, or who do not have a high school degree.

The contents of *Review of Adult Learning and Literacy, Volume 6,* do not necessarily represent the positions or policies of the U.S. Department of Education, nor are they endorsed by the federal government.

Review of Adult Learning and Literacy

VOLUME 6

Connecting Research, Policy, and Practice

Edited by

JOHN COMINGS
BARBARA GARNER
CRISTINE SMITH

A Project of the
*National Center for the Study
of Adult Learning and Literacy*

LEA LAWRENCE ERLBAUM ASSOCIATES, PUBLISHERS
2006   Mahwah, New Jersey   London

UNIVERSITY OF PLYMOUTH

9007857884

Copyright © 2006 by Lawrence Erlbaum Associates, Inc.

All rights reserved. No part of this book may be reproduced in
any form, by photostat, microform, retrieval system, or any other
means, without prior written permission of the publisher.

Lawrence Erlbaum Associates, Inc., Publishers
10 Industrial Avenue
Mahwah, New Jersey 07430

Cover design by Kathryn Houghtaling Lacey

ISBN 0–8058–5459–2 (cloth : alk. paper)
ISBN 0–8058–5460–6 (pbk)

Books published by Lawrence Erlbaum Associates are printed on acid-
free paper, and their bindings are chosen for strength and durability.

Printed in the United States of America
0 9 8 7 6 5 4 3 2 1

Contents

Foreword

In April 2000, the World Education Forum[1] in Dakar, Senegal, set six goals for achieving education for all. The goals encompassed the span of human life from early childhood through to the golden years. The fourth goal committed the world to "achieving a 50% improvement in levels of adult literacy by 2015, especially for women, and equitable access to basic and continuing education for all adults," while the sixth goal aimed at "improving all aspects of the quality of education and ensuring excellence of all so that recognized and measurable learning outcomes are achieved by all, especially in literacy, numeracy and essential life skills." About a year later, the United Nations General Assembly endorsed those goals and incorporated them into its Millennium Development Goals,[2] which aimed to reduce poverty, enhance health, and make good quality education universally available. Achieving the World Education Forum goal of halving current rates of adult illiteracy around the world by 2015 requires enabling some 400 to 500 *million* people, most of them women, to read, write, and manipulate numbers usefully—in other words, some 40 to 50 million people every year between now and the target date.

Let us not bother ourselves with yet another attempt to define literacy and numeracy. Let us just ask whether we know enough about adult learning and literacy to accomplish the goal within the next dozen years.

---

[1] *The Dakar Framework for Action, Education for All: Meeting Our Collective Commitments,* adopted by the World Education Forum (Dakar, Senegal, April 26–28, 2000), Paris, UNESCO, 2000, para. 7.

[2] United Nations General Assembly, Resolution A/56/326, September 6, 2001.

What prompts me to pose the question is information found in Volume 3 of NCSALL's *Review of Adult Learning and Literacy,* "The Year 2000 in Review." Although the *Review* deals mainly with the United States, and I have worked mainly in Africa and Asia, what Lennox McLendon and John Kruidenier observed resonates with my experience. Lennox noted that adult educators remain challenged to provide the data that Congress needs; John said that they have actually resisted collecting assessment data (p. 103). Both echo the experiences of UNESCO, the World Bank, and several governments, in trying to get adult educators to tell them in systematic, verifiable terms what works under what conditions, at what cost, and with what impact on personal fulfillment and family and community well-being. Can adult educators provide incontestable data to answer this question confidently: *What does it take to ensure that at least 65 out of every 100 fully able-bodied, nonliterate adults of average intelligence who enroll in a literacy education course master reading, writing, and numerical skills sufficiently to make a satisfactory difference to their lives?*

Active adult educators themselves have sufficient personal experience of working with people not to bother with the question. Whether we look at Bangladesh, Nicaragua, or Zimbabwe—not to mention the 50 states in America—we find educators, both professional and nonprofessional, who have seen how unschooled people benefit from and appreciate mastering literacy. These educators devote large portions of their lives to helping more people do the same. Whether these educators work for governments, nongovernmental organizations, community-based organizations, or on their own, in the United States or elsewhere, they educate with conviction, dedication, and perseverance. They do not need research and data to persuade them of the human value of what they are doing for their neighbors.

On the other hand, these educators certainly wish that they had more resources to educate more people more effectively. They also wish that obtaining resources were not such a continual struggle and drain on energy and even more on that very scarce resource—time. If they could demonstrate that their graduates contributed as much—and possibly more—to their society than equivalent investments in agriculture, small enterprises, better water supplies, more comprehensive health services, or better roads would, they might actually reverse the situation and find resources pursuing them for a change. Their allies—the education policymakers and planners in Bolivia, Nepal, Zambia, Washington, DC, and the 50 state capitals of the United States, who have the responsibility to achieve the Millennium Development Goals in their state or country—would be so grateful for demonstrations of effectiveness. Publications like this review would be just the place for assembling them. It could open ready access to clues for enabling committed adult educators to aid their adult learners to learn more effectively, both in the United States and around the globe.

—John Oxenham

Preface

The National Center for the Study of Adult Learning and Literacy and Lawrence Erlbaum Associates are pleased to publish the *Review of Adult Learning and Literacy, Volume 6: Connecting Research, Policy, and Practice* (formerly, *The Annual Review of Adult Learning and Literacy*). The *Review* aspires to serve as the source of record for the field of adult learning and literacy, reaching those policymakers, scholars, and practitioners who are dedicated to improving the quality of practice in adult basic education (ABE), adult English for speakers of other languages (ESOL), and adult secondary education programs.

Each *Review* begins with an overview of significant developments in the field of adult education and literacy during the year (in this case, 2003) and concludes with an essay and bibliography on a topic of current interest to the field (in this volume, broad-based organizing as a vehicle for promoting adult literacy). The chapters included in the core of the volume are both theoretical and practical, covering a wide range of topics critical to the success of adult education and literacy services in the United States.

In the foreword, international literacy expert John Oxenham muses on the role that accurate impact data could play in unleashing the resources, particularly financial, needed to provide adequate literacy services for the millions of people who need them around the globe. The *Review,* he points out, is just the place to publish such data, as well as to share information that enables educators to aid their learners more effectively.

In chapter 1, Noreen Lopez reviews the major events in the field of adult education and literacy in 2003, a year in which the field was saddened by the death of Senator Paul Simon, a major supporter of adult literacy. With much of the country focused on the war in Iraq, adult education received a small increase in federal appropriations. The National Institute for Literacy broadened its focus from adult literacy to literacy across the life span, and the ERIC Clearinghouses shut down operations due to changes in Department of Education mandates. The National Coalition for Literacy took steps to incorporate as a private nonprofit focused on raising awareness of and advocating for appropriate policies for adult literacy. The National Assessment of Adult Literacy collected data from a national representative sample of adults in an effort to provide an indication of the nation's progress since the first national adult literacy survey in 1992. Among other research reports published in 2003, NCSALL's "How Teachers Change" was released. Findings revealed that multiple factors interacted to influence how teachers change as a result of professional development; teachers who gained the most were those who, among other factors, worked more hours in adult education, had well-supported jobs, and had a voice in decision making in their programs.

In chapter 2, demographer Brad Edmondson describes the current and future characteristics of the low-literacy population in the United States, and considers how changes in this population might affect the provision of services for educating these adults. He examines trends among linguistically isolated households and Americans who have not completed high school, as they are described in census data from 1990 and 2000. He also describes the disabled population using data from the 2000 census. Drawing conclusions from this data, Edmondson writes that one major trend is the need for more diversified adult literacy services to respond to geographically diversified needs.

In chapter 3, Mary E. Curtis examines the role of vocabulary in adult basic education. Vocabulary—the extent of one's knowledge of word meanings—has long been recognized as a key factor in reading comprehension and as one of the most significant variables in the reading success of minority language learners. Curtis reviews the limited research that has been done on adult learners, and relevant K–12 research, to examine the link between vocabulary and comprehension, sources of vocabulary learning (context, morphology, and definitions), the nature of vocabulary learning, and effective approaches to teaching vocabulary. Her recommendations for improving policy and practice start with a research agenda that examines the relative importance for adults of what has been learned about vocabulary acquisition and instruction in K–12. In the policy arena, Curtis suggests that, given the importance of vocabulary, it should be more

greatly emphasized in assessment, and professional development to disseminate best practices in vocabulary instruction should link research and
practice.

In chapter 4, Diane J. Sawyer and M. Tara Joyce review the research on
spelling and its implications for adult basic education. In our society, poor
spelling can negatively influence perceptions of intelligence and even jeop-
ardize the poor speller's ability to succeed in the job market. Many adult
literacy learners cite spelling as a problem. Yet, Sawyer and Joyce reveal,
little if any research on spelling and the adult learner has been conducted,
nor is much professional development on spelling instruction offered to
adult basic educators. The authors trace the history of spelling instruction
in the United States and describe theories of, and research on, how people
learn to spell, concluding that, among other things, both visual and auditory systems play important roles and learning to spell proceeds in a predictable, developmental sequence. They examine the research on spelling
as it relates to subsets of adult learners: those with learning disabilities or
hearing impairments and those who are enrolled in English for speakers of
other languages. They provide specific recommendations for practice and
suggest that, given spelling's important role, adult-specific research and
policy be developed to address it.

In chapter 5, Kathleen M. Bailey writes about issues in teaching
speaking skills to adult ESOL learners. Just as instruction for adults on
strengthening vocabulary and spelling skills are research backwaters, the
development of English speaking skills—vital to adults as workers and
community members in the United States—is also a neglected area of
research. Bailey reviews the demographics of the ESOL population and
their needs, describes the components of spoken language and communicative competence, explains how speaking skills are currently taught
and assessed, and reviews educational standards related to the teaching of
speaking and promising curricular developments. In making recommendations for practice, Bailey points out that the complexity of spoken language means that teachers need solid knowledge and understanding about
the nature of speech and strong methodological skills for helping adult
ESOL learners develop their speaking skills.

In chapter 6, M Cecil Smith examines the preparation and stability
of the adult learning and literacy teaching workforce. He reviews what
the teacher workforce should look like in light of the K–12 research that
suggests that specific preparation within a teacher training program and
holding a teaching license are critical to student outcomes. The teacher
workforce now primarily consists of teachers prepared to teach K–12 who

receive some professional development in adult education. A sizable proportion of the teaching pool is employed part-time. The lack of a preservice certification system contributes to this, as does the lack of financial incentives. Smith turned to early childhood education, somewhat analogous to adult education as a marginalized field, for lessons on how to improve the teaching force. His recommendations include a call for research on characteristics of existing teachers, the connection between preparation and teacher quality, the factors that support retention of teachers, and the connection between teacher quality and retention. He concludes that policy changes should be geared toward developing a stable, highly skilled workforce of ABE teachers.

In chapter 7, Inez Bailey takes us to Ireland for an overview of its adult literacy system. She traces the history of adult literacy in Ireland, including the development of literacy as a very recent governmental priority that arose when the International Adult Literacy Survey, in 1995, showed that one in four of the Irish adult population scored at the lowest level of literacy on a scale of one to five. The survey also provided evidence that poor literacy skills among the adult population negatively affected family, community, and work life. Since then, numerous policy initiatives and dedicated funding from the government has permitted the adult literacy service to expand and improve, reaching a greater number of adults. This has been accomplished through three primary components: a national policy on adult education, *Learning for Life,* which is underpinned by a commitment to equality, and the understanding of lifelong learning as entailing a systemic approach; the first national strategy on adult literacy; and the inclusion of an adult literacy target in the National Anti-Poverty Strategy. She describes these components, the learner population, the teaching staff, and related organizations. Current issues are similar to those in the United States: a struggle to retain learner-centeredness amid a rapid growth in the population served, the need for coordination with other literacy services, staffing preparation and retention, accountability, and funding.

In chapter 8, Michael A. Cowan describes the role that broad-based organizing can play in promoting adult literacy. He defines community organizing as a deliberate effort to cross lines of race, class, religion, and geography to build organizations with sufficient power to stand for the whole and address "common-good" issues in local communities. This happens, he explains, not by bringing individuals together, but by connecting mediating institutions such as congregations, neighborhood associations, and other local voluntary associations. In his chapter, he identifies the role of adult literacy as one critical component of the effort to improve quality of life, locates broad-based community organizing within emerging theory and research on "social capital," describes how social problems gain public attention and attract resources, and offers suggestions for how to implement a metropolitan-wide, broad-based organizing effort on behalf of adult literacy. An annotated bibliography of key resources about the theory and practice of community organizing follows.

As this volume of the *Review* goes to press, members of the adult education and literacy field are enabling learners to participate as voters in a presidential election year, preparing to participate in a national gathering of researchers and practitioners in California, and going about their daily work of finding scarce dollars and stretching them to provide sound services. This volume of the *Review of Adult Learning and Literacy* is a tool that our colleagues in the field can use in their efforts to keep adult literacy at the forefront in policy arenas, to keep it relevant to the needs of learners, and to improve services based on solid information from research.

—John Comings
—Barbara Garner
—Cristine Smith
Editors

List of Tables and Figures

Tables

Figures

1

The Year 2003 in Review

Noreen Lopez

INTRODUCTION

The year 2003 was one in which any small gains in adult education were noteworthy as most of the nation was focused on the war in Iraq and the state of the economy. With large tax cuts and major increases in spending on the war effort, little federal money was left for increases in education funding, including adult education. Many adult education programs were fortunate to remain at a level of funding comparable to 2002. Lawmakers and the nation were not focused on reauthorizing legislation for welfare reform (Temporary Aid for Needy Families, TANF) and the Adult Education and Family Literacy Act (AEFLA), part of the Workforce Investment Act (WIA).

Despite this, there were successes in the policy arena of adult education. These included a moderate increase in federal appropriations; incorporation of field-recommended changes into the Senate version of WIA reauthorization; and, in the Senate version of TANF reauthorization, an increase in the amount of time states can count education toward meeting work requirements.

There were three national-level changes in organizations. The new Board of Directors for the National Institute for Literacy (NIFL) outlined its activities for literacy across the life span. In an effort to become a stron-

1

ger organization, the National Coalition for Literacy (NCL) incorporated and filed for tax-exempt status. The ERIC Clearinghouses shut down operations due to changes made by the Department of Education.

Individual transitions in the field of adult education included the appointment of a new assistant secretary of education for vocational and adult education. Also, the field lost a major supporter with the death of former Senator Paul Simon.

Discussions of practice were undergirded by a greater emphasis by the Department of Education on scientifically based research and evidence-based practice. All the while, local program personnel continued debates about testing, assessment, and the National Reporting System (NRS), while struggling with insufficient resources.

POLICY

Federal Appropriations

This section covers federal funding levels for fiscal year (FY) 2003 and 2004. Federal funding for adult education under WIA should be appropriated by September 30 of one year for the following program year. The appropriation for federal FY 2003 (October 1, 2002–September 30, 2003) is allocated to the states for the program year beginning July 1, 2003 and ending June 30, 2004. Therefore, any cut in appropriations for federal FY 2003 would be felt at the local level beginning in July 2003.

2003 Appropriations. The federal FY 2003 appropriations, which should have been approved by October 2002, were still in conference committee in late January 2003 while the government continued to operate under a continuing resolution. A continuing resolution allows federally funded programs to continue to operate at the same level as the previous year's appropriation level until Congress makes the final appropriation. Whereas the Senate bill proposed to cut adult education funding by 2.9% (or $16 million), the House bill proposed to maintain the same level of funding as FY 2002. In the end, the appropriation for adult education and literacy (including English Literacy/Civics funds) was reduced by only $4 million, for a total of $587.2 million, with $571.3 million for the state grants. The President signed it into law in February 2003.

At the same time that the federal appropriation was reduced, states were also beginning to feel the impact of the 2000 census data. The federal government allocates funds to the states based on the number of adults 16 years of age or older without a high school diploma who are no longer enrolled in school. Any shifts in population affect the allocation to the states by reducing or increasing the share of the appropriation. According to data available from the U.S. Department of Education, 20 states or outlying areas experienced an increase in their federal allocation and 39 suffered a decrease.

2004 Appropriations.   Even before the FY 2003 appropriations were finalized, the President presented his request for appropriations for FY 2004. The Administration requested $584 million for state grants (an increase of $13 million over FY 2003 appropriations), but included National Leadership Activities in that line item. The government had previously funded National Leadership Activities as a separate line item at $9.4 million. By November 2003, the House and Senate had passed different appropriation levels (Table 1.1) and, therefore, had to go to conference committee. In addition to working out differences in conference, Congress applied an across-the-board cut to discretionary programs, resulting in the amounts shown in the final column of Table 1.1. As with the FY 2003 appropriations, all budget figures should have been final by October 1, 2003, but were not, requiring a continuing resolution to provide for ongoing services.

Table 1.1 shows the final appropriations level for FY 2002 and FY 2003 (in millions), the Administration's FY 2004 requested level of funding, levels initially approved by the House and Senate, and the final Conference Report amount with the rescission as approved by the full House

TABLE 1.1
Federal Appropriations for the Adult Education
and Family Literacy Act and Even Start

Program & Activity	FY 2002 Final Approp.	FY 2003 Final Approp.	FY 2004 Request of President	FY 2004 House Floor	FY 2004 Senate Floor	FY 2004 Conference and Cut (Final)
State Grants	$575.000	$571.262	$584.300	$584.300	$571.262	$574.372
National Leadership	9.500	9.438	0	9.438	9.223	9.169
National Institute for Literacy	6.600	6.517	6.732	6.517	6.732	6.692
Even Start	250.000	248.375	175.000	250.000	175.000	246.910
Totals	841.100	835.592	766.032	850.255	762.217	855.143

and Senate and signed into law by the President in January 2004. The major source of local funds for adult education, the State Grants line item, reflects a slight increase over FY 2003, but is still less than FY 2002, for an overall loss in real spending power. These FY 2004 funds support the program year beginning July 1, 2004.

All these figures fall far short of the level of appropriations requested by the National Coalition for Literacy (NCL) as the level needed to adequately support the field. The NCL policy on appropriations (posted on their Web site at http://www.national-coalition-literacy.org/) indicates its goal as follows: State Grants $1 billion; National Leadership $30 million; the National Institute for Literacy (NIFL) $10 million; and Even Start $300 million.

Authorizing Legislation

2003 was an important year for reauthorizing two pieces of legislation that greatly affect the provision of adult education and literacy services. The most important is the federal Adult Education and Family Literacy Act, which is Title II of the Workforce Investment Act of 1998 (WIA). WIA legislation is the controlling legislation for the major funding of adult education, including the money for state grants, national leadership money for the Office of Vocational and Adult Education of the U.S. Department of Education, and the operations of the National Institute for Literacy.

There are at least four players in the development of any federal adult education legislation. One is the Administration, or office of the President, as represented by the Department of Education (USDE). Although the Office of Vocational and Adult Education within the USDE plays a major role in developing and carrying out policy in adult education, policy formulation is often directed by other policy staff within the Administration and Department of Education. Although the Administration cannot directly introduce legislation, it does work with members of Congress to incorporate Administration proposals into the bills introduced or to sponsor an Administration bill.

A second player is the Senate, and a third is the House of Representatives. The House and Senate often have different ideas about the legislation being proposed, and both have major influence in shaping it. When there are differences between the proposals from the two houses, a conference committee with representatives from both chambers of Congress resolves the differences. The Administration's policy is generally reflected in one or more of the bills drafted by the House or Senate.

The fourth player in the development of legislation is the field of adult education. The field is made up of individuals and organizations. Over the years, various organizations involved in adult literacy have worked together to present a unified voice to Congress on issues affecting adult education and literacy. One national organization whose membership is composed of these many organizations is the National Coalition for Literacy (NCL).

The Omnibus Literacy Legislation Concept Paper. In 2001, realizing that the Adult Education and Family Literacy Act would need to be reauthorized in 2003, the members of the NCL began identifying, and reaching consensus on, issues that should be addressed in any new legislation. The Coalition developed suggested legislative recommendations based on the National Literacy Summit Initiative Action Agenda developed in 2000. (For further information on the Summit Initiative, see Comings, Garner, & Smith, 2002, pp. 3–4.) The Coalition's goal was to recommend policy to Congress rather than merely react to policy proposals from the Administration and Congress. The Coalition finalized and approved the *Omnibus Literacy Legislation Concept Paper* in January 2003. In February, the Coalition distributed their four-page policy brief to all members of Congress. This brief outlined recommendations on reauthorization of the WIA and Temporary Aid for Needy Families (TANF) and appropriations for FY 2004. For TANF reauthorization, the NCL recommended that basic education be classified as "vocational education training" if it is part of an overall employment plan, extending the maximum time limit on vocational education training to 24 months, and limiting the power of the state executive branch in shifting funds from one service area to another under the legislation. The NCL made many recommendations on WIA reauthorization organized around the areas of access, quality, and resources. Some highlights include changes in One-Stop performance requirements, composition of workforce boards, definitions of eligible providers, funding criteria for adult education services, provisions on state leadership and professional development activities, technology use, the funding distribution formula, incentive grants, and national leadership activities. The appropriation recommendations are those cited earlier in the federal appropriations discussion as the goal of the NCL.[1]

---

[1] These resources can be found on the NCL Web site (http://www.national-coalition-literacy.org/) under Policy and Legislation.

Workforce Investment Act (WIA).   By March 2003, the House Sub-committee on 21st Century Competitiveness approved its version of a reauthorized WIA, The Workforce Reinvestment and Adult Education Act of 2003. The House approved the Act (HR 1261) on May 8, 2003. The House version renamed the Adult Education and Family Literacy Act the Adult Basic Skills and Family Literacy Education Act, which, as reported in a one-page National Institute for Literacy (NIFL) Policy Alert,[2] "requires focus on, and State demonstration of progress in, basic skills, such as reading, English language acquisition, writing, and mathematics." The Policy Alert further states that the bill also reauthorized the NIFL, but redirected its purpose to "provide national leadership in promoting reading research, reading instruction and professional development in reading based on scientifically based research. This purpose will be achieved primarily through information dissemination activities." The House version, therefore, also shifts NIFL's purpose from a focus on adult literacy (including reading, writing, speaking, and math literacy) to a focus on only reading but for children, youth, and adults.

Many of the proposals in HR 1261 reflected the Administration's policies on reauthorization. The Department of Education presented the Bush Administration's vision to the public in June in a paper entitled *A Blueprint for Preparing America's Future,*[3] which contained many of the ideas found in HR 1261. These ideas include: focusing on basic academic skills (as opposed to life skills or employability skills), emphasizing readiness for postsecondary education, promoting practice and professional development based on scientifically based research, expanding access through technology and distance learning, and opening up the provider system to a broader array of agencies, including for-profit entities and faith-based organizations. Accountability is emphasized at both the program and state level. The House version also eliminated the role of the USDE in funding national leadership activities through grants or contracts for "developing, improving and identifying the most successful methods and techniques for addressing the education needs of adults," and carrying out demonstration programs (Van Scoyoc Associates, 2003, pp. 34–36).

The Senate version (S.1627 The Workforce Investment Act Amendments of 2003) included the Administration's ideas from the *Blueprint* that would require states to develop state content standards. The Senate

---

[2] The Policy Alert is available at http://www.nifl.gov/nifl/policy/updates/03_05_15 .html.

[3] http://www.ed.gov/policy/adulted/leg/aeblueprint2.doc.

version also incorporated several of the recommendations in the NCL *Omnibus Literacy Legislation Concept Paper,* including, among other things, policy changes to increase state leadership funds from "not more than 12.5%" of the state allotment to "no more than 15%." State leadership funds finance activities such as professional development, technical assistance, evaluation, and technology assistance. Another NCL recommendation that was successfully incorporated was the inclusion, under National Leadership activities, of the option of supporting grants or contracts for capacity building in private, nonprofit organizations to help them meet requirements of the Act. Such assistance could help community-based organizations and other nonprofits compete more effectively for funding at the state level by helping them build their skills in areas such as data collection and record keeping, which are needed to meet requirements of the National Reporting System.

Both the House and Senate versions reflect greater emphasis on distance learning and technology when compared to previous legislation. State leadership activities now specifically allow for the development and implementation of distance learning, and national leadership activities permit the support and development of an entity that would produce and distribute technology-based programs and materials (Van Scoyoc Associates, 2003, pp. 20, 39). Both also present a major change in the role of the National Institute for Literacy, by changing its role to include support and dissemination of research on reading for children, youth, and adults. A major difference between the two in this area is that the Senate version retains much of the previous language allowing the Institute to address all areas of literacy, not just reading, whereas the House version specifically limits its focus to reading.

The NCL took the position that the Senate version of the reauthorization is preferable to the House version in many areas and urged its members and others to contact their representatives in Congress to advocate support of the Senate version. A conference committee was scheduled to meet in January 2004 to work out the differences and present a final bill to both houses. Members of the adult education community were particularly concerned about the threat to the NIFL and its focus on adult education and literacy. Much discussion took place on adult education electronic discussion lists (particularly the American Association for Adult and Continuing Education-National Literacy Advocate [AAACE-NLA] list), and a separate Web site was established to provide information to practitioners on the proposed legislative changes to the NIFL and to suggest ways to contact federal representatives.

Welfare Legislation.   The other major piece of legislation that greatly affects the provision of adult education services is Welfare, formerly TANF. The House passed their version of the reauthorization of this legislation, HR 4, the Personal Responsibility and Individual Development for Everyone Act (PRIDE), in 2003. The Senate's version passed in committee but must return to the full Senate for consideration in 2004. The NCL supported the Senate version because it has several provisions that are more favorable to adult education. One of these provisions allows states to count participation in adult literacy programs toward meeting work requirements for a period of 3 months in any 24-month period, and allows another 3 months if combined with work or work-readiness activities. The House version has a total maximum of 3 months. Although this time period is much shorter than the NCL desired, its inclusion reflects some level of success in educating members of the Senate about the need for adult literacy and English-language services for many welfare recipients.

PROGRAM ACCOUNTABILITY ISSUES

Despite the uncertainty concerning policy and funding, the work of the adult education field continues in classrooms and programs throughout the country. Discussions take place regularly on various discussion lists about issues of testing and accountability, often in relation to reporting for the National Reporting System (NRS). At various times during the year, a discussion of these issues, in some form, took place on the AAACE National Literacy Advocacy (NLA) List, the NIFL Assessment List, and the NIFL Equipped for the Future (EFF) List. Topics ranged from trying to find alternative assessments (as opposed to standardized tests) that would meet NRS requirements, to finding definitions for the subskills tested in one standardized test, to trying to understand the relationship of hours of instruction to progress made through the levels of the NRS. Overall, the discussions, which may or may not reflect the feelings of the field as a whole, show a general concern about the lack of adequate measures or tests of learning gain and a lack of a research base for understanding how various factors related to instruction (e.g., time, intensity, technology) affect those learning gains. These discussions reflect frustration among adult educators who feel pressured to be accountable without the resources to provide what they feel is more appropriate data.

As more programs have become involved in providing distance learning through technology, particularly video and the Internet, they are trying to address similar questions. How do you provide a standardized test to someone studying at a distance? How do you count "seat time" for someone using video or the Internet when the teacher is not there to actually view the time on task? These and other questions are being addressed by distance learning programs that are accountable for the learners they serve and must report such information to the NRS.

The number of adults served in programs is one of the easiest measures of accountability. However, there is always a significant time lag between the end of a program year and the availability of statistics on the number of learners served in that year. Although data for 2003 is not currently available, the statistics from the Department of Education for the most recent available year (program year July 2001–June 2002) show that 2,787,416 adults were served. The largest percentage (42%) of learners is English language learners (a total of 1,173,989), whereas ABE was 38% (1,067,597) and adult secondary education (ASE) 20% (545,830). Learners served under the English Literacy/Civics program are included in the English language numbers. This number reflects only those learners receiving services from programs that are funded under the Adult Education and Family Literacy Act or from state funds used for the purposes allowed under the Act. Other adults may receive comparable services through organizations not receiving state or federal funds under the Act (such as some volunteer groups, businesses, Job Corps programs, etc.), but no single agency is responsible for collecting such data.

ORGANIZATIONAL TRANSITIONS IN 2003

The National Institute for Literacy

The Adult Education and Family Literacy Act under WIA originally defined the role of the National Institute for Literacy (NIFL). When the No Child Left Behind (NCLB) Act of 2001 passed, and was signed into law January 2002, the role of the NIFL was expanded. As stated on the NIFL Web site (http://www.nifl.gov), "The AEFLA directs the Institute to provide national leadership regarding literacy, coordinate literacy services and policy, and serve as a national resource for adult education and literacy programs. The NCLB law directs the Institute to disseminate information on scientifically based reading research pertaining to children, youth, and adults as well as information about development and implementation of classroom reading programs based on the research."

During 2003, the NIFL continued to operate under the direction of its interim director, Sandra Baxter. President Bush appointed the 10-member board of directors of the NIFL in 2002, and they held their first meeting in March 2003. Because most board members had expertise in research and children's literacy and little experience with adult literacy, the National Coalition for Literacy made several contacts with members of the board. The Coalition wanted to encourage board members to retain adult literacy as a priority and focus and also to let the board know that the members of the NCL were anxious to assist them.

Based on notes taken by a representative of the NCL at the first NIFL board meeting, the board decided to focus its efforts on literacy across the life span. They also planned to focus on the following activities:

- Review and assess all current NIFL activities and products to fit the NIFL's focus.
- Conduct a search for an executive director (as required by law).
- Develop a strategic plan, starting with adult education and moving down the life span priority.
- Conduct policy analysis about literacy across the life span.
- Support the work of the Adult Literacy Research Network.[4]
- Comment on WIA reauthorization as it relates to adult education.

The NIFL has hosted a number of electronic discussion lists for the field of adult education. These have been an invaluable means of communication among teachers, administrators, and others. During 2003, many discussions centered on the proposed changes to the NIFL's role and other proposals in the reauthorization bills. Because the government funds these lists, the NIFL was concerned about possible violations of laws prohibiting the use of federal funds for lobbying. As a result of these concerns, Sandra Baxter posted a notice to all list users in July 2003 clarifying the use of

---

[4]The Adult Literacy Research Network is a partnership of the Office of Vocational and Adult Education (OVAE), the National Institute for Literacy (NIFL), and the National Institute of Child Health and Human Development (NICHD), formed to determine scientifically based reading instructional methods for low-literate adults. More information can be found at http://www.ed.gov/about/offices/list/ovae/news/alrn.html.

the lists. Her notice stated that lists could be used to discuss critical issues but not to disseminate messages that could be interpreted as lobbying, that is, "that are intended to influence or cause others to influence a member of Congress to favor or oppose legislation or an appropriation by Congress."[5] This generated a great deal of discussion on several lists regarding censorship, freedom of speech, and the importance of legislation and appropriations in any discourse over critical issues in the field. The two electronic listservs most involved in "policy" discussions removed their lists and archives from the NIFL server and established them elsewhere. The American Association for Adult and Continuing Education (AAACE) agreed to host the National Literacy Advocacy (NLA) list and a newly created broadcast list initiated by the NCL. ProLiteracy Worldwide now hosts the NCL member discussion list.

Two major long-term projects of the NIFL, the Equipped for the Future initiative and the Literacy Information and Communication System (LINCS), continued during 2003, with ongoing development and involvement by many partners throughout the United States. Despite transitions at the Institute, other work, such as the America's Literacy Directory, Partnership for Reading activities, and the Bridges-to-Practice project, continued.

The National Coalition for Literacy

Eleven national organizations concerned with adult literacy founded the National Coalition for Literacy in 1981. The NCL's purpose was to increase public awareness of the problem of adult literacy, answer questions and make referrals through a toll-free telephone number, and raise funds to support these and related efforts. The NCL was not incorporated and was an informal coalition of concerned organizations. Because it was not a 501c3 organization, one of its member organizations served as the recipient of any funds received. There were no dues and no staff.

As the organization grew over the years to include 30 to 35 national literacy organization members, its goals expanded, as did demands on the time of an all-volunteer membership to carry out its purpose and mission. Because it was not a nonprofit organization, it was often difficult to attract funders to support any of the projects that the NCL wanted to carry out. At the past several annual planning meetings, members discussed the

---

[5] See http://www.nifl.gov/nifl-assessment/2003/0068.html.

difficulties associated with this and suggested possible solutions. In 2002, the NCL commissioned a study of its options for the future. The report, prepared by Forrest P. Chisman of the Council for Advancement of Adult Literacy, was presented to the NCL membership in September 2002. Following discussions of the report, the membership voted to pursue incorporation and nonprofit status. Articles of Incorporation were filed in March 2003. The founding board adopted bylaws as a private nonprofit corporation in the District of Columbia in May 2003, and filed for tax-exempt status with the IRS. With its new status as a formal coalition of national dues-paying organizations and contributing organizations and individuals, the membership confirmed the new board of directors in September 2003. As the NCL moves forward, it is eligible to receive funds directly, hire staff, and more realistically carry out its purpose and goals.

One of the first actions the new Coalition took was to establish a broadcast electronic list, the NCL Update, to provide information updates on policy and legislation that affect adult and family literacy at the national level. Additionally, in an effort to support implementation of the Action Agenda at the local program level, the NCL received a small grant from the NIFL to gather and disseminate information on state and local efforts to help move the agenda forward in terms of access and resources. Information on the selected programs, what they did, and how well they worked is posted on the NCL Web site so other programs can benefit.[6]

ERIC Clearinghouse

At the end of December 2003, the ERIC Clearinghouse system (as it had been known since 1966) closed. As a result of a request for proposal issued by the Department of Education in the spring of 2003, starting in 2004 the Clearinghouse will function as an electronic database. This will eliminate its information and referral services and peer-reviewed educational publishing. One of the 16 clearinghouses around the country had been dedicated to providing information on adult and vocational education, and although there had been significant concerns expressed on the adult education electronic lists about the proposed change, and encouragement to respond to the draft changes, the shutdown proceeded in December 2003. A new contractor for all subject areas will be selected and initiated in 2004.

---

[6] http://www.national-coalition-literacy.org/stories/index.html.

INDIVIDUAL TRANSITIONS

U.S. Department of Education Leadership

In May 2003, Carol D'Amico resigned as assistant secretary of education for vocational and adult education. In September 2003, President Bush announced his intent to nominate Susan Sclafani to serve as the replacement. At the same time, he designated her as acting assistant secretary for the office until the Senate confirms the nomination. According to a September 3, 2003 press release from the Department of Education, prior to the nomination Sclafani served as a counselor to Secretary of Education Paige and advised him on all education issues and initiatives, including the No Child Left Behind Act. The press release also stated, "Prior to joining the Department of Education, Sclafani served as chief of staff for education services in the Houston Independent School District, where she represented the superintendent on education issues and coordinated activities of the departments directly involved in the education of children . . ."[7]

Champion of Adult Literacy

Adult education lost a great leader in December when former Senator Paul Simon of Illinois passed away. Senator Simon had been one of the few strong supporters of adult literacy and a sponsor of significant federal adult education legislation. As his obituary in the *Chicago Tribune* of December 9, 2003 related, he was modest, gracious, and willing to help ordinary citizens. In the Senate his colleagues saw him as a leader in education matters and someone able to achieve compromise on thorny issues. Many in the adult education field knew and admired him. Even after leaving the Senate he remained involved in and continued to influence adult literacy issues. He will be missed.

SIGNIFICANT EVENTS

According to a message from Thomas Sticht on the AAACE-NLA list August 19, 2003, the United Nations Literacy Decade was launched in February 2003, with the theme of "Literacy as Freedom." Unfortunately,

---

[7] Available at http://www.ed.gov/news/pressreleases/2003/09/09032003b.html.

the popular press and media in the United States have paid little attention to this announcement despite press releases and Web sites devoted to the issue by the United Nations, and a speech in New York by First Lady Laura Bush. A few education-related Web sites, such as the NIFL and the Literacy Assistance Center, have posted some information about United Nations Literacy Decade activities. However, a search of two top newspapers, *The New York Times* and *The Chicago Tribune,* and a Google search indicate that the U.S. media seemed to pay no attention to this announcement.

Apparently unrelated to the UN's Literacy Decade, two television networks produced media programs about the issue of adult literacy. One was an NBC Special Report by Tom Brokaw in August 2003 on "Adult Illiteracy: A Reaction." The broadcast generated some lively discussion on the adult education electronic discussion lists, with some people expressing disappointment about the use of the term "illiteracy" rather than "literacy," and the narrow focus on one group of learners with only one tutor. Others on the discussion list tried to highlight the positive aspects of the program, such as the fact that adult literacy got an hour of attention on national TV, the learners were treated with respect, and it highlighted some of the struggles and joys that learners experience.

HBO produced a documentary about a maximum-security prison literacy program in New Jersey that partners with a ProLiteracy affiliate, LVA Trenton, and recruits and trains prisoners to teach other prisoners. After a private screening of the film in New York City on September 16, the film aired on Cinemax on September 24. Although there were few comments on the electronic discussion lists about this documentary, Marsha Tait of ProLiteracy Worldwide stated that ProLiteracy Worldwide had reviewed the video and found it to be "a very respectful and credible treatment of the subject."

RESEARCH

Given the current emphasis in legislation and policy on scientifically based research, it would be inappropriate not to address the issue of research in adult education. This section highlights only a few of the long-term studies underway in 2003 that are using scientifically based research approaches and presents one study released in November. We encourage the reader to view the full reports and outcomes from such studies on the appropriate Web sites.

National Assessment of Adult Literacy

During 2003, the National Assessment of Adult Literacy (NAAL) assessed a national representative sample of adults in an effort to provide an indication of the nation's progress since the first national adult literacy survey in 1992. As indicated on the National Center for Educational Statistics Web site (http://nces.ed.gov/naal), the NAAL seeks to:

- Describe the status of adult literacy in the United States.
- Report on national trends.
- Identify relationships between literacy and selected characteristics of adults (such as gender, age, education level, language background, labor-force participation, income, welfare participation, and health).

The main data collection was conducted in 2003 with standard setting, analysis, and reporting scheduled for the period of January 2004 to May 2005.

NCSALL Lab Schools

Two research lab sites are currently part of the National Center for the Study of Adult Learning and Literacy's network. One is an ESOL lab site at Portland State University in Portland, Oregon; the other is an ABE lab site at Rutgers University in New Brunswick, New Jersey. Both lab sites are conducting high-quality research, including basic and applied research using both quantitative and qualitative methods, with a goal of also strengthening professional development systems. They will be disseminating research and professional development materials locally and nationally. These projects are investigating instructional approaches, student engagement, outcomes, and other aspects of adult education program participation. Information on these studies and other research through NCSALL can be found at http://www.ncsall.net/?id=22.

TECH 21

TECH 21 is a project of the National Center on Adult Literacy, in partnership with the Sacramento County Office of Education (SCOE) and the National Adult Education Professional Development Consortium (NAEPDC). It consists of a National Technology Laboratory for Literacy and Adult Education in Philadelphia, a companion technology lab in

Sacramento, a demonstration lab in Washington, DC, seven adult education program-based field sites nationwide, and an Internet portal. As the summary on the TECH 21 Web site indicates, at each of these field sites, learners and educators are learning how to use and participate in the development of information technology models for learning, instruction, and professional development. As research findings become available, they are posted on the Web (http://www.tech21.org). During 2003, two studies related to ESL instruction were made available, as well as reports on teachers' use of resources for distance learning.

Project IDEAL

In 2001, 12 states joined together in Project IDEAL, a multistate collaborative effort organized by the Teaching, Learning, and Technology Program at the University of Michigan's Institute for Social Research (ISR). In 2003, three additional states joined Project IDEAL. Project IDEAL is developing effective distance learning models for adult learners. The staff of Project IDEAL provides technical support in the areas of teacher training, research design, data collection, data analysis, and reporting. The project has developed a *Handbook of Distance Education for Adult Learners* that shares many of the findings to date. It is available, along with other resources from the project, on their Web site: http://www. projectideal.org.

How Teachers Change—Final Research Report

How Teachers Change: A Study of Professional Development in Adult Education was sponsored by NCSALL and conducted in three New England states between 1998 and 2000. The study investigated how adult education teachers changed after participating in one of three professional development models. The sample consisted of 100 men and women. The findings focus on the change teachers experienced, which roles changed (as teacher, program member, learner, or member of the field), what factors interacted to influence teacher change, and whether the kind of support teachers had in their job affected the change. Researchers found that most teachers changed, at least minimally, and changes were most often seen in their role as a classroom teacher. Multiple factors interacted to influence teacher change, and teachers who gained the most were those who, among other factors, worked more hours in adult education, had well-supported jobs, and had a voice in decision making in their programs. The full report, a summary report, and a research brief are all available at http://www. ncsall.net/index.php?id=29.

Establishing an Evidence-Based Adult Education System

At the close of 2003, adult education still lacks any definitive research on effective program models. An Occasional Paper published in September 2003 by NCSALL calls attention to this and offers a possible solution. This paper, *Establishing an Evidence-Based Adult Education System,* available on the NCSALL Web site (http://www.ncsall.net/index. php?id=26/), makes a cogent argument for an approach to developing an adult education system that rests on "a foundation of the best available empirical evidence and practitioner knowledge." Of course, this would require substantial funding at a time when appropriations are not keeping pace with costs.

CONCLUSION

The growth and maturation of adult education as a professional field has been evidenced in many ways throughout 2003. The incorporation of the National Coalition for Literacy was finally accomplished, setting the stage for its more active involvement in policy, communications, and leadership at the national level. The Omnibus Literacy Legislation concept paper marks one of the few times the field has taken the initiative to draft legislation, rather than merely react to legislation. The support for evidence based research and efforts in more multiyear research demonstrates the field's desire to find answers to difficult questions that are not based on theory or experience alone and that can improve practice.

Although the field has had only moderate success in influencing legislation and appropriations, it is important that the struggle continue. Fortunately, there are many in the field who, like Senator Paul Simon, are champions of adult literacy. They will not give up easily.

REFERENCES

Comings, J., Garner, B., & Smith, C. (Eds.). (2002). *Annual Review of Adult Learning and Literacy* (Vol. 3). San Francisco: Jossey-Bass.

Van Scoyoc Associates. (2003). Side-by-Side Comparison of Proposals to Reauthorization of the Adult Education and Family Literacy Act. Paper prepared for the American Library Association. Available online at: http://www.caalusa.org/titleIIsidebysideala.pdf.

2

Demographic Change and Low-Literacy Americans

Brad Edmondson

INTRODUCTION

More than one fifth of Americans over the age of 16 have marginal read-ing and math skills, according to the 1992 National Adult Literacy Survey (NALS). The 21% to 23% of adults who scored in the lowest level of the NALS[1] would likely be able to pick out key facts in a newspaper article, but they would not be able to draft a letter explaining an error on their credit-card bill. This group includes a subset of roughly 4% of adults who are unable to perform even the simplest literacy tasks.

---

[1] NALS, a project of the U.S. Department of Education's National Center for Education Statistics, was based on 1-hour surveys with a nationally representative sample of 13,600 Americans aged 16 and older, conducted during the first 8 months of 1992. Twelve states surveyed an additional 1,000 adults each to create comparable data for those states, and 1,100 inmates were surveyed in 80 federal and state prisons. Adults received proficiency scores along three 500-point scales, which reflect varying degrees of skill in prose, docu-ment, and quantitative literacy. A score of 225 or lower put the respondent in Level 1; a score of 376 to 500 put the respondent in the highest level, Level 5.

The socioeconomic characteristics of this low-literacy population are changing. Much of the research done on this group by social science professionals offers a detailed examination of one aspect of the lives of low-literacy Americans, such as the composition of their families or their transportation arrangements, and how these aspects affect literacy. Although this kind of work is useful, it does not give us an overall portrait of the low-literacy population, or explain how and why it is changing. The purpose of this chapter is to describe the current and future characteristics of the low-literacy population in the United States, and to consider how changes in this population might affect the provision of services for educating these adults. This chapter describes trends among linguistically isolated households and Americans who have not completed high school, as they are described in census data from 1990 and 2000. It also describes the disabled population using data from the 2000 census.[2] In addition, the chapter describes two major demographic trends and discusses the various implications of these trends for future research and policy development in literacy education.

This chapter does not consider demographic trends among Americans who scored in Level 2 of the NALS, even though Level-2 skills are widely considered insufficient for many kinds of skilled employment. The chapter is also too brief to do justice to every nuance and countertrend contained in the complicated relationship between demographics and literacy. The author's goals are to give a broad outline of the demographics of low-literacy Americans, and also to suggest the directions of demographic and geographic change for this group over the next two decades.

The best way to begin to understand this group is to take a step back and put it in a larger social context. Like most population groups, low-literacy Americans are profoundly affected by long-term demographic trends. During the last half of the 20th century, two of these trends had powerful effects on the composition of the low-literacy population. The first change is the baby-boom generation, a huge cohort of 77 million Americans born between 1946 and 1964, which continues to transform our society as it

---

[2] Disability data from the 1990 and 2000 censuses are not comparable because each census measures disability differently. Disability data in 2000 measures the population aged 5 and older with a "sensory disability" (blindness, deafness, or a severe vision or hearing impairment) and a "physical disability" (a condition that substantially limits basic physical activities such as walking or climbing stairs). It also measures the number of Americans aged 5 or older and aged 16 or older with disabilities related to mental functioning, self-care, leaving the home, and employment. The 1990 census measured the population with disability limits to mobility, self-care, or employment.

moves through the life cycle. The second trend is a wave of international immigrants that has moved into certain states, especially California, Texas, and Florida, since 1980. The aging of the baby-boom generation and the influx of immigrants have strong relationships with three demographic variables that are significantly correlated with low literacy: linguistic isolation, disability, and educational attainment.

According to the U.S. Census Bureau, a linguistically isolated household is one in which all members aged 14 and older have at least some difficulty with English. According to the NALS, 25% of Level-1 respondents in 1992 were foreign-born; many foreign-born Americans are likely to have limited English-language skills. As the foreign-born population increases, linguistic isolation will likely be a more common characteristic of the low-literacy population.

Disability is another demographic variable associated with low literacy. More than one quarter (26%) of the NALS Level-1 respondents had physical, mental, or health conditions that kept them from participating fully in work, school, housework, or other activities, and 19% reported having visual difficulties that affect their ability to read print. A factor closely related to disability is age: Older adults are much more affected by disability than younger adults are, and the elderly are also more likely to have limitations in cognitive abilities. One third of the NALS Level-1 adults in 1992 were aged 65 or older.

Age and disability may become more important contributors to the low-literacy population as the huge baby-boom generation ages. Through the sheer weight of their numbers, baby boomers have transformed consumer markets and public policy as they moved through the life cycle. In 2004, the eldest baby boomers were aged 58 and the youngest were 40. In the next two decades, the number of Americans suffering from disabilities related to sensory and cognitive decline could increase as baby boomers move into their 60s and 70s.

The third demographic connection to low literacy is also the most important one. It should hardly be surprising that Americans with weak literacy skills are also likely to have relatively few years of formal education. In fact, more than six in ten adults who scored within Level 1 in the 1992 NALS (62%) had not completed high school. Educational attainment has an overarching importance in determining literacy. In fact, increasing educational attainment dramatically reduces the likelihood that a person will experience linguistic isolation or age-related disability. To judge the most likely changes in the demand for literacy education, it is important to remember that all three of these demographic factors will be working together.

IMMIGRATION TRANSFORMATION

In 1965, just as the baby boom ended, Congress passed an Immigration Act that made it easier for people from non-European countries to move to the United States. After the act was passed, the number of people who moved to America and got permanent work visas started edging up. Since 1980, the number of legal immigrants to the United States has averaged about 850,000 a year. Another 8 to 10 million immigrants may be in the United States illegally (Fix & Passel, 2001). Immigration now accounts for one third of U.S. population growth, and about 11.5% of U.S. residents, or 32.5 million people, were foreign-born in 2003. In 1960, just 5.4% (9.7 million) were foreign-born.

Immigrant Characteristics

Recent immigrants to the United States are likely to share several demographic characteristics. For example, most of them come from Latin America and Asia. In 2000, 20% of legal immigrants to the United States came from Mexico, 11% came from the Caribbean, and 16% were born in Central and South America. About one third of immigrants came from Asian countries, and just one fifth came from Europe, Canada, or Africa.

Many recent immigrants tend to be young. More than half of foreign-born Americans are between the ages of 20 and 44, whereas only one third of the general population falls between these ages. The relative youthfulness of foreign-born Americans means that immigrants tend to be family builders. In fact, immigrants have an added incentive to set up households and bear children after they arrive in the United States, because any child born on U.S. soil is legally a U.S. citizen. As a result, immigrants often boost the population twice: once by arriving, and once again by having more children than native-born Americans do. The average lifetime number of children borne by Hispanic women living in the United States is 2.9; for non-Hispanic White women, the average is 2.1 children. This statistic means that non-Hispanic Whites in America no longer contribute much to population growth. By bearing an average of 2.1 children, non-Hispanic White women are merely replacing themselves and their partners. As time goes on, the population boost provided by immigrants and their children will account for a higher and higher share of America's population growth.

Within the foreign-born group, legal aliens are younger than are naturalized citizens. Almost two thirds of legal aliens (62%) were between the ages of 20 and 44 in 2002, compared with 39% of naturalized citizens and 34% of native-born Americans. The likely reason is the high number of young-adult immigrants since 1990 that have yet to receive their citizenship. In contrast, naturalized citizens are heavily concentrated in the prime working ages. Almost three quarters of naturalized citizens (73%) are aged 25 to 64, compared with just 50% of native-born Americans and 68% of legal aliens. Extending literacy education to recent immigrants might encourage more of them to work toward gaining U.S. citizenship in the hope of achieving the employment gains and other social benefits associated with obtaining one's citizenship.

A final distinguishing characteristic of immigrants is the fact that most of them come to the United States to find jobs (see Capps, Fix, Passel, Ost, & Perez-Lopez, 2003), especially if those jobs are near family members or friends. Because most of the job creation in the United States happens in the largest metropolitan areas, most immigrants have settled there. As the immigrant population continues to grow, however, it is becoming a factor in suburbs and smaller cities as well.

How Immigration Changes Communities

The combination of high immigration and low fertility among native-born Americans has been a factor for more than 20 years, which is long enough to have an impact on other demographic characteristics, such as race. Out of every nine babies born in America, three are born to immigrants and two are Hispanic, Asian, or African American; only four of the nine are non-Hispanic white babies. Demographers use the term *minority majority* to describe a condition when all the minority groups added together—African American, Hispanic, Asian, and the rest—add up to a majority of the population. As the 21st century proceeds, the minority majority is likely to move through the life cycle, just as the baby-boom generation did.

One area where the immigration and differential fertility trends have had a measurable impact is the complex of metropolitan areas around New York City. Every year, about one quarter to one third of people immigrating to the United States pass through New York City, and many of them stay in the region, making it the most ethnically diverse region of the United States. The five counties that make up New York City, plus Hudson County, New Jersey, registered a minority majority in the 2000 census. If current immigration and fertility trends continue, five more counties in the region will achieve minority majority status by the year 2025.

Other areas are also undergoing a demographic transformation due to the impact of immigrants. The state of California reached a minority majority in 2000, due to continued immigration from Latin America and Asia. The state of Texas is projected to reach a minority majority in 2015, due to continued immigration from Mexico. Many of the nation's largest cities, including Detroit, Chicago, and Atlanta, have also been profoundly affected in recent years by immigration from Latin America and Asia (U.S. Bureau of the Census, 2003).

As the immigration and differential fertility trends account for a larger share of America's population growth, smaller cities are also being affected. Many of these places have had very few immigrants until recent years, so a relatively small number of new arrivals can produce a rapid growth rate. However, as the stream of immigrants continues, these small numbers will quickly become much larger.

In 1990, about one third of the population in Jefferson County, Alabama—which includes the city of Birmingham—was African American. However, during the 1990s, carpet mills and other manufacturing plants in the Southeast began hiring laborers from Mexico, Central America, and Asia. As a result, the Hispanic population of Birmingham quadrupled during the 1990s, from 3,800 in 1990 to 12,600 in 2000. In 2000, 42% of the population of Jefferson County belonged to a minority group, with Hispanics and Asians accounting for almost all of the population increase. African Americans and Whites have gotten used to living near each other in southern cities like Birmingham. The next generation of Birmingham residents may inherit a truly multicultural city, with pockets of White, African American, Mexican, Central American, and Asian residents.

The rapid growth of ethnic neighborhoods can happen anywhere, and it sometimes happens for surprising reasons. Fargo, North Dakota has about 90,000 residents. Northern European farmers arrived there about 140 years ago and planted wheat, and the ethnic mix did not change much for the next 130 years. In 1990, only about 260 Fargo residents were African American, but in 2000 that number quintupled to about 1,250. A local church began sponsoring refugees from Somalia in the early 1990s, and those refugees wrote home to tell their family members that North Dakota had cheap housing, plentiful food, and jobs: things that Somalia did not have. In places like North Dakota, where the overwhelming majority of residents are native-born, even small numbers of non-English-speaking immigrants may have a large impact on the demand for literacy training.

Why Immigration Will Continue

In the 2000 census, Hispanics made up 13% of the U.S. population, African Americans 12%, non-Hispanic whites 69%, Asians about 4%, and American Indians and other races about 2%. In 2025, if current trends continue, non-Hispanic whites will make up only 62% of the U.S. population. African Americans will increase to 13% of the population, Hispanics will be 18%, and Asians will be about 6%. Of course, these forecasts could change if Congress decides to drastically restrict the flow of immigrants, but that is unlikely to happen. Large numbers of immigrants will continue to come to the United States for the foreseeable future, for reasons of both supply and demand.

On the supply side, conditions such as famine, war, and dictatorship in a large number of unfortunate countries result in waves of refugees leaving their home countries for the United States. Since 1985, about 100,000 people a year have been granted political asylum in the United States (INS, 2002). And even in relatively stable countries such as Mexico and China, where asylum is not the ordinary reason for immigration, the economic benefit of moving to the United States can be compelling.

The demand side reveals even more powerful reasons why immigration will continue. If our borders were suddenly closed to new immigrants, the United States would immediately experience severe labor shortages in low-wage industries like agriculture, hospitality, and food processing. We would also see shortages in high-wage industries such as software design and entertainment (INS, 2002). America's economic leaders know that immigration is crucial to economic growth in this country, and they are using their influence to ensure that our borders remain open.

Immigration and Income

Opponents of immigration warn that keeping our borders open will worsen social problems in the United States by increasing the numbers of unemployable people and driving down wages. Yet only one portion of the foreign-born population is unskilled. In fact, the educational attainment of foreign-born Americans looks like a reverse bell curve. There are many unskilled low-wage workers among the foreign-born, but there are also many very highly skilled, highly paid immigrants working as software engineers, set designers, and physicians.

One study found that even a large influx of unskilled immigrants might not have any measurable effect on a city's wage levels. In the summer of

1980, during the Mariel boatlift, about 125,000 Cuban immigrants arrived in Miami. This represented a 7% increase in the size of Miami's labor force. Moreover, most of the new arrivals were unskilled. Yet an analysis of unemployment levels and wages in Miami and three other metropolitan areas between 1976 and 1984 found that this influx did not increase unemployment or decrease wages for other workers in Miami (Card, 1990). The Mariel boatlift study concluded that Miami's unique characteristics, such as a large number of jobs for unskilled workers and a large network of services for non-English speakers, might have caused the rapid absorption of workers.

More recently, another study found evidence that Hispanic immigrants have driven down wages for low-skilled jobs in the largest U.S. metropolitan areas. This study compared 1990 census data from 38 metropolitan areas with large concentrations of immigrants and found that immigrant men who have been in the United States for less than 5 years have a disproportionate impact on wages in the industries where they hold jobs (Catanzarie, 2003). Although recent immigrant men did not comprise more than 5% of the population in any of the metropolitan areas she studied, Catanzarie found that this group often comprised more than one quarter of the labor force in what she calls "brown collar" occupations,[3] such as janitor, roofer, construction worker, gardener, and dishwasher. When many Hispanic immigrants work in a given occupation, she says, the job will pay less than others that require similar skills but employ fewer recent arrivals.

Hispanic immigrants drive down wages for the simple reason that they are willing to work for less, says Catanzarie. They are willing to work for less because they live at the margins of society. Hispanic immigrants are unlikely to defend their rights in the workplace because many of them are living in the United States illegally. Even legal immigrants are at a severe disadvantage if they lack English literacy skills. Providing amnesty for illegal aliens, enforcing minimum-wage standards, and implementing other measures designed to raise the social status of immigrant workers would also benefit native-born workers in the same industries, she says.

Foreign-born Americans with low incomes already dominate literacy education in many areas, and their numbers will likely increase in years

---

[3] Catanzarie defines "brown collar" as "occupations where immigrant Latinos are overrepresented, largely in low-level service, construction, agriculture, and manufacturing jobs, including waiters' assistants, gardeners and groundskeepers, cooks, farm workers, and painters, in metropolitan areas such as Anaheim–Santa Ana, Chicago, Fresno, Jersey City, Los Angeles, New York City, and San Diego" (Catanzarie, 2003, p. 1).

to come. It is important to remember, however, that they are only one segment of the entire foreign-born population. Only 34% of U.S. households headed by a foreign-born person have incomes of less than $25,000, compared with 29% of all U.S. households. Some low-income households headed by a foreign-born person contain multiple earners working for very low wages; in households like these, the combined income may conceal the very low per capita earnings of each worker. But still, households like these are only one segment of a large, diverse, and growing population group.

In fact, immigrants to the United States are concentrated at both the low and high ends of the income scale because the rewards of immigration from Asia and Latin America are greatest for the least-skilled and the most-skilled workers. A Central American farmer with only a few years of schooling has limited job options if he moves to the United States. But even if the wages of the menial job he can get are low by U.S. standards, he will earn much more washing dishes in Los Angeles than he would in Mexico City. At the other end of the skills spectrum, a software engineer educated in India will earn much more in Boston than he would in Bombay. However, a middle-class office worker in Seoul will not see a huge boost in his standard of living if he moves to San Francisco, and the relatively smaller rewards for this worker are likely to be outweighed by the considerable cost and disruption of moving to America.

Limits of Demographic Data

The low-income, little-educated segment of the foreign-born is the segment that concerns literacy educators. This segment is highly concentrated within specific groups. For example, Hispanic foreign-born households are among the poorest in America. More than four in ten (42%) Hispanic foreign-born households earned less than $25,000 in 2001. Within the Hispanic foreign-born group, South-American-born householders are the least likely to have low incomes, with 31% earning less than $25,000 a year. Central-American-born families are more likely to be poor (39% earning less than $25,000), Caribbean-born Hispanics are even more likely (44%), and Mexican-born Hispanics are most likely to have low incomes (45%).

Although broad statements like these are useful for surveying the field, it is dangerous to rely on them when making program or policy decisions. Significant differences are hidden within broad categories. For example, the Caribbean population includes some of the nation's poorest groups:

37% of Dominicans, Haitians, and Puerto Ricans in the United States live in poverty. However, the Caribbean designation also includes the wealthiest Hispanic subgroup, Cubans, with only 20% living in poverty. Cubans are relatively more affluent than other Caribbean subgroups for several reasons, including the relatively high educational attainment of 1960s refugees from Castro's regime and strong support networks among Cuban Americans in Miami. Within the Cuban subgroup, poverty is much higher among those living in Jersey City, New Jersey than it is among those living in Miami. Poverty is almost nonexistent among Miami Cubans who have lived in the United States for more than 10 years.

Another important limiting factor on census statistics is that they miss significant portions of low-income and minority groups. The error rate is extremely high for Mexicans and Central Americans because so many immigrants from these countries—as many as four million, by some estimates—are in the United States illegally, and are therefore likely to avoid U.S. government employees carrying clipboards (Fix & Passel, 2001). For all of these reasons, it is crucial for educators to go beyond demographics and understand the literacy effects of immigration one household at a time.

LINGUISTIC ISOLATION

A major implication of the immigration trend that is of interest for literacy educators is that it results in a significant share of households in many parts of the United States having difficulty with English. More than one in five households in Miami do not have a member who understands English well, for example. That proportion is one in seven in Jersey City, New Jersey. It is not just a problem in big cities, either: More than one in ten households in Garden City, Kansas speaks Spanish but not English, because a big meat-packing plant, which is just outside of town, employs a large number of Spanish-speaking immigrants.

According to the Census Bureau, a U.S. household is in "linguistic isolation" if none of its members over the age of 14 speaks English "very well." Households in this category grew rapidly in the 1990s, according to the decennial census counts of 1990 and 2000. While the total number of U.S. households increased 15%, from 92 million to 105.5 million, the number of households in linguistic isolation increased 49%, from 2.9 million to 4.3 million. The proportion of all U.S. households in linguistic isolation increased almost a full percentage point during the 1990s, to 4.1%.

Isolation Concentration

Linguistic isolation is geographically concentrated. Half of all isolated households in the United States are in 3 states: California (with 1.1 million isolated households), New York (with 545,000), and Texas (533,000). Isolated households make up more than 5% of all households in 10 states, but they make up less than 2% of the population in 27 states. The 10 states with the highest proportion of isolated households are also the states that were most affected by immigration in the 1990s: Arizona, California, Florida, Hawaii, Nevada, New Jersey, New Mexico, New York, Rhode Island, and Texas.

States with the lowest proportion of linguistically isolated households, such as West Virginia (where 0.3% of households do not speak English) and Montana (0.7%), tend not to have large metropolitan areas or other places where a stranger can quickly find a job. Some states with moderate rates of linguistic isolation are actually comprised of a large metropolitan area where many immigrants settle, surrounded by an expanse of rural and small metropolitan areas where nearly everyone speaks English. In Illinois, for example, an average of just 2.2% of households have difficulty with English, but the linguistic isolation rate within Illinois ranges from 4% in the city of Chicago to just 0.1% in rural Woodford County. Linguistic isolation is found wherever new immigrants are found.

Linguistic isolation is also concentrated by native language. The proportion of non-English-speaking households in the United States that speak Spanish[4] increased from 54% in 1990 to 59% in 2000, due to the dominance of low-income families from Mexico and Central America in the immigrant stream of the 1990s. The number of linguistically isolated Spanish-speaking households increased 61% during the 1990s, from 1.6 million to 2.6 million. There are nine states where the vast majority of linguistically isolated households are Spanish-speaking: In Arizona, Arkansas, Colorado, Florida, Idaho, Nevada, New Mexico, Texas, and Wyoming, the Spanish-speaking proportion is 70% or greater.

Arkansas is the only state on that list that is neither a major immigrant center (such as Texas and Florida) nor a former territory of Spain. Moreover, only 36% of Arkansas' non-English-speaking households were Spanish-speaking in 1990. However, during the 1990s, a stream of Mexican and Central American workers began flowing into Arkansas to take jobs in services and manufacturing, such as textile mills. The number of Hispanic

---

[4]In the 2000 census, the Spanish-language category also includes those who speak Ladino.

households in Arkansas increased more than 50% during the 1990s, from 19,000 to 41,000, whereas the total number of households in the state increased just 17%. This trend was apparent throughout the Southeast. The number of Hispanic households in North Carolina increased from 69,000 to 170,000, and the number of Spanish-speaking linguistically isolated households in North Carolina increased from 5,000 to 44,000. In Georgia, the overall number of Hispanic households increased from 71,000 to 181,000, and the number of such households having trouble with English increased from 8,000 to 44,000. Literacy educators in the Southeast must adjust their programs to serve this new population.

Asian Isolation

Linguistically isolated households that speak an Asian language are even more geographically concentrated than are Spanish-speaking isolated households. There are 805,000 U.S. households that speak an Asian language[5] but have difficulty with English: 37% of them (301,000 households) are in California, and another 12% (98,000) are in New York. The number of Asian-speaking isolated households increased 55% during the 1990s, which is similar to the rate of increase for Spanish-speaking isolated households. There was also a similar broadening of the Asian-speaking isolated population into new areas during the 1990s. There were 11 states where the number of linguistically isolated Asian-speaking households more than doubled: Connecticut, Delaware, Florida, Georgia, Kentucky, Nebraska, Nevada, New Hampshire, North Carolina, South Carolina, and South Dakota. This list includes major immigration centers (Florida) and southeastern centers of manufacturing employment (Georgia, Kentucky, the Carolinas), but it also reflects the spread of recent immigrants away from major immigration centers (e.g., from New York City to Connecticut, or from California to Nevada).

Why was there rapid growth in Asian-isolated households in Nebraska, New Hampshire, and South Dakota? The answers are not clear, but the absolute numbers are small enough that it could be due to changes in just a few neighborhoods. In Nebraska, the number of Asian-isolated households increased from 798 to 1,852; in New Hampshire, from 513 to 1,091; and in South Dakota, from 193 to 427.

---

[5] In the 2000 census, Asian languages include Chinese, Korean, Japanese, Vietnamese, Hmong, Khmer, Lao, Thai, Tagalog or Pilipino, the Dravidan languages of India (such as Telegu, Tamil, and Malayalam), and other languages of Asia and the Pacific, including the Philippine, Polynesian, and Micronesian languages.

The proportion of Asian households that are linguistically isolated ranges from 13% (in Wyoming) to 39% (in New York), but in most states the proportion is between 20% and 30%. Moreover, the proportion of all Asian households in the United States that are linguistically isolated declined during the 1990s, from 30% to 29%. The reason is that Asian immigration to the United States in the 1990s was not dominated by a stream of people with little formal education, as Hispanic immigration was. Asian immigrants to the United States were far more likely than Hispanic immigrants to have the equivalent of a high school diploma or some college experience.

The influence of Asian immigrants was strong in neighborhoods like Oak Tree Road in Iselin, New Jersey, an aging area of strip shopping centers that was transformed during the 1990s by Asian-Indian shopkeepers. Relatively few of Iselin's newcomers needed literacy training, however. Asian households that are isolated tend to be concentrated in areas with all-encompassing Asian neighborhoods, such as New York's Chinatown.

Indo-European Isolation

About 6.38 million U.S. households speak a non-English language that is neither Spanish nor Asian. This group includes 5.51 million households that speak an Indo-European language other than Spanish, and 869,000 households that speak some other language, such as an African or Native American tongue.[6] The number of U.S. households that speak a non-English language that is neither Spanish nor Asian increased 20% during the 1990s, and the proportion that are linguistically isolated increased slightly, from 14% to 15%.

About 855,000 households in the United States contain Indo-European language speakers who have trouble with English. They are concentrated in New York (with 174,000 Indo-European isolated households), California (113,000), Florida (69,000), Illinois (68,000), New Jersey (56,000), and Massachusetts (52,000). This list reflects the tendency of European immigrants to settle in Northeastern and Midwestern cities. Some of the

---

[6] In the 2000 census, "Other Indo-European languages" includes most languages of Europe and the Indic languages of India. These include the Germanic, Scandinavian, Romance (excluding Spanish), Slavic, Celtic, Greek, Baltic, and Iranian languages. The Indic languages include Hindi, Gujarathi, Punjabi, and Urdu. "All other languages" includes languages that are Uralic, such as Hungarian; Semitic, such as Arabic and Hebrew; languages of Africa; native North American languages, including the American Indian and Alaska native languages; and some indigenous languages of Central and South America.

linguistically isolated Indo-European households are immigrants from former Soviet-bloc countries who came to America when the Soviet Union collapsed in 1989–1990. However, a large proportion of this group are probably foreign-born Americans who have been in the United States for many years and have never learned English, relying instead on family and neighborhood connections to get by.

The future size of the linguistically isolated population depends as much on the success of literacy training programs as it does on demographic trends. So far, the success of literacy education for immigrants has depended largely on the education they receive before they arrive in the United States. Immigrants who arrive in the United States before the age of 12 eventually acquire English literacy skills that are comparable to native-born Americans, according to an analysis of NALS data by Greenberg and her colleagues (Greenberg, Macias, Rhodes, & Chan, 2001). Immigrants who arrived after age 12 and had substantial levels of formal education in their native countries were also likely to become biliterate. However, teenaged and adult immigrants who arrived in the United States with low levels of formal education were found to have low rates of participation in classes that would have improved their English skills, according to the study.

Whether or not the linguistically isolated population grows in the next decade depends on whether or not literacy educators can find ways to extend English training to the largely unserved group of recent immigrants who have had little formal education of any kind, and who may be unable to read or write in their native languages. A key question for literacy educators is whether their teaching methods take into account the varying levels of literacy in their students' native languages.

DISABILITY

More than one quarter of the NALS Level-1 population (26%) in 1992 had physical, mental, or health conditions that kept them from participating fully in work, school, housework, or other activities. In addition, 19% of NALS Level-1 respondents reported having visual difficulties that affect their ability to read print. Unfortunately, the 1990 and 2000 censuses measured disability differently, so we cannot use this data source to measure trends in the disabled population. However, the 2000 census counted 49.7 million people with some type of long-lasting condition or disability, which is almost one in five Americans aged 5 and older (19.3%).

The 2000 census measured disability in several ways:

- 9.3 million people had a sensory disability involving sight or hearing.
- 21.2 million had a condition that limited basic physical activities such as walking, lifting, or carrying.
- 12.4 million had a physical, mental, or emotional condition that limited their ability to learn, remember, or concentrate.
- 6.8 million had a physical, mental, or emotional condition causing difficulty in dressing or getting around inside the house.
- 21.3 million people aged 16 to 64 had a condition affecting their ability to work at a job. These 21.3 million people represented almost one in eight Americans aged 16 to 64.

The disabled population is spread much more evenly across the United States than are recent immigrants, but there are some regional patterns worth noting. The five states with the highest rates of disability among the population aged 5 and older are all in the Deep South and Appalachia: West Virginia (24.4% have a disability), Kentucky (23.7%), Arkansas (23.6%), Mississippi (23.6%), and Alabama (23.2%). The state with the highest proportion of elderly residents, Florida, ranks sixth (22.2%). This is remarkable, because disability rises sharply with age. Whereas 19.3% of all Americans are disabled, 41.9% of those aged 65 and older have some form of disability.

Disability and Education

The distinguishing characteristic of the five highest-disability states, other than their location in the South, is low educational attainment. All five are among the top seven U.S. states with the highest proportion of adults who have not completed high school. In contrast, Florida's elderly population is far above the national elderly averages for affluence and education.

States with the lowest disability rates are also among those with the highest rates of educational attainment. The state with the lowest disability rate—Alaska, where just 14.9% of the population aged 5 and older has a disability—also has the highest rate of high school graduation, with 86.8% of state residents aged 18 and older having a high school diploma. The other states in the top five for low disability rates—Utah, Minnesota, Wisconsin, and Nebraska—all have graduation rates that are far above the national average. The most likely explanation is that higher educational attainment creates opportunities and awareness that reduce the incidence of long-term disability.

The education connection remains strong for disability rates within the older population segment. The top five states with the highest proportion of disabled among the population aged 65 and older are Mississippi, Alabama, Kentucky, Arkansas, and West Virginia. The five states with the lowest elderly disability rate are Wisconsin, Minnesota, Connecticut, Nebraska, and Delaware.

The education–disability connection is not as strong for one type of disability that is directly associated with low literacy, however. The proportion of adults who suffer from a sensory disability (sight and hearing) is 2.3% in the working ages (16 to 64) and 14.2% among the elderly (aged 65 and older). The population of sensory-disabled Americans closely follows overall population distribution patterns. The top five states for the total number of sensory-disabled persons are also the top five for total population: California, Texas, Florida, New York, and Pennsylvania. However, within the disabled population, the numbers show a different pattern.

Within the overall total of disabled persons, the proportion that has sensory difficulties is 12% for working-age Americans and 34% for the elderly. The state with the highest rate of sensory difficulties within the disabled population is Alaska, where 21% of the working-age disabled and 45% of the elderly disabled have sensory problems. Other states with the highest proportion of sensory disability also tend to have low overall disability rates, including Wyoming, Montana, and Idaho. Although these proportional differences are relatively small, they are intriguing.

Disability and Aging Boomers

The five most populous states also have the largest absolute number of residents with mental disability, defined as chronic difficulty with concentrating, remembering, or learning. Mental disability may become more important to literacy educators as the baby-boom generation ages. The proportion of all adults who suffer from a mental disability is 3.8% in the working ages but 10.8% for those aged 65 and older, due to a rapid increase in the incidence of Alzheimer's Syndrome and other forms of cognitive decline that are due to organic brain disorder. The big question, for both literacy educators and for society in general, is whether these rates will hold steady or decrease when the aging baby-boom generation pushes the number of elderly American to historic highs.

The Census Bureau projects that the total U.S. population will increase about 4% in each 5-year period between 2005 and 2025 but that the population aged 65 and older will increase much more rapidly, due to the steady movement of the baby-boom generation into this group. The population aged 65 and older is projected to increase 9% between 2005 and 2010, 16% between 2010 and 2015, 17% between 2015 and 2020, and 17% between 2020 and 2025. The number of elderly Americans is projected to increase from 35 million in 2000 to 62.6 million in 2025, when the baby-boom generation will be between the ages of 61 and 79. If the rates of mental disability hold steady, the number of elderly Americans who will be unable to think clearly would increase from 3.6 million in 2000 to 6.7 million in 2025.

The future may not conform to this straight-line projection, however. Numerous gerontological studies have found that a person's likelihood of developing mental disability in old age can be greatly reduced by regular physical activity, proper diet, and regular exposure to new experiences and mental challenges. Researchers are also finding that the likelihood that a person will follow these good health practices into old age is closely related to their educational attainment. The more education a person has, the better their health practices are likely to be.

High educational attainment is one of the defining characteristics of the baby-boom generation. Thanks to the rapid postwar expansion of higher education, boomers became the first U.S. generation to send a majority of their members to college—and the shift has become the rule for generations following the baby boom. Fifty-seven percent of baby boomers and younger adults (aged 25 to 54) have attended some college. Among today's adults aged 65 and older, only 35% have attended college.

The number of elderly Americans who suffer from a mental disability will almost certainly increase in the next two decades, simply because of a huge increase in the elderly population. However, the rate of elderly mental disability is also likely to go down, due to the fact that the generation currently entering old age has followed better health practices throughout their lives. Under these conditions, a small increase in the number of mentally disabled elderly adults would constitute a huge victory.

The proportion of adults aged 65 and older who participate in Adult Basic Education (ABE) programs is currently very low. As the baby boomers create a new generation of elderly with higher educational attainment, the utilization of ABE programs among the elderly may remain at a low level. Yet the number of elderly adults who suffer from cognitive impairment due to organic brain disorders will also certainly increase, given the rapid increase in the elderly population. Under these conditions, we can expect increased need for forms of ABE that work closely with gerontologists and physicians to help formerly capable adults cope with cognitive losses associated with aging.

HIGH SCHOOL DROPOUTS

Educational attainment is the demographic characteristic with the greatest correlation to literacy. Almost two thirds of NALS Level-1 respondents (62%) have not completed high school. Other factors are also associated with low literacy, such as disability and linguistic isolation, but the correlation between these factors and literacy problems decreases as a person's educational attainment increases.

The good news for literacy educators is that gains in the educational attainment of Americans during the last half of the 20th century were remarkable. In 1950, 67% of Americans aged 25 and older did not have a high school diploma, including 69% of men and 65% of women. Massive public investment in education drove the proportion of dropouts to 57% of all adults aged 25 and older in 1959, 47% in 1968, 37% in 1975, 27% in 1984, and 16% in 2002, according to the Current Population Survey. The gender gap has also been erased: according to the Current Population Survey, 84% of all men and 84% of all women over age 25 are now high school graduates (including GED holders).

However, the rate of increase in the proportion of high school graduates began slowing in the 1980s, and between 1993 and 2002 the rate increased only four percentage points. Perhaps this means that the curve of high school graduation rates is becoming asymptotic as it approaches 100%. The remaining 16% of American adults who are high school dropouts may form a hard core that will be particularly tough to reach.

It is also possible that the plateauing of the proportion of high school graduates is due in part to the fact that literacy education programs have not adapted to a changing client base. The wave of immigration that began in the 1980s has created a new core population of low-literacy adults, and literacy educators face new challenges in helping them achieve high school graduation or its equivalent. For example, looking at state rankings of the proportion of high school dropouts in different age groups shows the shift in characteristics of the low-literacy population. In 1980, when America's 14 million foreign-born residents comprised just 6% of the U.S. population, high school dropouts were most prevalent in southern states that had been struggling for generations with entrenched poverty. Although these same southern states still have the highest dropout proportions, a new generation of adults with little formal education has emerged in states that are accepting large numbers of immigrants.

Dropout Geographics

The America that is emerging is a land where low-literacy groups persist—and even grow—while the bulk of the population grows more educated. Between 1990 and 2000, the number of Americans aged 25 and older increased by 23.3 million. However, the national number of high school dropouts decreased by 3.6 million, as older adults with less education died and were replaced by a new generation of elderly that had more education.

The dying-off of less-educated elderly combined with growth in the number of less-educated immigrants produced large shifts in state educational attainment levels during the 1990s. The national proportion of high school dropouts among all adults aged 25 and older decreased from 25% in 1990 to 20% in 2000, according to the decennial censuses.[7] Moreover, the dropout proportion decreased in every state, but it dropped 10 percentage points (from 36% to 26%) in Kentucky, and it dropped nine percentage points in Mississippi, Tennessee, Arkansas, and West Virginia. Meanwhile, the proportion dropped only one point (from 24% to 23%) in California, and only two points in Alaska, Nevada, Arizona, and Colorado.

The shift is also apparent in the numbers for different racial and ethnic groups. Between 1990 and 2000, the proportion of African Americans aged 25 and older who are high school dropouts decreased nine percentage points, from 37% to 28%, but the proportion of dropouts among Asian adults decreased only two points, from 22% to 20%, and the proportion among Hispanics also decreased only two points, from 50% to 48%.

In the next few decades, the interplay of generational transition and immigration should dampen the demand for literacy education in Southeastern states and increase it in the Southwest and in the nation's largest

---

[7]The 2000 census estimate of the proportion of adults who are high school graduates is drawn from a sample of one U.S. household in seven. The 2002 Current Population Survey (CPS) estimate of the high school graduate proportion cited earlier, which is substantially different from the 2000 census estimate, is drawn from a much smaller group—a nationally representative sample of 60,000 households. Moreover, the census estimate is for the year 2000, and the CPS estimate is for 2002. The two sources are not comparable.

urban areas, where low-literacy immigrants congregate. These two trends should also decrease the need for literacy education among the African American population, where educational attainment is increasing rapidly, while increasing the need for literacy education among the Hispanic population where educational attainment has been stable or declining.

SUMMARY OF FINDINGS

One effect of changing demographics should be growing regional diversity in the types of literacy services that will be in demand. English for Speakers of Other Languages (ESOL) programs will be the dominant need in areas where large numbers of immigrants are displacing an aging native-born population, such as in California and the urban Northeast. Both basic literacy and ESOL will be in demand in Florida, where a native-born population with aging-related losses in cognitive ability is combined with a large number of immigrants. Also, literacy educators in areas of the United States where the population is stable and "aging in place," including most nonmetropolitan areas, will need to develop programs in tandem with gerontologists to serve elderly clients whose life skills are compromised by age-related organic brain disorders.

Immigration Isolation

Immigration has been an important component of population growth in the United States for more than 20 years; in fact, immigrants and their children now account for most of America's population growth. The immigration wave has several points of significance for literacy educators. First, more than 80% of recent immigrants come from countries where English is not the native language. Second, immigrants tend to be young adults who seek employment and raise families. Third, a large segment of recent immigrants to the United States has arrived with little in the way of formal education or job skills. Fourth, immigration can change the population characteristics of a city or neighborhood relatively rapidly, so providers may not notice that new needs have arisen in their communities.

Immigration is likely to continue at high levels for two reasons: first, because it is an essential source of workers in many industries, and second, because for the indefinite future the United States will remain a very attractive place for immigrants for both economic and sociopolitical reasons. However, research indicates that low-wage, unskilled immigrants drive down wages in industries where they congregate. This happens for two reasons: They will accept lower wages, and lax enforcement of labor laws allows employers to pay them less than minimum wage. It follows that literacy education and other efforts to "mainstream" unskilled immigrants could be an effective component in campaigns to increase wages in construction, hospitality, agriculture, and other industries.

The number of households that do not have a member who speaks English increased from 2.9 million in 1990 to 4.3 million in 2000. "Linguistic isolation" is a geographically concentrated phenomenon. Half of all U.S. households in isolation are in California, New York, and Texas, yet more than half of U.S. states do not have significant clusters of isolated households. Six in ten linguistically isolated households speak Spanish, and growth in Spanish-speaking isolated households has been particularly rapid in the Southeastern states such as North Carolina and Georgia.

Disability

The proportion of adults who have a disability increases sharply with age, but it also appears that disability rates are sharply lower among elderly populations that have high educational attainment. In the future, two countervailing trends will determine the impact of disability on literacy education. First, the number of elderly Americans will increase rapidly in the next 20 years, as the huge baby-boom generation (now aged 40 to 58) moves through the last third of its life. Yet baby boomers have much higher educational attainment than previous generations did, and boomers have also shown a strong lifelong interest in exercise, proper diet, and other forms of preventive health care.

As the number of elderly Americans increases, it is safe to assume that there will be some increase in the number of elderly whose literacy skills are compromised due to cognitive decline. Yet the improved health status of elderly Americans is also likely to mitigate this increase. The complex and unprecedented nature of the aging baby boom makes it impossible to say exactly how much the improving health status of elderly Americans will benefit society in the next two decades. This phenomenon, which was named "the compression of morbidity" by Dr. James Fries of Stanford University in 1980, has become one of the hottest research topics in the field of gerontology (Fries, 1980; Olshansky, Hayflick, & Carnes, 2002). Literacy educators should follow this research closely.

Educational Attainment

The best demographic indicator of literacy is the high school graduation rate, and the proportion of U.S. adults with high school diplomas increased sharply between 1950 and 1990. However, the rate of increase slowed markedly in the 1990s, as a large number of immigrants with little formal education entered the United States. Because the flow of low-skill immigrants and the aging of less-educated generations are both likely to continue, literacy educators should notice a shift in the characteristics of their clients in the next few years. States that have had extremely high dropout rates, such as Alabama and Kentucky, are seeing dramatic gains in educational attainment as less-educated generations die off. At the same time, states that are accepting large numbers of low-skill immigrants, such as Texas and California, are seeing little or no improvement in the proportion of adults who have a high school diploma.

CONCLUSION

In the next two decades, changes in the low-literacy population in the United States will be driven by two long-term demographic shifts. The first is the aging of the baby boom, a generation that is much more educated than preceding generations were. The baby boom is a massive population phenomenon, and the striking gain in educational attainment among boomer cohorts will drive the overall number of low-literacy adults down as they replace less-educated generations. Although boomers will acquire more disabilities as they age, they may not acquire as many disabilities as their parents did. The disabilities of aging baby boomers should be lessened by the higher educational attainment of this generation, which leads to better preventive health practices.

While boomers replace the low-literacy elderly, a second demographic shift is creating new challenges for literacy educators. The least-educated segment of immigrants to the United States are forming a new core of workers with little formal education in states like California, Texas, Nevada, and Florida. The gap in educational attainment between some new immigrants and the mainstream is daunting. According to the U.S. Department of Education's Office of Educational Research and Improvement (1999), the "status drop-out rate" for all 25- to 34-year-olds—that is, the proportion that was neither enrolled in school nor had graduated from high school—was 11.9% in 1997. However, the rate was 30.8% for 25- to

34-year-olds who were born outside the United States, and it was 60% for foreign-born Mexicans in this age group. By way of contrast, the status dropout rate for foreign-born Asians aged 25 to 34 was below the national average (10.7%).

The challenges involved in reaching these new clients are considerable. Many low-wage immigrants are here illegally, and therefore they avoid any programs or classes that appear to involve government employees. Even those willing to participate may have less than the equivalent of an elementary-school education. Yet the challenge must be met. One of the most cherished aspects of life in the United States is giving people who were born in poverty the opportunity to acquire a good job, a home of their own, and a better life for their children. To keep this dream alive, new methods must be found to bring a new generation into the mainstream.

REFERENCES

Capps, R., Fix, M., Passel, J., Ost, J., & Perez-Lopez, D. (2003, October). *A profile of the low-wage immigrant workforce.* Washington, DC: The Urban Institute.

Card, D. (1990, January). The impact of the Mariel boatlift on the Miami labor market. *Industrial and Labor Relations Review, 43*(2), 245–257.

Catanzarie, L. (2003). Wage penalties in brown-collar occupations. *Latino Policy & Issues Brief,* 8, September 2002, Chicano Studies Research Center, University of California Los Angeles. See also "Hispanic Newcomers Skew Wages," *The Wall Street Journal,* August 19, 2003, p. 2.

Fix, M., & Passel, J. (2001, August 2). *U.S. Immigration at the beginning of the 21st century: Testimony before the Subcommittee on Immigration and Claims, Committee on the Judiciary, U.S. House of Representatives.* Washington, DC: The Urban Institute.

Fries, J. F. (1980). Aging, natural death, and the compression of morbidity. *New England Journal of Medicine, 303,* 130–135.

Greenberg, E., Macias, R., Rhodes, D., & Chan, T. (2001, August). *English Literacy and Language Minorities in the United States,* NCES 2001-464. Washington, DC: National Center for Education Statistics.

Immigration and Naturalization Service. (2002). *2002 Yearbook of Immigration Statistics,* Tables 4, 5. Springfield, VA: National Technical Information Service.

Olshansky, S. J., Hayflick, L., & Carnes, B. A. (2002). Position Statement on Human Aging. *Science of Aging Knowledge Environment 2002,* p. 9-9.

U.S. Bureau of the Census. (2003). Projected state populations by sex, race, and Hispanic origin, 1995–2025. Washington, DC: Author.

U.S. Department of Education's Office of Educational Research and Improvement. (1999). High School Dropouts by Race-Ethnicity and Recency of Migration. In *The Condition of Education: 1999.* Washington, DC: National Center for Education Statistics.

3

The Role of Vocabulary Instruction in Adult Basic Education

Mary E. Curtis

My goal in this chapter is to review theory and practice related to vocabulary learning in adult literacy learners and to draw some implications for research, policy, and practice. Vocabulary—the extent of one's knowledge of word meanings—has long been recognized as a key factor in reading comprehension (Davis, 1944). Vocabulary knowledge has also been identified as one of the most significant variables in the reading success of minority language learners (Fitzgerald, 1995). Given the central role of vocabulary in reading, along with the large percentage of English-language learners enrolled in ABE programs, it is surprising how few studies have focused on vocabulary acquisition and instruction in adult literacy learners.[1] However, a much more extensive body of work describes

---

[1] Among the nearly 900 journal articles listed in ERIC that deal with reading/literacy in adult basic education, only 24 (about 3%) focus on vocabulary. Such a small number does not necessarily indicate less awareness about the importance of vocabulary in ABE, as less than 4% of the articles about reading/literacy in secondary education focus on vocabulary. Similarities in relative emphasis aside, however, more than 400 journal articles have been published about vocabulary at the secondary level.

the vocabulary knowledge and skills of children and young adults, along with information about the factors that seem to influence vocabulary growth (e.g., see Baumann, Kame'enui, & Ash, 2003; National Reading Panel, 2000; RAND Reading Study Group, 2002). As a point of departure, therefore, I rely on this research to identify trends in theory, research, and vocabulary practices that hold promise for adult literacy learners.[2] For purposes of this discussion, unless otherwise noted, I use "adult literacy learners" to refer to all adults—those who are learning to read in their native language as well as those who are English-language learners.

THE LINK BETWEEN VOCABULARY AND COMPREHENSION

Vocabulary and reading comprehension are highly correlated (about $r = .75$ for 14-year-olds and $r = .66$ for 17-year-olds), making vocabulary among the best single predictors of comprehension (Thorndike, 1973). This finding is true for children and, although we have no empirical data to prove this, we can assume that it is true for adults as well. A variety of hypotheses have been offered to explain the correlation (e.g., see Anderson & Freebody, 1981; Mezynski, 1983; and Ruddell, 1994). Each explanation suggests a very different avenue for vocabulary instruction. In this first section, four of these hypotheses are introduced, and the potential relationships that exist among them during acquisition of reading skills are discussed. In the sections that follow, issues of how and what vocabulary should be taught are addressed in more detail.

Two of the hypotheses posit a causal relationship between vocabulary and comprehension. According to the first hypothesis, the extent of one's knowledge of word meanings directly affects how much is understood. Because vocabulary controls comprehension, to improve understanding it is necessary to increase the number of word meanings that are known. This hypothesis is often referred to as the *instrumental hypothesis* (Anderson & Freebody, 1981).

A second hypothesis contends that comprehension ability affects vocabulary size. The more opportunities provided for reading, the better one is at understanding what is read, and the better one is at understanding, the more likely new word meanings will be learned. In other words, improve-

---

[2] See Gillespie (2001) and Kruidenier (2002) for examples of how this approach has been used previously to inform overviews of adult literacy research and practice.

ment in vocabulary is a consequence—not a cause—of comprehension. I refer to this as the *byproduct hypothesis.* (See Ruddell, 1994, for a similar explanation—one she calls "a comprehension-process view.")

Two other hypotheses about the relationship between vocabulary and comprehension point to their link with a third factor. The first such hypothesis suggests that vocabulary and comprehension are correlated because both are connected to the extent of background knowledge a reader has about what is being read. Once a relevant knowledge base has been built, both vocabulary and comprehension will be improved. This is commonly known as the *knowledge hypothesis* (Anderson & Freebody, 1981).

According to a fourth hypothesis, vocabulary and comprehension are related because both reflect an individual's overall competence with language. As learners develop linguistically, their vocabulary and comprehension abilities improve. This I refer to as the *language proficiency hypothesis.* (See Stahl, 1999, for a description of a somewhat related view, one that accounts for the relationship between vocabulary and comprehension in terms of their relationship to "general ability," or intelligence.)

Hypotheses like these are important because one's view about the nature of the relationship between vocabulary and comprehension has implications for instruction. For instance, if the instrumental hypothesis is correct, comprehension should be improved by teaching word meanings. If any of the other hypotheses are correct, however, word-meaning instruction will not in itself improve comprehension. Instead, instruction focusing more directly on promoting linguistic knowledge and use (language proficiency hypothesis), or increasing topical knowledge (knowledge hypothesis), or providing opportunities for understanding (byproduct hypothesis) would improve reading.

Studies conducted with students in Grades K–12 support each of these hypotheses, leading the RAND Reading Study Group to conclude that:

> the relationship between vocabulary knowledge and comprehension is extremely complex, confounded as it is by the complexity of relationships among vocabulary knowledge, conceptual and cultural knowledge, and instructional opportunities. (RAND, 2002, p. 35)

Complex as the relationship may be, however, there is reason to believe that these hypotheses may be—to some extent, at least—developmentally related. That is, all of them may in fact be "true," but at different points in reading development.

Consider the situation for children just beginning to read. By the end of the primary grades, children can decode and understand about 3,000 words, although they recognize the meaning of about 9,000 words when heard (Chall, 1983). Young children who are learning to read are much better at listening comprehension than they are at reading comprehension. Moreover, at this age, the extent of oral language experience still has a sizeable impact on growth in knowledge of word meanings and ability to understand (Biemiller, 1999). For adults at this stage of reading development (learning to decode), the language proficiency hypothesis seems to be the best explanation for the correlation between vocabulary and comprehension.

Once children have learned to decode, the number of words that they can read and understand begins to affect directly their ability to comprehend (Beck, Perfetti, & McKeown, 1982; Chall, Jacobs, & Baldwin, 1990). At this point in reading development, vocabulary takes on a causal role in reading comprehension. To improve their comprehension ability, adults at this stage must acquire new vocabulary knowledge (i.e., the instrumental hypothesis).

By middle school, the extent to which children have been exposed to written language becomes a significant factor in their vocabulary growth (McBride-Chang, Manis, Seidenberg, Custodio, & Doi, 1993; Nagy, Anderson, & Herman, 1987). What has been comprehended as a result of wide and varied reading determines opportunities for incidental learning from context, a situation consistent with the byproduct hypothesis. Adults at this stage need to read many different types of text, and read more.

By adolescence, the conceptual knowledge readers have about topics has an increasingly greater influence on how well they understand and acquire new concepts from what they read (Bulgren, Deshler, Schumaker, & Lenz, 2000). As school-related content-area reading tasks increase, background knowledge assumes an increasingly important role in the ability to understand the link between vocabulary and comprehension (i.e., the knowledge hypothesis). Adults at this stage must use reading to learn.

In adult literacy learning research, less curiosity about the nature of the relationship between vocabulary and comprehension is apparent than in the K–12 literature. Even so, connections with each of the aforementioned hypotheses can be found. For instance, approaches to adult reading instruction that emphasize the use of personal experiences and listening, speaking, and writing (Taylor, 1992) would seem to be based on the language proficiency hypothesis.

The view that vocabulary enables comprehension (the instrumental hypothesis) seems to be the basis for recommendations that vocabulary words should be taught to adult English-language learners "roughly in order of their frequency of occurrence, with high frequency words being learned first" (Laufer & Nation, 1999, p. 35).

Other second-language researchers such as Singleton (1999) argue that vocabulary is best taught not as knowledge of individual word meanings but through instruction in comprehension of the context in which word meanings are integrated (the byproduct hypothesis). Reading comprehension's impact on vocabulary growth may also help to explain why, by the time the fifth-grade reading level is reached, the extent of vocabulary knowledge of ABE students is no greater than children who read at the same level (Greenberg, Ehri, & Perin, 1997).

The notion that domain knowledge influences the ability to comprehend and acquire new vocabulary (the knowledge hypothesis) would seem to be the foundation for content-based approaches to literacy development in adults. According to Sticht (1997), for example, young adults in a remedial reading program who lacked knowledge relevant to what they were reading required an 11th-grade "general reading" ability to comprehend with 70% accuracy. However, when learners had high amounts of knowledge about what they were reading, they were able to comprehend with 70% accuracy with only sixth-grade "general reading" ability.

More research is needed to establish how the relationship between vocabulary and comprehension might differ in adults learning to read from the relationship for children learning to read, and whether the relationship changes for adults as reading ability develops. What is evident at present is that one's view about the nature of the relationship has significant implications for practice, affecting what the focus of vocabulary instruction will be, as well as what ultimately is learned. Research on these topics is examined in the next sections.

SOURCES OF VOCABULARY LEARNING

Although relatively little has been written about vocabulary learning for ABE students, several aspects of vocabulary have been suggested as important for instruction within the literatures on K–12 students and second-language learners. Three of these aspects have to do with sources of vocabulary learning. The first concerns the use of context—recognizing clues that signal the meaning of unknown words, as well as the words that can signal relationships among ideas in a text. A second aspect involves the use of morphology—identifying word parts that can be used in making inferences about the meaning of unknown words. A third is concerned with word definitions—understanding what they consist of and producing them.

Contextual Analysis

Virtually every discussion of vocabulary instruction for struggling readers includes recommendations for teaching students how to use context and word parts to figure out the meaning of unknown words. Techniques like these make sense, particularly given the consensus that most of the word meanings we know have been acquired incidentally, using context and morphemic/structural analysis while we read (Graves & Watts-Taffe, 2002; Stahl, 1999). Aside from a logical connection, however, little research exists to support the assumption that specific instruction in teaching students how to use word and context clues is beneficial for increasing students' vocabulary size.

Contextual analysis refers to use of the syntactic and semantic clues found in context to derive word meanings. For instance, notice how the comparison used in the following sentence could help a reader determine something about the meaning of the underlined word: *Mary's quietness was in sharp contrast to Mike's vociferousness.* A number of clues of this sort have been identified (e.g., see Johnson & Pearson, 1984), and training in how to use and apply them can lead to improvements in an adult's ability to learn word meanings from context (Sternberg, 1987).

Outside of the laboratory, however, the kinds of texts used in school, as well as those that readers encounter in everyday life, do not always afford the opportunity to use contextual clues successfully because sentences do not always offer clear clues to meaning (Beck, McKeown, & McCaslin, 1983; Schatz & Baldwin, 1986). Moreover, vocabulary instruction that focuses on context can be especially problematic for students who have reading difficulties. In order to improve vocabulary using these techniques, students must have a base of word meanings on which to build and the ability to recognize and use the context clues expressed in what is read. Like their younger counterparts, less-skilled adolescent and adult readers have without a doubt acquired much knowledge about word meanings via incidental encounters with words in context. Frequently, however, their base of word knowledge is tied to specific contexts and characterized by experiences with words that tend to be aural in nature, rather than written. Consider, for example:

... the man who assumed that *beneficial* must have something to do with money because he remembered that there used to be a company called "Beneficial Finance." Or the teen who defined ancestor as "one of your relatives who you don't see too much." Or the student who said a controversy was "something to do with government." Or the one who said about desist, "My high school teacher used to say that—cease and desist—I think it means sit down, shut up, and pay attention." (Curtis, 1997, pp. 81–82)

Kuhn and Stahl (1998) analyzed the results from 14 studies designed to teach students how to derive meaning from context. Their conclusion was that providing learners with opportunities to engage in wide and varied reading at a challenging level is as effective in building vocabulary as instruction with context clues per se.

Still another way in which contextual analysis is involved in word knowledge and text comprehension is via the category of words known as *signal words.* Signal words, such as *similarly* and *nevertheless,* help point out the connections among ideas in a text. Understanding (and use) of signal words improves steadily throughout adolescence (Nippold & Schwarz, 1992), although many less-skilled readers do not realize any benefit from them, either because they fail to attend to them, or because they fail to understand their meaning (Harris & Sipay, 1990).

In its review of studies of vocabulary instruction at the K–12 level, the National Reading Panel made little if any reference to signal words and their instruction. However, in the area of writing, teaching students to use signal words to combine sets of sentences into increasingly complex structures has been shown to improve the quality of their written products (see Hillocks & Smith, 2003 for a review). Comprehension may be improved by a similar instructional approach, particularly for students who lack understanding of the textual "road map" provided by this category of words. Signal words also occur quite frequently over a wide range of academic texts, making them good candidates for instructional focus with learners seeking to improve their content-area literacy skills (Coxhead, 2000).

In summary, the limitations in vocabulary knowledge and weaknesses in comprehension characteristic of learners who struggle with reading often prevent much growth in word meanings via a contextual approach (Curtis & Longo, 1999). In particular, less-skilled readers have been shown to have a tendency to focus too narrowly on some aspects of the context while missing others, and to have problems separating the meaning of the context from the meaning of the word itself (Beck, McKeown, & Kucan, 2002; Curtis, 1987). Instead, reading widely—especially materials that include challenging words—may be a more effective approach for incorporating context in vocabulary learning. In addition, instructional focus on those words that have meaning within the context of other words—signal words—may improve comprehension and written expression (see also Tuley, 1998).

Morphological Knowledge and Skills

As grade level increases, instances of basic morpheme patterns (i.e., prefixes, suffixes, roots) of Latin and Greek origin become more frequent in content-area textbooks. These tend to be patterns that older students with reading difficulties are unfamiliar with, both because they lack knowledge of the meanings of word parts and because they have had limited experience using the parts they know as a way to derive the meaning of unfamiliar words (Henry, 1999, 2003).

Knowledge of common English suffixes (such as -tion, -ment, and -less) grows considerably between fourth grade and high school, and is related to reading comprehension in children (Nagy, Diakidoy, & Anderson, 1993) and in adult English-language learners (Qian, 1999). Children's awareness of the structure of words also seems to be significantly related to their ability to define them (Carlisle, 2000), although many high school students remain unaware of how word parts can help in deriving meaning (Stahl, 1999). Success in reading is also tied to the ability to use clues to meaning found when words from different languages share the same or similar form and have at least one sense in common (i.e., cognates). For instance, bilingual Hispanic children who varied in their proficiency in reading English also varied in the extent to which they took advantage of cognates as aids in comprehension (Garcia, 1991).

Not surprisingly, then, vocabulary instruction that teaches the meaning of common roots, prefixes, and affixes as an aid in determining the meaning of words is recognized as a basic instructional method in a number of texts written for practitioners (e.g., see Blachowicz & Fisher, 2002; Stahl, 1999), as well as in reviews of vocabulary research studies (e.g., see the report of the National Reading Panel, 2000). What is surprising, however, is the paucity of research evidence supporting the effectiveness of morphemic analysis instruction as a way to improve vocabulary and comprehension (Baumann et al., 2002). In part, this may be because studies of morphemic analysis instruction have tended to be short-term, limiting their impact to a study of the transfer of the particular roots and affixes taught, rather than allowing for a long-term assessment of the value of morphemic analysis as a strategy for independent word learning (Baumann, Edwards, Boland, Olejnik, & Kame'enui, 2003). In addition, however, morphemic analysis is now viewed by many experts as helpful, but not sufficient in and of itself, for improving comprehension (Baumann et al., 2003).

Morphology has also been implicated in adult literacy learners' difficulties with spelling (Viise, 1996; Worthy & Viise, 1996). As Shaughnessy (1977) summarized the situation:

> Aware that things often have to change when letters are added at the beginnings or ends of words, students are not prepared to make these changes deliberately. Here again their unfamiliarity with the "carpentry" of words keeps them from being able to apply some of the useful rules for affixation, which requires the perception of syllables and stress and an understanding of the way certain letters . . . affect the pronunciation of vowels. (p. 171)

In summary, little evidence exists in support of direct instruction in particular root words or affixes as an effective approach for improving vocabulary and comprehension. Discussion of morphological features of words may be a useful component of vocabulary instruction for both children and adults, however, and attention to prefixes, suffixes, and roots may lead to improvements in spelling for adult literacy learners.

Definitional Skill

The way in which readers define words changes significantly during reading development (McGhee-Bidlack, 1991; Nippold, Hegel, Sohlberg, & Schwarz, 1999). Whereas younger children (and less-skilled readers) define words in terms of functions (*"You sit on a chair"*) and specific contexts (*"my rocking chair"*), more proficient readers produce definitions that contain information about category memberships and essential features (*"A chair is a seat for one person; it has four legs and a back"*).

In the case of familiar words, increased understanding of what constitutes an appropriate definition appears to underlie the difference in the way that younger and older students define words. With less familiar words, though, differences in categorical and feature knowledge about the words themselves seem to play a role in how words are defined (Nippold, 1998). For instance, with abstract words like *idleness,* Nippold and her colleagues (1999) found that 6th- and 9th-grade students produced less complete definitions ("It's like laziness—just sitting around all day and doing nothing") than did 12th-grade students and college students ("It's associated with a state of laziness or lack of productivity; isn't necessarily a negative thing, though—could also be a state of relaxation or rest").

The ways in which words are defined has significance in vocabulary learning for at least two reasons. First, as illustrated earlier with the words *beneficial, ancestor, controversy,* and *desist,* a learner's definition of a word often reflects the extent to which he or she is having difficulty separating the meaning of that word from the context in which it occurs. And second, appropriate definitions—those that contain information about essential features and category memberships—provide learners with the basis they need for understanding and building new relationships among words and concepts. For example, although a functional definition of *chair* and *couch* would be the same—a place for people to sit—a more formal definition of each word's meaning would make apparent the similarities and differences between them, thereby facilitating understanding of new vocabulary, like *divan* or *pew.*

Research on definitional skill has also called our attention to the differences that exist between the kinds of definitions helpful for vocabulary learning and the kinds of definitions found in most dictionaries (McKeown, 1993). As Beck et al. (2002) and others have pointed out (see also Miller & Gildea, 1987), dictionaries tend to use vague language and fail to specify how the target word differs from other similar words (e.g., *couch: an article of furniture used for sitting or reclining*). In contrast, based on her research, McKeown (1993) found that in order for definitions to be instructionally effective, they should: (a) pinpoint a word's meaning by explaining its typical use, and (b) use language that is readily accessible.

Summing up, understanding the nature of word definitions and the ability to produce them are skills related to growth in reading ability. Although these aspects of vocabulary learning are yet to be examined in any depth in adult literacy learners, it seems likely that a significant relationship exists for this population as well, as they develop their ability to read. Of particular importance for older learners may be finding ways that tools like dictionaries can be used effectively to arrive at adequate definitions for word meanings that are unknown (Blachowicz & Fisher, 2002).

In this section, three aspects of vocabulary representing sources of vocabulary learning—contextual analysis, morphological knowledge and skills, and definitional skill—were described. In the section that follows, two additional aspects of vocabulary suggested as important for instruction within the literatures on K–12 students and second-language learners are discussed. These aspects—breadth and depth of knowledge about word meanings—have to do with the nature of vocabulary learning.

THE NATURE OF VOCABULARY LEARNING

Vocabulary breadth and depth are dimensions of a person's vocabulary repertoire. *Vocabulary breadth* refers to the number and kinds of word meanings known. *Vocabulary depth* refers to the flexibility and precision of word-meaning knowledge.

Breadth of Vocabulary

The breadth of a learner's word knowledge (also referred to as vocabulary size) is the number of words for which the individual has at least some familiarity with their meaning. Simply put, vocabulary breadth is important because the more word meanings learners know, the easier it is for them to acquire new ones.

Estimates of the number of words known by the time students reach high school vary widely, ranging anywhere from 15,000 to 45,000 root words (Biemiller, 1999; Biemiller & Slonim, 2001; Stahl, 1999). Regardless of the figure we accept, breadth of vocabulary clearly grows tremendously during the years between kindergarten and 12th grade. For instance, in typically developing readers, vocabulary size more than doubles between the 6th and 12th grades. This is not so for older learners with reading difficulties, however. Studies of vocabulary size in adolescent poor readers are sparse, but clinical work suggests that as many as one out of every two teens may have vocabularies that are weak enough to cause comprehension problems (Curtis & Longo, 1999). Greenberg et al. (1997) found that ABE students reading at the 3rd- and 4th-grade levels had larger vocabularies than children reading at the same levels; however, by the 5th-grade reading level, no differences between the children and adults were found. Inner-city adults seeking help from a literacy program have also been shown to have vocabularies well below average (Gottesman, Bennett, Nathan, & Kelly, 1996).

In another study of low-literacy adults, Davidson & Strucker (2002) also found that knowledge of word meanings was an area of great need. The expressive vocabularies of their study participants averaged below the 7th-grade level, and their receptive vocabularies (as measured by the PPVT–III[3]) were below the 10th percentile of the norming population.

---

[3] The Peabody Picture Vocabulary Test–Third Edition (PPVT–III) is an individually administered test of listening (receptive) vocabulary. A learner is shown four pictures and asked to indicate (verbally or nonverbally) the picture that best represents a word spoken by the examiner (Dunn & Dunn, 1997).

Davidson and Strucker (2002) examined the reading errors of native and nonnative speakers of English. They found that native speakers made twice as many real-word substitutions (e.g., saying "property" for *prosperity*) as nonnative speakers, whereas nonnative speakers made nearly three times as many phonetically plausible substitutions (e.g., saying "so-litary" for *solitary*) as native speakers. Given that the native speakers had larger English vocabularies than did the nonnative speakers, this pattern of results suggests that breadth of vocabulary knowledge affects not only comprehension, but can also affect word recognition, at least among ABE learners.

Depth of Vocabulary

Knowledge of word meanings is rarely (if ever) an all or nothing matter. Depth of vocabulary refers to how much learners know about the meanings of the words they are familiar with, along with the connections that exist among the word meanings they know.

Developing depth of vocabulary knowledge is the process of clarifying and enriching the meanings of known words and building interconnections among them. To illustrate, consider Fig. 3.1. In this example, depth of vocabulary knowledge about the target word (stretch) refers not only to how much is known about the meaning of that word (i.e., its link to the meanings of exercise and extend), but also to the interconnections that exist between the meanings of those words and other words that are related (e.g., practice, exert, taut, etc.).

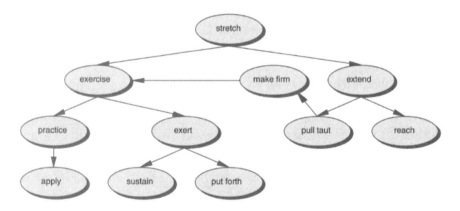

FIG. 3.1.   Example of a semantic map.

Like breadth of vocabulary, depth of vocabulary knowledge changes with development. One aspect of vocabulary depth has to do with acquisition of new meanings for known words. For example, by 4th grade, 90% of children know that list can mean "to write down in order," but it is not until college age that a majority know that it can also mean "to tilt" (Dale & O'Rourke, 1981). Among native and nonnative speakers, the more word meanings one knows, the more one tends to know about the meanings of known words (Curtis, 1987; Qian, 1999).

Knowledge about categories of words has also been shown to change as a function of development. For example, understanding of words used to make distinctions among cognitive states such as knowing and believing and inferring becomes more precise with age and literacy development (Booth & Hall, 1994; Nippold, 1998). Adult literacy learners, on the other hand, often tend to be inflexible in their use of words. For example, Byrne, Crowe, Hale, Meek, and Epps (1996) found that adults with low literacy levels seemed unable "to appreciate that one word may have more than one meaning, and that more than one word can be used to express the same meaning" (p. 43).

Another aspect of vocabulary depth that changes as a function of development is the level of abstractness that learners use to characterize word relationships. For instance, when Anglin (1970) gave the same set of words to children and adults and asked them to sort them based on similarity in meaning, younger children put together words based on thematic, concrete relationships (like putting eat with apple, and cold with air), whereas adults grouped them based on more abstract categories, like parts of speech (e.g., eat with live and cold with dark).

A useful framework for thinking about these differences in depth as well as breadth of word meaning knowledge is Dale's (1965) "stages of word knowledge." According to Dale, four stages of comprehension are involved in word knowledge: words whose meanings are known (Stage 4); words whose meanings are recognized in some contexts but not others (Stage 3); words that have been seen or heard, but whose meanings are not known (Stage 2); and finally, words that have never been heard or seen before (Stage 1).

Vocabulary breadth refers to the number of words in Stages 3 and 4—that is, words for which a learner has at least a minimum amount of knowledge about their meanings. Vocabulary depth refers to words that are in Stage 4—words for which a learner has sufficient knowledge of their meanings to understand and use them in a variety of contexts and to recognize their relationships to other words.

Although instruction that leads to Stage 3 knowledge is usually sufficient for demonstrating that a word is known (particularly when knowing is measured by a typical multiple-choice test), instruction that leads to Stage 4 knowledge is required to improve comprehension (Curtis, 1987).

EFFECTIVE APPROACHES
TO TEACHING VOCABULARY

Arriving at conclusions about effective vocabulary instruction in low-literacy adults has proven to be difficult (Kruidenier, 2002). A handful of studies have found that vocabulary increases as a result of instruction (Byrne et al., 1996; Gold & Johnson, 1982; Lazar, Bean, & Van Horn, 1998; McDonald, 1997; Nickse, Speicher, & Buchek, 1988; Philliber, Spillman, & King, 1996). However, those studies do not identify specific approaches, nor do they include control groups in their design. One study found no effect of literacy instruction on vocabulary (Venezky, Bristow, & Sabatini, 1994). In another study—the only one that used a control group—reading vocabulary improved, but oral vocabulary did not (Gold & Horn, 1982).

Even so, from work done with children and adolescents, we can identify some general principles of vocabulary instruction that seem likely to be applicable to adult literacy learners as well. These include emphasis on direct instruction, differentiation of word meanings, promotion of word consciousness, and engagement in wide reading.

Direct Instruction in Word Meanings

After reviewing the research on vocabulary learning, the National Reading Panel concluded that direct instruction was highly effective for vocabulary learning. Indeed, many experts now recommend vocabulary instruction that is intensive—that is, new word meanings are introduced, learners are provided with multiple opportunities to actively process and extend those meanings, and precise and sophisticated use of the word meanings is encouraged (Beck et al., 2002; Curtis & Longo, 2001; Stahl & Fairbanks, 1986). Such an approach would seem to be particularly important for adult learners, who have missed out on so many opportunities throughout the years to acquire vocabulary knowledge (Greenberg et al., 1997).

In a recent discussion of the challenges associated with direct vocabulary instruction, a panel of experts concluded that, "Effective vocabulary instruction presupposes choosing the right words to teach" (RAND Reading Study Group, 2002, p. 36). Beck and her colleagues have described a scheme—called *word tiers*—that helps in thinking about which words should be part of general vocabulary instruction (Beck et al., 2002). In tier one are basic words like *store* and *girl* and *truck.* Tier two consists of more abstract words that are common in a variety of school subjects, like *complex* and *consequence.* In tier three are words that are of low frequency and are associated with specific domains, like *trajectory* and *photosynthesis.* (See also Laufer & Nation, 1999, who distinguish among high-frequency words, high-utility academic vocabulary, and domain-specific technical vocabulary.)

Because words in the first tier occur so frequently in spoken language, not much instructional time usually needs to be spent on teaching their meanings, especially to native-language speakers. English-language learners—particularly those in the initial stages of language development—may need more assistance, depending on native-language skills and cultural considerations (Ernst-Slavit, Moore, & Maloney, 2002).

Words in tiers two and three are ones associated with academic language. Because of their connection with specific domains of knowledge, tier-three words are often best taught within the particular content area in which they occur. Due to the high utility of tier-two words, however, direct and systematic vocabulary instruction that incorporates them can have a powerful influence on students' vocabulary development, and as a result, comprehension. This seems so especially for English-language learners, where deep and extensive experiences with vocabulary words seem to produce the best results (Gersten & Jiménez, 1994).

When making choices about which word meanings to teach, teachers most often select vocabulary words from the texts that students are reading. Work with adolescents with reading difficulties suggests that a much broader approach can be effective (Curtis & Longo, 2001). Meanings to be taught can be expanded beyond those that appear in the learners' reading materials. All that is required is that the instructed word meanings be related to what students are reading, and that learners receive guidance in their application of those meanings. (For example, even though the word *decision* does not appear in the current paragraph, the meaning of *decision* does apply, providing an opportunity to teach its meaning.) Similarly, research shows that grouping words thematically is not necessary if vocabulary instruction is varied and rich (see Stahl, 1999 for a summary of this work). In fact, learners can often be hindered in building their own connections among meanings when those connections are built for them a priori.

Word lists have a long tradition as tools to help teachers make decisions about which words to teach. For instance, in the introduction to their *Teacher's Word Book,* Thorndike and Lorge (1944) wrote:

> A teacher should decide, concerning many words which occur in books or articles to be read by the class, whether to have the class learn the word well enough so that the ability to know the sound and the important meaning or meanings of the word when they see it will be a permanent part of their stock of word knowledge, or merely inform them of its meaning temporarily so that they can understand and enjoy the reading matter in which it occurs. (p. x)

More recent lists suitable for use with adult literacy learners include the most frequently used high-utility words (Corson, 1997; Coxhead, 2000), as well as words important for survival and success (Davis & McDaniel, 1998).

Differentiating Word Meanings

Highlighting distinctions among word meanings can enhance the success of vocabulary instruction. This sort of semantic analysis—whether it involves comparison, classification, analogical reasoning, or figurative language—has been found to be among the most powerful strategies teachers have for enhancing student reading achievement (Marzano, Pickering, & Pollock, 2001). For instance, to build rich and interconnected networks of word meanings, open-ended analogies—analogies with more than one correct answer (e.g., *confine : fences :: constrict: ?*)—seem to work particularly well. With more than one correct answer, learners can be encouraged to make their reasoning explicit, providing opportunities for discussion of additional relationships among meanings to be discovered and evaluated (Curtis & Longo, 2001).

Techniques that involve graphic representations of the relationships among word meanings are also effective tools for promoting discussion of similarities and differences. For example, semantic mapping involves making a visual representation of the relationships that exist among vocabulary words and concepts, along with the categories in which they fit. (The schematic of *stretch* and related words shown earlier is an example of a semantic map.) Semantic feature analysis involves building a matrix that identifies both the common and unique characteristics (or features) of words that belong to a particular category (Johnson & Pearson, 1984). For example, a semantic feature analysis for the concept *game* is shown in Fig. 3.2. Via semantic feature analysis, students learn which characteristics are defin-

Concept: game Examples:	rules	uniforms	ball	points	dice	strikes	league
football	+	+	+	+	−	−	+
golf	+	−	+	+	−	−	+
Monopoly	+	−	−	+	+	−	−
bowling	+	+	+	+	−	+	+
baseball	+	+	+	+	−	+	+
cribbage	+	−	−	+	−	−	−
pool	+	−	+	+	−	−	−

FIG. 3.2. Semantic feature analysis of the concept "game."

ing attributes (i.e., common to all examples of a concept—like *rules*) and which ones are specific to particular examples (like *ball*).

Semantic mapping and semantic feature analysis have both been shown to be more effective techniques for secondary-school students who are learning content-area concepts than simply providing the students with the definitions of the concepts (Bos & Anders, 1992). A drawback of both techniques is that their effectiveness depends on the teacher being present and the material being suited to being introduced in a certain way. In other words, they are strategies for teaching, not activities that can be student initiated and student directed (Weinstein & Mayer, 1986).

Analogical reasoning and graphic representation have both been combined in a technique known as *concept anchoring,* an instructional tool designed to improve secondary school students' comprehension of complex concepts (Bulgren et al., 2000). Concept anchoring connects new information to what is already known via a visual display that relates key characteristics of the new concept to similar characteristics of a familiar one. For instance, the workings of a camera (a familiar object) would be used to teach about the functioning of the human eye (a new concept). When compared to what they learned from a more traditional, lecture-style presentation of information, Bulgren and his colleagues found that high school students at all ability levels (including students with learning disabilities) had improved understanding of new concepts when a concept-anchoring approach was used.

Word sorts are another technique that has been suggested as effective for adult learners in promoting discussion of classification of words and their defining characteristics (Olle, 1994). In a word sort, students are presented with a set of words (e.g., food-related terms) written on cards and they are asked to sort the words into columns. Teachers can provide learners with the categories to use, or ask them to establish their own categories (see also Blachowicz & Fisher, 2002). Regardless of the approach used, students should be asked to explain why they sorted the words in the ways that they did.

Promoting Word Consciousness

Increasingly, vocabulary experts have been pointing to the importance of nurturing students' awareness of and interest in words and their meanings (Anderson & Nagy, 1996). Graves and Watts-Taffe (2002) describe five approaches to fostering consciousness about words in learners. The first involves modeling enthusiasm for and skill in using words adeptly. The second has to do with providing opportunities to experience pleasure from manipulating the looks, sounds, and meanings of words. The third entails involving learners in instructional activities where "rich, precise, interesting, and inventive use of words is valued" (p. 150). The fourth consists of encouraging students to engage in research projects that investigate words and their meanings. The fifth involves providing instruction that enhances students' understanding of the complexity of word knowledge and vocabulary learning.

As noted by the RAND Reading Study Group (2002), research has yet to demonstrate the specific role that word consciousness plays in vocabulary learning and any subsequent improvement in comprehension. Practitioners, however, have identified techniques that lead to positive results when they are part of a program of vocabulary instruction. For example, encouraging struggling adolescent readers to report "sightings" of vocabulary words (Beck et al., 2002) in newspapers and magazines and on television, and to use their vocabulary words in both speaking and writing motivates them to generalize vocabulary learning and see it as something that is not purely academic (Curtis & Longo, 1999). Vocabulary self-selection, where students and the teacher are all responsible for nominating potential vocabulary words for further study, has also been shown to increase engagement (Haggard, 1982; Ruddell & Shearer, 2002). Awareness of relationships among cognates—words similar in form and meaning in different languages, like *rhyme* and *rima,* and *excellent* and *excelente*—is a specific type of word consciousness that has significance for English-language learners (RAND, 2002).

Engaging in Wide Reading

The importance of the role of wide and varied reading in the development of vocabulary knowledge has long been recognized and is well documented (e.g., see Anderson, Wilson, & Fielding, 1988; Cunningham & Stanovich, 1991). Significantly, however, engaging in reading alone is not always sufficient to improve word knowledge, especially with regard to vocabulary learning in students with reading difficulties (Jenkins, Stein, & Wysocki, 1984). Growth in vocabulary for these students seems to require that reading be followed by other activities that extend their understanding, such as discussion of what has been read (Stahl & Clark, 1987). In particular, the greatest gains seem to occur when learners have opportunities to engage in activities that promote their understanding and elaboration of contextual use of meanings (Anderson & Nagy, 1996).

Learners also seem to retain meanings of new vocabulary best when they are encouraged to generate their own elaborations of context (Curtis & Longo, 2001). For example, when introducing word meanings, learners should be directed toward coming up with contexts already familiar to them in which the new words can be applied. Once meanings have been introduced, students should be provided with multiple opportunities (via discussion and writing activities) to apply the new word meanings. In this way, vocabulary instruction is always occurring in context, but the emphasis is on helping the learner make inferences about contexts in which word meanings fit (rather than asking them to make inferences about word meanings from context they have been given).

RECOMMENDATIONS FOR RESEARCH, POLICY, AND PRACTICE

As noted at the outset, few studies exist in the area of vocabulary acquisition and instruction in adult basic education. Consequently, first steps toward improving policy and practice will require development of an agenda for research. Many avenues are possible, but the ones with most promise may be those that build on what has already been learned from existing K–12 research.

For instance, researchers have suggested a number of hypotheses to account for the relationship between vocabulary and comprehension in children. Research to establish (a) the relative importance of each of these hypotheses in understanding the link between vocabulary and comprehension among adult learners, and (b) whether some of these hypotheses have more relevance than others at certain points in adult reading development could provide useful information for informing policy and practice. Additional research would study which word meanings and vocabulary skills produce the greatest impact for ABE literacy learners. Research could also determine if different words or skills are more appropriate for some learners than for others or at some points in reading development more than others.

Better understanding about the cumulative effects that reading difficulties can have on adults' vocabulary knowledge and word learning would be beneficial as well. Among children with reading problems, for example, struggles with word identification result in an inability to develop fluency in word recognition. Lack of fluent word recognition then causes these students to avoid reading, which in turn leads them to miss out on opportunities to develop vocabulary knowledge. Generally referred to now as the "Matthew Effect" (Stanovich, 1986)—good readers continue to get more and more skilled, poor readers continue to fall farther and farther behind—interactions like these appear to be fertile areas for further exploration among adult learners.

Investigation concerning the impact that social class and language differences have on the interaction between vocabulary and comprehension in adult learners may also yield important results. Among economically disadvantaged children, for example, growth in knowledge of word meanings begins to decelerate at about the fourth-grade level, followed by word recognition and spelling, and finally, by the ability to comprehend text (Chall, Jacobs, & Baldwin, 1990). Chall and others (Becker, 1977, and Biemiller, 1999) have concluded that these children need more intensive interventions focusing on vocabulary if they are to have any chance at keeping up with their more advantaged peers. The same trends may hold for adult literacy learners. If this is the case, the instructional implications may be the same or different. Similarly, vocabulary seems to play a greater role in the comprehension skills of children who are proficient bilingual readers than it does for proficient monolingual readers (Jiménez, Garcia, & Pearson, 1995). The same may be true for the development of reading skills of ABE learners.

Better tools for identifying which ABE literacy learners might benefit from a vocabulary intervention, as well as for assessing how much growth results, would also advance the field. At present, success on most standardized vocabulary tests requires only minimal knowledge about word meanings (Curtis, 1987). As a consequence, if the purpose is to obtain a rough estimate of the range and level of a learner's vocabulary knowledge, then tests of this sort can be helpful. However, if the purpose is to understand how well learners know the meanings of words that are familiar to them, and how proficient they are in using their vocabulary knowledge when comprehending, other measures will need to be developed.

Finally, as recognized by the National Reading Panel (2000), the role that technology can play in improving vocabulary learning and instruction for all learners is in its infancy, but would seem to hold particular promise for the needs of adult literacy learners. The capability for building adults' background knowledge via multimedia "texts" and for improving vocabulary knowledge via digital texts already exists. In addition, however, computers would seem to be the optimal way to customize the vocabulary knowledge and skills that adult learners need. Technology would afford ways to provide the multiple opportunities needed to experience new word meanings in a variety of contexts, and to ensure that vocabulary knowledge and skills are introduced and learned in active and generative ways.

Concerning policy, at least two important implications can be drawn from the literature on vocabulary learning in adult literacy learners. The first has to do with the ways in which the success of adult literacy programs is measured. Based on the descriptions of programs contained in the literature, instructional impact frequently is assessed using tools that estimate gains in "total reading"—a composite of vocabulary and comprehension. Identifying and disseminating best practices in vocabulary, however, will necessitate use of assessments that more directly measure relevant kinds of word-meaning knowledge and skills in ways that will be useful to teachers.

The second implication for policy has to do with professional development. As research identifies the processes and practices that teachers can use to promote vocabulary learning, technical assistance will be required so that program personnel can become familiar with the research and its implications for vocabulary instruction.

Finally, with regard to the vocabulary practice, no definite conclusions can be drawn, due to the paucity of research on what works with adult literacy learners. From my clinical work, though, I would venture to predict the following. Too many adults with a history of reading difficulties are getting caught in the following predicament: Their lack of vocabulary knowledge is causing them comprehension problems, and their comprehension problems are preventing them from overcoming their vocabulary deficits. For many of these learners, a multistage approach to vocabulary instruction may be required. For example, to teach students the meaning of the word "persistent," teachers could take the following approach:

1. Stage One: Teachers use direct instruction to introduce word meanings, and then solicit examples from learners of familiar contexts in which those meanings could apply (e.g., Can you think of a time when

you were persistent? Do some occupations require more persistence than others?).

2. Stage Two: Teachers guide learners through further understanding and application of the new word meanings with oral and written activities that extend the meanings (e.g., Can persistence ever be extinguished? Could persistence ever be a barrier to success?).

2. Stage Three: Teachers provide learners with independent opportunities to use their new understanding (e.g., When reading the following article about the Wright Brothers, think about the role that persistence played in their accomplishments.).

It is this sort of intensive vocabulary instruction identified as effective with younger readers—instruction that helps them focus on creation of meaningful contexts that make connections to what they already know—that may be the only way to help adult learners to turn their situation around.

ACKNOWLEDGMENTS

I am grateful to Margaret McKeown and Daphne Greenberg for their comments on an earlier version of this chapter.

REFERENCES

Anderson, R. C., & Freebody, P. (1981). Vocabulary knowledge. In J. T. Guthrie (Ed.), *Comprehension and teaching* (pp. 77–117). Newark, DE: International Reading Association.

Anderson, R. C., & Nagy, W. E. (1996). Word meanings. In R. Barr, M. L. Kamil, P. B. Mosenthal, & P. D. Pearson (Eds.), *Handbook of reading research* (Vol. II, pp. 690–724). Mahwah, NJ: Lawrence Erlbaum Associates.

Anderson, R. C., Wilson, P. T., & Fielding, L. G. (1988). Growth in reading and how children spend their time outside of school. *Reading Research Quarterly, 23,* 285–303.

Anglin, J. M. (1970). *The growth of word meaning.* Cambridge, MA: MIT Press.

Baumann, J. F., Edwards, E. C., Boland, E. M., Olejnik, S., & Kame'enui, E. J. (2003). Vocabulary tricks: Effects of instruction in morphology and context on fifth-grade students' ability to derive and infer word meanings. *American Educational Research Journal, 40,* 447–494.

Baumann, J. F., Edwards, E. C., Font, G., Tereshinski, C. A., Kame'enui, E. J., & Olejnik, S. (2002). Teaching morphemic and contextual analysis to fifth grade students. *Reading Research Quarterly, 37,* 150–176.

Baumann, J. F., Kame'enui, E. J., & Ash, G. E. (2003). Research on vocabulary instruction: Voltaire redux. In J. Flood, D. Lapp, J. R. Squire, & J. M. Jensen (Eds.), *Handbook
of research on teaching the English language arts* (pp. 752–785). Mahwah, NJ: Lawrence Erlbaum Associates.

Beck, I. L., McKeown, M. G., & Kucan, L. (2002). *Bringing words to life: Robust vocabulary instruction.* New York: Guilford.

Beck, I. L., McKeown, M. G., & McCaslin, E. S. (1983). Vocabulary development: All
contexts are not created equal. *Elementary School Journal, 83,* 177–181.

Beck, I. L., Perfetti, C. A., & McKeown, M. G. (1982). Effects of long-term vocabulary
instruction on lexical access and reading comprehension. *Journal of Educational Psychology, 74,* 506–521.

Becker, W. C. (1977). Teaching reading and language to the disadvantaged: What we have
learned from field research. *Harvard Educational Review, 47,* 518–543.

Biemiller, A. (1999). *Language and reading success.* Cambridge, MA: Brookline Books.

Biemiller, A., & Slonim, N. (2001). Estimating root word vocabulary growth in normative
and advantaged populations: Evidence for a common sequence of vocabulary acquisition. *Journal of Educational Psychology, 93,* 498–520.

Blachowicz, C., & Fisher, P. J. (2002). *Teaching vocabulary in all classrooms.* Upper Saddle River, NJ: Merrill Prentice Hall.

Booth, J. R., & Hall, W. S. (1994). Role of the cognitive internal state lexicon in reading
comprehension. *Journal of Educational Psychology, 86,* 413–422.

Bos, C. S., & Anders, P. L. (1992). Using interactive teaching and learning strategies to
promote text comprehension and content learning for students with learning disabilities. *International Journal of Disability, Development and Education, 39,* 225–238.

Byrne, M. E., Crowe, T. A., Hale, S. T., Meek, E. E., & Epps, D. (1996). Metalinguistic
and pragmatic abilities of participants in adult literacy programs. *Journal of Communication Disorders, 29,* 37–49.

Bulgren, J. A., Deshler, D. D., Schumaker, J. B., & Lenz, B. K. (2000). The use and effectiveness of analogical instruction in diverse secondary content classrooms. *Journal of
Educational Psychology, 92,* 426–441.

Carlisle, J. F. (2000). Awareness of the structure and meaning of morphologically complex
words: Impact on reading. *Reading and Writing, 12,* 169–190.

Chall, J. S. (1983). *Stages of reading development.* New York: McGraw-Hill.

Chall, J. S., Jacobs, V. A., & Baldwin, L. E. (1990). *The reading crisis: Why poor children
fall behind.* Cambridge, MA: Harvard University Press.

Corson, D. (1997). The learning and use of academic English words. *Language and Learning, 47,* 671–718.

Coxhead, A. (2000). A new academic word list. *TESOL Quarterly, 34,* 213–238.

Cunningham, A. E., & Stanovich, K. E. (1991). Tracking the unique effects of print exposure in children: Associations with vocabulary, general knowledge, and spelling. *Journal of Educational Psychology, 83,* 264–274. Cambridge, MA: Brookline Books.

Curtis, M. E. (1987). Vocabulary testing and vocabulary instruction. In M. G. McKeown
& M. E. Curtis (Eds.), *The nature of vocabulary acquisition* (pp. 37–51). Hillsdale, NJ:
Lawrence Erlbaum Associates.

Curtis, M. E. (1997). Teaching reading to children, adolescents, and adults: Similarities
and differences. In L. R. Putnam (Ed.), *Readings on language and literacy* (pp. 75–88).
Cambridge, MA: Brookline Books.

Curtis, M. E., & Longo, A. M. (1999). *When adolescents can't read: Methods and materials that work.* Cambridge, MA: Brookline Books.

Curtis, M. E., & Longo, A. M. (2001). Teaching vocabulary to adolescents to improve comprehension. *Reading Online, 5*(4). Available from http://www.readingonline.org.

Dale, E. (1965). Vocabulary measurement: Techniques and major findings. *Elementary Education, 42,* 895–901, 948.

Dale, E., & O'Rourke, J. (1981). *The living word vocabulary.* Chicago: World Book.

Davidson, R. K., & Strucker, J. (2002). Patterns of word-recognition errors among adult basic education native and nonnative speakers of English. *Scientific Studies of Reading, 6,* 299–316.

Davis, A. P., & McDaniel, T. R. (1998). An essential vocabulary: An update. *Reading Teacher, 52,* 308–312.

Davis, F. B. (1944). Fundamental factors of comprehension in reading. *Psychometrika, 9,* 185–197.

Dunn, L. M., & Dunn, L. M. (1997). *Peabody Picture Vocabulary Test* (3rd ed.). Circle Pines, MN: American Guidance Service.

Ernst-Slavit, G., Moore, M., & Maloney, C. (2002). Changing lives: Teaching English and literature to ESL students. *Journal of Adolescent & Adult Literacy, 46,* 116–128.

Fitzgerald, J. (1995). English-as-a-second-language learners' cognitive reading processes: A review of research in the United States. *Review of Educational Research, 1995, 65,* 145–190.

Garcia, G. E. (1991). Factors influencing the English reading test performance of Spanish-speaking Hispanic students. *Reading Research Quarterly, 26,* 371–392.

Gersten, R., & Jiménez, R. (1994). A delicate balance: Enhancing literature instruction for students of English as a second language. *The Reading Teacher, 47,* 438–449.

Gillespie, M. K. (2001). Research in writing: Implications for adult literacy education. In J. Comings, B. Garner, & C. Smith (Eds.), *Annual Review of Adult Learning and Literacy* (Vol. 2, pp. 63–110). San Francisco: Jossey-Bass.

Gold, P. C., & Horn, P. L. (1982). Achievement in reading, verbal language, listening comprehension, and locus of control of adult illiterates in a volunteer tutorial project. *Perceptual and Motor Skills, 54,* 1243–1250.

Gold, P. C., & Johnson, J. A. (1982). Prediction of achievement in reading, self-esteem, auding, and verbal language by adult illiterates in a psychoeducational tutorial program. *Journal of Clinical Psychology, 38,* 513–522.

Gottesman, R. L., Bennett, R. E., Nathan, R. G., & Kelly, M. S. (1996). Inner-city adults with severe reading difficulties: A closer look. *Journal of Learning Disabilities, 29,* 589–597.

Graves, M. F., & Watts-Taffe, S. M. (2002). The place of word consciousness in a research-based vocabulary program. In A. E. Farstrup & S. J. Samuels (Eds.), *What research has to say about reading instruction* (3rd ed., pp. 140–165). Newark, DE: International Reading Assocation.

Greenberg, D., Ehri, L. C., & Perin, D. (1997). Are word reading processes the same or different in adult literacy students and third–fifth graders matched for reading level? *Journal of Educational Psychology, 89,* 262–275.

Haggard, M. R. (1982). The vocabulary self-selection strategy: An active approach to word learning. *Journal of Reading, 26,* 203–207.

Harris, A. J., & Sipay, E. R. (1990). *How to increase reading ability* (9th ed.). New York: Longman.

Henry, M. K. (1999). A short history of the English language. In J. Birsh (Ed.), *Multisensory teaching of basic language skills* (pp. 119–139). Baltimore: Brookes.

Henry, M. K. (2003). *Unlocking literacy: Effective decoding and spelling instruction.* Baltimore: Brookes.

Hillocks, G., & Smith, M. W. (2003). Grammar and literacy learning. In J. Flood, D. Lapp, J. R. Squire, & J. M. Jensen (Eds.), *Handbook of research on teaching the English language arts* (pp. 721–737). Mahwah, NJ: Lawrence Erlbaum Associates.

Jenkins, J. R., Stein, M. L., & Wysocki, K. (1984). Learning vocabulary through reading. *American Educational Research Journal, 21,* 767–787.

Jiménez, R. T., Garcia, G. E., & Pearson, P. D. (1995). Three children, two languages, and strategic learning: Case studies in bilingual/monolingual reading. *American Educational Research Journal, 32,* 67–97.

Johnson, D. D., & Pearson, P. D. (1984). *Teaching reading vocabulary.* New York: Holt, Rinehart and Winston.

Kruidenier, J. (2002). *Research-based principles for adult basic education reading instruction.* Washington, DC: The National Institute for Literacy.

Kuhn, M. R., & Stahl, S. A. (1998). Teaching students to learn word meanings from context: A synthesis and some questions. *Journal of Literacy Research, 30,* 119–138.

Laufer, B., & Nation, P. (1999). A vocabulary-size test of controlled productive ability. *Language Testing, 16,* 33–51.

Lazar, M. K., Bean, R. M., & Van Horn, B. V. (1998). Linking the success of a basic skills program to workplace practices and productivity. *Journal of Adolescent and Adult Literacy, 41,* 352–362.

McBride-Chang, C., Manis, E. R., Seidenberg, M. S., Custodio, R. G., & Doi, L. M. (1993). Print exposure as a predictor of word reading and reading comprehension in disabled and nondisabled readers. *Journal of Educational Psychology, 85,* 230–238.

McDonald, B. A. (1997). The impact of content-based instruction: Three studies. *Focus on Basics,* 1(D).

McGhee-Bidlack, B. (1991). The development of noun definitions: A metalinguistic analysis. *Journal of Child Language, 18,* 417–434.

McKeown, M. G. (1993). Creating effective definitions for young word learners. *Reading Research Quarterly, 28,* 16–31.

Marzano, R. J., Pickering, D. J., & Pollock, J. E. (2001). *Classroom instruction that works: Research-based strategies for increasing student achievement.* Alexandria, VA: Association for Supervision and Curriculum Development.

Mezynski, K. (1983). Issues concerning the acquisition of knowledge: Effects of vocabulary training on reading comprehension. *Review of Educational Research, 53,* 253–279.

Miller, G. A., & Gildea, P. M. (1987). How children learn words. *Scientific American, 257,* 94–99.

Nagy, W. E., Anderson, R. C., & Herman, P. A. (1987). Learning word meanings from context during normal reading. *American Educational Research Journal, 24,* 237–270.

Nagy, W. E., Diakidoy, I. N., & Anderson, R. C. (1993). The acquisition of morphology: Learning the contribution of suffixes to the meanings of derivatives. *Journal of Reading Behavior, 25,* 155–170.

National Reading Panel (2000). *Teaching children to read: An evidence-based assessment of the scientific research literature on reading and its implications for reading instruction.* Washington, DC: National Institute of Child Health and Human Development.

Nickse, R. S., Speicher, A. M., & Buchek, P. C. (1988). An intergenerational adult literacy project: A family intervention/prevention model. *Journal of Reading, 31,* 634–642.

Nippold, M. A. (1998). *Later language development* (2nd ed.). Austin, TX: Pro-Ed.

Nippold, M. A., Hegel, S. L., Sohlberg, M. M., & Schwarz, I. E. (1999). Defining abstract entities: Development in pre-adolescents, adolescents, and young adults. *Journal of Speech, Language & Hearing Research, 42,* 473–482.

Nippold, M. A., & Schwarz, I. E. (1992). Use and understanding of adverbial conjuncts: A developmental study of adolescents and young adults. *Journal of Speech & Hearing Research, 35,* 108–118.

Olle, R. D. (1994). Word sorts: Vocabulary development with adult literacy learners. *Journal of Reading, 38,* 230–231.

Philliber, W. W., Spillman, R. E., & King, R. E. (1996). Consequences of family literacy for adults and children: Some preliminary findings. *Journal of Adolescent and Adult Literacy, 39,* 558–565.

Qian, D. D. (1999). Assessing the roles of depth and breadth of vocabulary knowledge in reading comprehension. *Canadian Modern Language Review, 56,* 282–307.

RAND Reading Study Group (2002). *Reading for understanding: Toward a R & D program in reading comprehension.* Santa Monica, CA: RAND.

Ruddell, M. R. (1994). Vocabulary knowledge and comprehension: A comprehension-process view of complex literacy relationships. In R. B. Ruddell, M. R. Ruddell, & H. Singer (Eds.), *Theoretical models and processes of reading* (4th ed., pp. 414–447). Newark, DE: International Reading Association.

Ruddell, M. R., & Shearer, B. A. (2002). "Extraordinary," "tremendous," "exhilarating," "magnificent": Middle school at-risk students become avid word learners with the Vocabulary Self-Collection Strategy (VSS). *Journal of Adolescent and Adult Literacy, 45,* 352–363.

Schatz, E. K., & Baldwin, R. S. (1986). Context clues are unreliable predictors of word meanings. *Reading Research Quarterly, 21,* 439–453.

Shaughnessy, M. P. (1977). *Errors and expectations: A guide for the teacher of basic writing.* New York: Oxford University Press.

Singleton, D. (1999). *Exploring the second language mental lexicon.* Cambridge: Cambridge University Press.

Stahl, S. A. (1999). *Vocabulary development.* Cambridge, MA: Brookline.

Stahl, S. A., & Clark, C. H. (1987). The effects of participatory expectations in classroom discussion on the learning of science vocabulary. *American Educational Research Journal, 24,* 541–556.

Stahl, S. A., & Fairbanks, M. M. (1986). The effects of vocabulary instruction: A model-based meta-analysis. *Review of Educational Research, 56,* 72–110.

Stanovich, K. E. (1986). Matthew effects in reading: Some consequences of individual differences in the acquisition of literacy. *Reading Research Quarterly, 21,* 360–406.

Sternberg, R. J. (1987). Most vocabulary is learned from context. In M. G. McKeown & M. E. Curtis (Eds.), *The nature of vocabulary acquisition* (pp. 89–105). Hillsdale, NJ: Lawrence Erlbaum Associates.

Sticht, T. G. (1997). The theory behind content-based instruction. *Focus on Basics, 1* (D).

Taylor, M. (1992). The language experience approach and adult learners. *Eric Digest* (Report No. EDO-LE-92–01). National Center for ESL Literacy Education. (ERIC Document Reproduction Service No. ED350887)

Thorndike, E. L., & Lorge, I. (1944). *The teacher's word book of 30,000 words.* New York: Teachers College Press.

Thorndike, R. L. (1973). *Reading comprehension education in fifteen countries: An empirical study.* New York: Wiley.

Tuley, A. C. (1998). *Never too late to read: Language skills for the adolescent with dyslexia.* Baltimore: York Press.

Venezky, R. L., Bristow, P. S., & Sabatini, J. P. (1994). Measuring change in adult literacy programs: Enduring issues and a few answers. *Educational Assessment, 2,* 101–131.

Viise, N. M. (1996). A study of the spelling development of adult literacy learners compared with that of classroom children. *Journal of Literacy Research, 28,* 561–587.

Weinstein, C. E., & Mayer, R. E. (1986). The teaching of learning strategies. In M. C. Wittrock (Ed.), *Handbook of research on teaching* (pp. 315–327). New York: Macmillan.

Worthy, J., & Viise, N. M. (1996). Morphological, phonological, and orthographic differences between the spelling of normally achieving children and basic literacy adults. *Reading and Writing, 8,* 139–159.

4

Research in Spelling: Implications for Adult Basic Education

Diane J. Sawyer
M. Tara Joyce

Literacy has been likened to a societal currency (Kirsch, Jungeblut, Jenkins, & Kolstad, 1993). In this chapter, we consider how spelling ability might contribute to the value of that currency and the ways in which adult basic literacy instruction can support that contribution. Over the last few centuries, society has been increasing the value it places on accurate spelling, and spelling difficult words has now become a mark of a good education. Gerber and Hall (1987) noted, "The ability to spell is still imbued by an admiring public with connotations of studiousness, literacy, and intelligence" (p. 34). In the United States, the fact that we hold an annual National Spelling Bee in Washington, DC, attests to the cultural value that is placed on correct spelling, for its own sake, even today.

A recent study revealed that the perception, among their peers, of college students' writing ability and even of intelligence is negatively affected by the presence of a large number of spelling errors in a piece of writing (Kriener, Schnakenberg, Green, Costello, & McClin, 2002). Schramm and

Dortch (1991) found that even two misspellings in a resume substantially reduced the likelihood that a job seeker would be granted an interview. Accurate spelling is a criterion for employment even for blue-collar jobs. A cursory Internet search of position announcements, as well as of general information provided on the Web sites of employment agencies, showed that (a) various state agencies note accurate spelling as a criterion for many job postings, including entry-level positions, and (b) agencies that provide advice and assistance for job seekers note accurate spelling as a critical consideration in preparing cover letters, applications, and memos. One agency describes spelling ". . . as a reflection of one's competence and commitment to quality" (http://www.employmentreview.com).

A needs-assessment survey of adults with low literacy skills found that 65% cited spelling as a significant problem in their lives (Hoffman et al., 1987). The results of this survey suggest that spelling instruction should be a specific component of the curriculum in ABE classes. Proficient spelling does appear to contribute to enhanced workplace opportunities as well as to self-actualization.

This chapter reviews the research about spelling (related to K–12 and adult students).[1] The research base contributes to our understanding of spelling as a skill having personal and social value, as a language-based process that follows a developmental path, and as a curricular component within adult literacy education. We then discuss the implications of the research for adult literacy education practice, policy, and further research.

SPELLING INSTRUCTION
IN HISTORICAL PERSPECTIVE

Throughout much of the early history of the United States, spelling instruction was inextricably bound to reading instruction. In the early colonial period, children learned letter names first, then learned to spell and pronounce letter couplets, syllables, and multisyllable words. Spelling was not intended to teach meaning, and accurate spelling, in and of itself, was the desired goal.

It was not until the mid-1800s that critics began attacking spelling instruction for failing to give attention to word meaning as well as accu-

---

[1] It is necessary to include K–12 research because there is very little research on spelling of low-literate adults. Much of the adult research discussed here relates to low-literate, rather than proficient, adult spellers.

racy of spelling. These critics believed that spelling should serve written communication and, therefore, it was important to recognize and understand the meanings of words one could spell. During the mid-to-late 1800s, several vocal advocates called for the reform of English spelling. In the main, they proposed altering the alphabet or creating an entirely new alphabet (Balmuth, 1982). Within this movement, Dr. Edwin Leigh's efforts are noteworthy—he might be considered the father of the phonics approach to spelling instruction. Leigh modified letter features to cue different pronunciations. For example, the soft sound of *TH* (as in *thin*) might have a line drawn through it to visually cue the distinction of the soft sound from the hard or voiced sound of *TH* (as in *they*). The program developed by Leigh retained conventional spellings but, for the first time, the sound a letter represented, not its name, was the entrée to reading and spelling words. The sound of each letter was pronounced and then blended together to produce the word. For example, when seeing *CAT* the child now pronounced the sound of each letter */kuh/-/a/-/tuh/* and blended or fused these sounds into the complete word */cat/.* Similarly, when spelling a word that was pronounced orally, the child first isolated the individual sounds and then coded each sound with the appropriate letter or combination of letters.

During the first half of the 20th century, advocates of spelling reform in the United States focused on development of a functional spelling vocabulary by identifying specific words to teach and determining when (in what grades) to teach them. Choosing which words to teach was rooted in the frequency of their occurrence in the writing of children and adults (Hodges, 1977).

In the latter half of the 20th century, research in the field of linguistics began to reveal that English orthography (the spelling patterns) represented logical and predictable relationships rooted in semantics (word meaning) as well as phonology (speech sounds). Extensive research conducted within this linguistic framework supported the conclusion that English spelling represented a morphophonological system, wherein the letter symbols relate to the speech units of the language but the structural or meaning units (e.g., roots and affixes) determine spelling and pronunciation—the words look similar even if they are pronounced differently (Crowder & Wagner, 1992). Subsequently, as an outgrowth of extensive research conducted in the McGuffey Reading Clinic at the University of Virginia, an approach to spelling instruction was developed that elucidated three layers of information in the spelling system: the alphabetic or letter–sound layer; the pattern layer (which links variant spellings of a sound to its position in a syllable); and the meaning layer (which links the spelling of different words that are related in meaning, such as *human* and *humane;* Henderson & Templeton, 1989 as cited in Templeton & Morris, 2000). Teachers using this approach initiate instruction with letter–sound associations, use word sorting to help students recognize different ways (patterns) to spell some sounds (i.e., different spellings of the long sound of *"e"* as in *beet, meat, key, believe*), and teach how spelling patterns are used to inform pronunciation (e.g., *stop, stopping* where doubling the consonant preserves the short sound of the vowel; *mine, mining* where dropping the *e* and adding *ing* maintains the long vowel sound, as well as meaning).

In the latter decades of the 20th century, educational theorists were divided in their opinions of the "best" way to develop skill in reading and spelling. Generally speaking, the advocates of various approaches could be separated into two camps — those advocating "bottom-up" approaches and those advocating "top-down" approaches. Bottom-up approaches emphasized learning about print features as they relate to sound and meaning. Letter–sound approaches (phonic rules) and word-family (analogy) methods are illustrative of the bottom-up approach to both reading words and spelling words. Top-down approaches focused on the learner's knowledge about the world as each learner interacted with the orthography to communicate through print. The goal of reading was to construct meaning by drawing on one's own reservoir of experiences that could be related to the text created by the author. The principal focus of writing was on the content of the message. Among beginning spellers, for example, teachers' acceptance of "invented spelling" encouraged students to create their own ways to spell so that they were free to focus on the meaning and message, rather than on form. In invented spelling "kak" would be an acceptable rendering for "cake" or "cr" for "car," as these spellings preserved the sequence of sounds as well as a reasonable representation of letter–sound correspondence. Therefore, it was possible for a reader (the teacher or another student) to decode the intended message. In time, the beginning writer was expected to recognize that the spelling he or she used for a given word was different from that used by others — in books, on charts, when reading the work of others in the class — and would adopt the standard form.

This brief overview of spelling instruction in the United States since colonial times reveals a repeating cycle of debate and change. Successive changes have served to bring instruction more in line with the functional utility of accurate spelling. Only recently, however, has debate spawned research that places the learner and the learning process at the core of the issues being debated. The next section reviews research that addresses different theories to account for the underlying mechanisms that support proficient spelling, as well as those that attempt to explain how one learns to spell.

Becoming Proficient in Spelling

Rote memorization was the dominant approach to learning to spell throughout much of U.S. history because the way words were spelled was considered illogical and unpredictable. In the latter half of the 20th century, the field of linguistics ushered in a new view of language as a highly regular, rule-governed system (Chomsky, 1968; Chomsky & Halle, 1968). In this view, the language learner did not learn by imitating adults. Rather, the learner, in a rich language environment, actively abstracted rules about the structure and organization of language and applied them in novel situations. A child's progress in learning the implicit rules that guide the formation of sentences or word forms could be inferred from the errors made in production. For example, a child who used *goed* for *went* or *runned* for *ran* was applying the regular rule for forming past-tense verbs, but had not yet recognized or internalized irregular forms. In this context, Read (1975) analyzed the spelling attempts of young children and concluded that their spelling "inventions" reflected their current knowledge of the orthography and the rules that had been abstracted about the spelling system. For example, if "kk" is used to spell "cake," we can infer that the child has isolated two separate sounds in the word but that there is still some confusion about the distinction between letter names and letter sounds when coding the separate sounds. The letter name is used to code the first sound the student isolated, /kay/, but the letter sound associated with the same letter was used to code the second sound, /kuh/. Knowledge of the orthography is still emerging ("c" and "k" can both code the /kuh/ sound), while knowledge of a basic spelling rule (a vowel appears in every word) has not yet been abstracted from involvement in literacy acts. Sawyer (2003, personal observation) saw a similar example. An adult with very low literacy skills spelled "ruin" as "run." Here, the first syllable was coded correctly, but the letter name for "n" was used to code the last syllable /en/ (the student pronounced the word as "roo-en").

In the latter half of the 20th century, the field of cognitive science was focusing on the underlying mental processes that account for or explain behavior. Learned behavior was assumed to involve a process of abstracting information from experience that was then consolidated into general rules or logically derived plans for behavior. Work in linguistics and cognitive science converged, resulting in a definition of the learner as an active participant in developing an understanding of his environment and in interacting within it. From these two fields, four principal theories of spelling emerged. Two—dual-route theory and connectionist theory—attempt to describe the mental processes underlying proficient spelling. Two others—stage (or phase) theory and constructivist theory—attempt to explain how skilled spelling develops over time. In an attempt to assess the viability of a given theory, researchers often conceptualize a model or hypothetical flow diagram that specifies the elements of the theory and how they would relate if the theory were to be supported. Research studies are then designed to determine if the functions and relationships essential to the theory can be supported with evidence gleaned from these studies. Models provide a vehicle for testing the validity of a theory.

No theory has yet fully explained the mental processes involved when we spell a word, or has described how we acquire the ability to apply those processes. However, a substantial body of research is associated with each of the theories and this permits consideration of the relative value of each for spelling instruction in ABE classes.

Dual-Route Theory of Efficient Spelling.   The dual-route theory assumes that two separate and independent routes to storing and retrieving information are essential for spelling (Coltheart, 1978). The phonological route involves establishing and recalling the association or correspondence of sounds, letter clusters, and syllables with graphemes. The orthographic route involves direct access to lexical units (whole words in a mental dictionary) stored in memory. Dual-route models are descriptions of what and how each separate route contributes to correct spelling. Such models propose that, to spell words following regular letter–sound spellings, people tap into the phonological route. However, the direct lexical access route is used to spell irregular words. Over time, and with much experience with written language, the orthographic representations of many more words come to be stored in a personal lexicon—a mental dictionary. In other words, through the process of learning, words that were originally accessed via phonological processing may subsequently be accessed directly through the orthographic route. Direct access to the lexicon permits faster reading and more fluent spelling, bypassing the time-consuming process of converting sounds to letters and letter sequences. The phonological route places a heavy load on phonological processes including phoneme awareness, sound sequencing, and auditory memory. The lexical route puts the burden on visual memory.

Leong (1998) specifically tested the relative contribution to spelling that was derived from strategies that tapped into each route. One hundred and fifty students in Grades 3 through 6 were given lists of words to spell. Some words were phonologically regular (could be spelled by mapping each sound to a letter or common letter cluster) but others were not. Leong concluded that each route was equally important in achieving accurate, efficient spelling. He recommended that teachers deliver explicit instruction in both phonological and orthographic structures in order to develop the connections between phonologic and orthographic segments essential for effective spelling. Similarly, in a longitudinal study of spelling (in Grades 1 through 4), Wagner and Barker (1994) found that children's spelling of nonsense words reflected the joint influences of orthographic and phonological knowledge (such as remembering to code a long vowel sound in a word using a final *e*) as well as of phonological memory (coding all the component sounds present in the word). Individual differences in early spelling performance could be attributed to differences in phonological awareness (including the ability to isolate all sounds in a spoken word and retain the sequence while writing the letters to represent those sounds) that were constant across developmental levels from Grades 1 through 4. Nonsense words provide a unique window on spelling skill for they force the speller to draw on general knowledge of the orthographic and phonologic structure of pronounceable syllables that is independent of specific words they have learned to read or spell previously. Wagner and Barker concluded that both phonological and orthographic knowledge affect spelling performance among normally progressing students and that these systems are integrally related.

Weekes (1994) identified proficient adult spellers who demonstrated a preference for the lexical-access (visual) strategy when reading single words. Adults showing this preference generally recognized the words quickly and did not resort to sounding them out. Weekes then examined their spellings of regular, nonsense, and irregular words. These adults were superior to nonlexical (phonological) readers when spelling irregular words (words that do not adhere to the one sound, one letter pattern) and about equal to nonlexical readers on nonsense-word spelling (nonsense words generally adhere to common letter–sound associations). This finding was not expected as one would anticipate that users of the phonological strategy would have the advantage when spelling nonsense words because nonsense words have not been previously seen or read and cannot be stored in a personal lexicon. Weekes suggested that this, and earlier studies he cited, lends support to the basic assumptions of the dual-route

theory of normal spelling because lexical readers were efficient in the use
of both visual and phonological routes when spelling. However, it has been
documented that unfamiliar words can be, and often are, spelled by referring to a known word that contains a similar sounding chunk. For example,
if one knows how to spell "pant," it is relatively simple to generalize from
this to the correct spelling of the nonsense word "zant" if the letter–sound
correspondence for /zz/ is well established (Goswami, 1988).

Kamhi and Hinton (2000) reviewed a host of studies of spelling development and concluded that poor spellers follow a different developmental
path from good spellers. They rely on visual strategies, remembering how
words look rather than how sounds are spelled, and that reliance on visual
strategies is a consequence of limited phonological knowledge. When we
consider adults in ABE classes, limited phonological knowledge might
arise from previously limited educational opportunities. However, such
limitations may also be present due to cognitive processing deficits. That
is, speech sounds may be coded imperfectly in memory, making it difficult to map a letter or letter-string onto a phonemic unit reliably (e.g.,
confusion of f/th sounds in phonological memory can affect the spelling of
words such as "deaf" for "death" or "thin" for "fin"). The review provided
by Kamhi and Hinton (2000) raises two important issues for adult literacy
providers concerned with developing skill in spelling. First, reliance on
memorizing the spelling of specific words can promote reliance on visual
cues and word-specific knowledge. This is a relatively inefficient strategy
because memory cannot support retention of all the words one needs to
learn to be effective in written communication. Second, many adults with
language-based learning disabilities have inefficient phonological processing systems and poor phonological memory. Therefore, it would seem that
effective instructional approaches in ABE classes must seek to maximize
interactions among the visual and auditory systems. For example, words
identified for spelling study might be used in a sentence, meanings and
possible synonyms discussed, and phrases in which the words commonly
appear might be elicited and written on the board and in notebooks with
the target word underlined or highlighted. The target word might then be
spelled aloud as each letter is written on the board and in the notebook.
Students might then write a phrase or sentence that helps to fix the use of
the word in memory.

Fischer, Shankweiler, and Liberman (1985), in a study of college students, concluded that poor spelling was due to failure in acquiring the generalizations that describe the regularities of English spelling at all levels—
phoneme, morpheme, and derivational, that is, forms derived from a root

such as *skate* to *skating*. Such regularities apply to conversion rules (rules that govern the relationship between sounds in spoken words and the way letters are used to code those sounds—coding a long vowel, plural forms, past tense forms, etc.) and thus emphasize the role of the phonological route. Interventions that might flow from these conclusions would logically focus on enhancing phonological knowledge—phonological awareness and phonics. For example, Kitz and Nash (1992) reported that training college students who were poor readers to use letter–sound spelling strategies resulted in improved reading rate, comprehension, and spelling.

Holmes and Ng (1993) conducted a series of experiments involving spelling among college students that led to a very different set of conclusions. In those studies, the greatest difference in the spelling performance was that good spellers were more familiar with low-frequency words that were almost exclusively dependent on word-specific knowledge (e.g., *bourgeois*) learned by rote. Poor spellers in these studies also appeared to have less reading experience (exposure to words in print). However, differences between the groups were explained not in terms of reading experience but in terms of failure to attend to and use all of the cues available when reading a word (a partial-analysis strategy). The researchers concluded that this failure to process all available cues when reading placed limitations on the information that was accessible in their lexicon to support spelling.

Burt and Fury (2000) built on the work of Holmes and Ng. They assessed and compared spelling, vocabulary, reading comprehension, reading experience (inferred from a student's recognition of the author of popular books), and reading accuracy for a sample of 100 university students. They found that reading experience and word reading accuracy (evidence of direct recognition of a word stored without resorting to decoding) contributed to the prediction of spelling performance, above and beyond the contribution of reading comprehension and vocabulary. This finding was consistent with earlier work (Cunningham & Stanovich, 1990) that examined these skills among middle-school students. Cunningham and Stanovich concluded that spelling is rooted in word-specific knowledge and that their study suggests the preeminence of a single route for spelling, rather than a dual route, because greater experience with whole words through reading appeared to give rise to better spelling performance.

Taken together, the findings of the studies reported here suggest that efficient spelling draws on competencies in both the phonological and orthographic systems and that poor spelling may result from limitations in either or both systems.

Connectionist Theory of Efficient Spelling.   Connectionist theory holds that the lexical and phonological systems interact. Limitations in the phonological processing system affect one's ability to establish associations with the orthography. It is widely accepted that awareness of the sound structure of language—including skills of rhyming, blending, and segmenting syllables and phonemes in words—is essential for establishing the conceptual link between letters and sounds (the alphabetic principle; National Reading Panel Report, 1998). Van Orden, Bosman, Goldinger, and Farrar (1997) suggest that the strong connections between letters and phonemes explain why the majority of spelling errors are phonologically acceptable. Accurate spelling requires that one generate letter sequences out of phonologic and semantic data. In English, the sound-to-spelling relationship is relatively complex. Thus, reliance on phonological data permits several spellings for the same sound unit (e.g., *rows, rose*). Connectionist models (designed to describe and document interactions between the two systems) focus on the associations between phonology and orthography (Seidenberg & McClelland, 1989). These models describe learning as the adjustment of connection strengths between an actual pattern of activity (e.g., a spelling error) and a target pattern (e.g., accurate letter–sound association or the association of letter patterns with meaning).

Ehri (2000) describes such connections in her work. She used the term *amalgam* to explain how the spelling of a word is remembered:

> When readers see and pronounce words, their knowledge of the alphabetic system is activated and computes connections between graphemes in the spellings and phonemes detected in the pronunciation of the words. Repetition of this process a few times bonds the spelling of the word to its pronunciation and meaning in memory, forming an amalgam. (p. 22)

Ehri makes two important points: (a) reading and spelling are closely related processes and probably should be integrated for instruction, and (b) strengthening connections between the pronunciation and spelling of some irregularly spelled words by exaggerating the pronunciation to match the spelling (e.g., pronounce the *t* in *listen*) will better fix the visual form in memory. The latter point receives some support from a study by Dietrich and Brady (2001). They found that adult poor spellers more often misspelled words that they mispronounced. This suggests that poor phonological representations in memory, resulting from mispronunciations in normal speech, may contribute to poor letter–sound knowledge, which then results in misspellings. This conclusion is consistent with that of Kamhi and Hinton (2000), who attribute spelling that relies on memory of the way a word looks to limitations in phonological knowledge.

Read and Ruyter (1985), in their study of 50 men with low literacy skills, were able to better define the precise aspects of phonological processing deficits (knowledge about phonology) that interfere with the development of strong associations between letters and sounds. When performance on a number of tasks was compared to that of normally achieving children reading at the same grade levels as the men, the men were found to have poor phoneme segmenting skills and short-term memory. They did better than children when reading and spelling exception words—those rooted in experience with the orthography (e.g., *court, anxious*)—but much worse when decoding and spelling nonsense words (e.g., *nath, frug, phong*)— tasks that are dependent on phonological processes. The use of sound-to-spelling strategies was barely evident. The authors concluded that these men could not create and maintain an accurate phonological representation of a word in memory, analyze it into phonemes, and relate these to spellings beyond the beginning of a word. Due to the fact that they were adults, the authors conclude that phonological processing deficits in the study subjects cannot be attributed to a slower rate of development (maturational lag). One could not expect that these skills will develop naturally, with time. Thus, direct instruction would likely be necessary to address these deficits.

In their review of literature on learning to read, Perfetti and Marron (1995) concluded that training in phonological awareness is an appropriate beginning point for adults across a wide range of literacy skills, including spelling. They proposed that this training must be combined with direct instruction that builds on the alphabetic principle (understanding that speech sounds link with letters of the alphabet to spell a word) if instruction is to be effective.

In their series of three studies of spelling among university students, Holmes and Caruthers (1998) offered a somewhat different explanation. They maintained that, among normal readers, there is a common representation that underlies both reading and spelling. Because the subjects in their studies (the sample sizes ranged from 44 to 97) could read words they could not spell correctly, the authors concluded that a partial-cue strategy could support recognition but not production. Stated another way, the students gathered sufficient graphic cues through reading experience to recognize a word in print but did not input sufficient visual details or features of that word to establish fully specified networks of grapheme–phoneme connections that permit the detailed rendering required for accurate spelling. In this situation, spelling must rely more on how a word sounds than how it looks. Unlike the men in the study by Read and Ruyter, the students in this study evidenced the ability to create a strong phonological representation for words in memory. However, this was not sufficiently well supplemented with a store of visual details to support accurate spelling of exception words—those words that are not spelled as they sound (e.g., *love, chief, social,* etc.). Why the phoneme–grapheme representations might not be well established is open to interpretation. Could it be the result of limitations in the phonological processing system, in cursory visual analysis of print features, or in amount of attention required to integrate the two systems? This issue has relevance for instruction but has yet to be resolved.

Embedded in connectionist theory is the concept of spelling by analogy (Goswami, 1988; Nation & Hulme, 1998). This involves spelling unfamiliar words based on a part shared with a known word. For example, if one can pronounce and spell *cat,* one can use that knowledge to spell *rat, brat,* and even *attic.* Nation and Hulme (1998) found that even 6-year-olds could use this strategy if phoneme–grapheme correspondences were fairly well established. In a related study, they found that children who were skilled at segmenting phonemes in a word were more likely to use the analogy strategy when spelling than were those with less well-developed segmenting skills.

We can infer from research related to models of connectionist theory that learning to read and spell are probably mutually facilitative and that acquiring the underlying networks of association between spoken and written language requires many experiences to cement the auditory and visual representations for words, as well as the linkages between them. Then, a massive amount of practice is required to extract the regularities and to establish stable encoding behavior. In the course of normal development, extensive involvement in reading and spelling activities is generally sufficient to support such learning. However, when students continue to struggle, a more direct approach may be useful. One approach that has been suggested as especially facilitative of this learning process is the multisensory teaching method. In this approach, all senses are brought to bear in acquiring letter–sound correspondences, sound–spelling patterns, and spelling–meaning structures in simultaneous reading–spelling instruction programs. Although there is little research that examines the efficacy of such programs (see Fulk & Stormont-Spurgin, 1995, for a review), reports of clinical studies suggest they are effective in addressing the needs of students with learning disabilities (International Multisensory Structured Language Education Council, 1995). Successful applications of multisensory teaching programs have also been reported for adults with low literacy skills (Post, 2000), college students who are poor readers and spellers (Wilson, 1998), at-risk high school students (Sparks, Ganshow, Pholman, Skinner, & Artzer, 1992), and learning-disabled delinquents (Simpson, Swanson, & Kunkel, 1992).

Stage or Phase Models of How Spelling Is Learned. Stage models are related to dual-route theory but build on the Piagetian theory of cognitive development. Piagetian theory holds that qualitatively different skills characterize successive stages of cognitive development. Stage models seek to describe the qualitative differences that develop as complex skills are acquired. When applied to the acquisition of reading and spelling, stage models describe a learner's progress through stages of knowledge about the orthography and how this knowledge relates to the phonological system. At each stage, the learner constructs rules to organize and define the regularities embedded in the orthography.

Frith (1980, 1985) proposed a phase or stage model of reading and spelling development that describes three hierarchical levels of competence essential to support the acquisition of literacy: the logographic phase, the alphabetic phase, and the orthographic phase. In the logographic phase, children use visual cues and symbols to read and spell (e.g., drawing a heart to say "I love you," or recognizing a favorite cereal by the color or pictures on the box). Children might recognize whole words by their shape or special letter features. Adults who function at this stage (those at Level 1 or beginning English-language learners) recognize traffic signs, packaging logos, and the like, but do not always recognize the printed words within these materials when they are presented independent of the full context.

Frith characterized the alphabetic phase as representing a shift from primarily visual cue use to learning a phonological recoding system. In order to support the transition into this phase, refinement of phonological awareness skills—rhyming, blending, phoneme segmentation—is critical. As noted previously, the ability to segment the separate sounds in a word is considered essential in order to establish sound–letter mapping and phoneme–grapheme sequencing for spelling production. Frith suggests that reading and spelling at the alphabetic phase primarily involves sequential recoding (letters to sounds; sounds to letters) of words where there is a one-to-one match between letters and sounds (e.g., the sounds, /p/-/i/-/n/ may be spelled using the letters p-i-n). At this stage, words such as "late," which require knowledge about the final *e* rule to change the sound of the vowel, would not be consistent with the student's knowledge about how the orthography works to cue the representation of a sound. The work of other researchers lends support to Frith's hypothesis regarding the importance of phoneme segmenting and letter–sound coding at this stage of literacy acquisition. Ehri and Wilce (1987) found that students who could not decode words learned to read more words when they were trained to spell words phonetically than when trained to use letter–sound associations only. That is, among children who were nonreaders, those who were taught letter–sound correspondences as they learned to spell words (e.g., *man* = /mm/-/a/-/nn/) were able to read untaught words more readily than those who learned individual letter–sound pairings (e.g., /m/, /f/, /a/, /p/, /n/) and were asked to apply that knowledge to reading words containing those sounds (e.g., *man*). Segmenting and coding phonemes (oral to written representations) was a superior strategy for learning to read words. Share, Jorm, MacLean, and Matthews (1984) found that the two best predictors of reading achievement after 1 year of instruction were letter-name knowledge and phoneme segmentation measured before instruction. Similarly, Greenberg, Ehri, and Perin (1997) found that adults in literacy classes, matched for reading level with third, fourth, and fifth graders, were severely deficient in phonological processing (phoneme segmenting and deletion) and that this contributed to limitations in reading and spelling words. Spelling was the weaker skill among adults, due to weaker integration of knowledge about word reading with knowledge about spelling.

In the orthographic phase, Frith (1980, 1985) suggests that reading and spelling require a shift from primarily phonological recoding to the integration of phonological and orthographic knowledge. Grapheme–phoneme correspondences are consolidated into patterns that occur across words (e.g., the final *e,* multiletter blends, morphemic units that mark number or tense, etc.). Patterns of letters become part of the generalized knowledge of how sound and meaning are accounted for in the English spelling system. A study by Lennox and Siegel (1996) lends support to this shift in focus. Average spellers showed little gain in phonological task scores after fifth grade but visual task scores improved dramatically. In contrast, poor spellers continued to show gains in phonological scores beyond fifth grade and scores in visual tasks remained low. Poor spellers had less well-developed phonological skills, early on, to support spelling and were slow in shifting from a letter–sound strategy to a more efficient spelling pattern strategy.

Other researchers have also proposed stage models of spelling (Gentry, 1981; Henderson, 1985). Henderson further differentiated the phases proposed by Frith (into five rather than three) and more fully specified the hierarchy of concepts that must be learned and consolidated in order to move from one stage to the next (Ehri, 1994). Detailed descriptions of the skills hierarchy supports both diagnostic assessment—to determine where on the continuum instruction should focus—and identification of the specific skills and concepts that must next be developed. Bourassa and Treiman (2001) reviewed recent literature on spelling development and spelling disabilities. Within the general framework of a three-stage model, they conclude that spelling disability might arise as a consequence of incomplete mastery of skills (e.g., phonological awareness, awareness of letter forms and names) and knowledge (e.g., orthographic and morphological rules) at any stage. They urge fine-grained analysis of spelling errors to determine differences between normally developing students and those with spelling disabilities to identify the focus for remediation.

Fresch (2001) applied a stage-model approach to interpret data collected during a longitudinal study involving one child's journal entries from kindergarten through fourth grade. These entries provided a window on the child's developing knowledge. Fresch found that the spontaneous spelling productions could be characterized, from kindergarten through third grade, according to the hierarchical five-stage model (Henderson, 1985) of knowledge about word structure. She suggests that journal entries are a source for analyzing students' word knowledge, planning individual instruction, and assessing progress over time.

Within the conceptual framework of stage models of spelling acquisition, learning to spell has been described as a process of moving from spelling to represent sound to spelling to represent meaning (Templeton, 2002). To assess where on this continuum a student's skill development might be, Ganske (2000) designed lists of words to permit an inventory of concepts about spelling that span the process continuum. Such an inventory permits direct teaching of the specific concepts each student is ready to learn. To help students learn the critical concepts necessary for success at each stage, researchers at the University of Virginia developed activities that involve sorting and categorizing words by features of sound or meaning to help students discover the rules that relate letters and letter sequences to sound and meaning (Bear, Templeton, Invernizzi, & Johnston, 2000). For example, one group of students might receive a set of words that require sorting according to categories that will help to support recognition of different ways to spell the long *a* sound (final *e, ay, ai*). At the same time, another group may be working on sorts that reveal distinctions in the sound of a vowel within open or closed syllable patterns (e.g., *ma-ple* vs. *mat-ter*), while a third group is working on sorts to reveal the effect of adding "*ing*" to words ending in a consonant or in final *e*. During the sorting activity, the teacher can observe the ease or difficulty of the task for each student and ask questions to assess a student's ability to articulate a generalization discovered through the sorting task (e.g., doubling a final consonant before adding "*ing*" is necessary to preserve the short sound of the vowel). In this way, the teacher can determine which students need more practice, as well as who may be ready to move on to learning a new concept. Word-sorting activities provide the means to effectively individualize instruction within a group of students and to chart individual progress.

To examine the utility of a stage-model approach in adult literacy classes, Bear, Truex, and Barone (1989) used a spelling inventory to determine the stage of spelling development of 32 adult students. They wanted to determine if the developmental sequence observed among children would hold for adult learners. Additionally, the researchers wished to determine how well a spelling inventory worked, compared to a word-recognition measure, in determining level of skill attainment. A strong correlation was obtained between spelling scores on the inventory and word-recognition scores. However, word-recognition scores offer insights into the grade level of material that might be used for instruction, but not what skills to specifically teach. The spelling inventory provides an entry point for systematically expanding students' knowledge about word structure to improve both reading and spelling. The authors concluded that adult spelling development follows a pattern similar to that observed in children and that assessment of spelling stage is a useful tool to differentiate instruction for clusters of students in adult literacy classes. Two other studies also support the conclusion that adults and children follow the same developmental path toward correct spelling. Viise (1995) and Worthy and Viise (1996) examined the spelling errors of adult literacy learners and elementary students, matched for achievement. Both groups demonstrated the same patterns in their mastery of spelling features. Unlike the children, however, the spelling errors of adults suggested both phonological coding deficits and difficulty with word endings in general. Word endings (suffixes) signal a change in meaning. Difficulties that are specific to the spelling of word endings suggest a specific difficulty with understanding and use of the morphology or meaning system of the language. In her review of research, Ehri (1991) concluded that learning to spell evolves through a combination of processes including inductive learning (abstracting generalizations from experiences with words), scaffolding (building new insights on previously mastered concepts), and explicit teaching. To support student progress through the various stages of spelling acquisition, instruction must be sequential (from letter–sound patterns, to rule-governed patterns, to meaning-based patterns) and systematic. Instructional manuals such as *Words Their Way* (Bear et al., 2000) support this approach.

The Constructivist Theory of How Spelling Is Learned. The field of psycholinguistics, a blend of theories about the development of cognition and language, provided the foundation for the constructivist theory of literacy acquisition (see Sawyer, 1991 for a detailed discussion). The theory is based on two principal assumptions. The first is that the individual actively constructs knowledge out of the full range of prior experiences in his or her environment. What one learns depends, in part, on the knowledge and experience that is already in place to support new learning. Provided with rich experiences, children naturally abstract the pertinent details they are ready to attend to, work out an understanding of these details, and build them into systems of understanding about the world. The second assumption is that the process of constructing knowledge is most effectively supported through authentic or real-world (as opposed to contrived) experiences. Within this framework, reading and writing personally meaningful texts are the experiences out of which both word recognition and spelling develop.

The constructivist theory presumes that skill with written communication develops much the same as for oral communication—the impetus is the personal drive to communicate. Students learn to read by reading themselves and by seeing reading modeled by others; they learn to spell by writing their own messages and reading messages written by others. Within the framework of a model derived from constructivist theory, teachers initially encourage invented spelling to support communication. Correct spelling is expected to evolve through purposeful attention to words the person specifically wants to learn, and through repeated exposure to frequently used words encountered when reading text or the written messages of others. Orthographic units, whether whole words or spelling patterns, are the predominant focus. Specific and formal instruction involving subskills associated with the alphabetic system, outside the context of purposeful reading and writing, is not an acceptable practice within this theoretical framework.

The whole-language approach to literacy acquisition is the prominent illustration of a constructivist model in practice. This approach incorporates a collaborative process to support learning in which teachers model reading and writing and become partners with students in developing communication skills through supportive questioning or by supplying important pieces of information about the system of written communication as needed (e.g., correctly pronouncing a word a child has misread only when the error affects meaning, or writing the correctly spelled word under a word a child has written using invented spelling), to meet the learner's personal communication intentions. As with learning oral communication, this approach assumes that such personally meaningful interactions with print will lead students to acquire the knowledge, rules, and conventions needed to accomplish their communication goals using the print medium. This emphasis on interactions with personally meaningful material contrasts with more traditional approaches that employ a common text for reading skill development or a workbook containing writing exercises (copying sentences; filling in blanks; writing a paragraph based on a provided sentence stem). Key to success within the whole-language approach is structuring supportive learning opportunities that focus on knowledge and skills that are within the learner's "zone of proximal development" (Vygotsky, 1962). Teachers should organize knowledge, skills, and content to establish the most receptive climate for specific new learning. The learner's current knowledge, skills, and interests must determine what information or strategy the teacher selects to model or teach in supporting the learner's communication needs of the moment (see Sawyer, 1991). This places a tremendous responsibility on the teacher to effectively assess individual communication competencies, identify knowledge and skills that would be most helpful, and structure literacy activities that support learning within the zone of proximal development.

Tompkins (2002) describes a one-semester intervention program for 24 seventh-grade poor readers that emphasized a constructivist approach called *process writing*. Students' reading levels ranged from first to sixth grade. Tompkins found that spelling was the most severe mechanical problem the students had. Sixty-seven percent spelled phonetically, with skills at the first- to third-grade level. Although some improvement in spelling was noted at semester end, spelling remained a serious problem. On average, students gained one grade level on an inventory of spelling development. However, one third of the students had made no progress in spelling by the end of the study. Tompkins does not describe any specific instruction provided to support spelling. Any gains made were apparently the result of personal discoveries students might have made. Despite the measured gains some students did demonstrate, error analysis suggested that the phonological and orthographic cueing systems were generally not being integrated.

Butyniec-Thomas and Woloshyn (1997) specifically examined the effects on spelling of explicit instruction (subword and whole-word strategies), whole-language instruction (target words used to complete writing activities), and the two in combination. Explicit instruction alone, or in combination with whole-language instruction, yielded growth among third-grade students that was superior to that of the whole-language approach alone. Results of this study and the Tompkins study already discussed suggest that learning to spell effectively among older poor spellers is, at best, likely to be a slow and undependable process within a constructivist framework.

Two extensive reviews of research on spelling instruction cast further doubt on the efficacy of an exclusively naturalistic approach to spelling acquisition as embodied in the whole-language approach. Graham (2000) reviewed more than 60 research studies of spelling and spelling instruction, which involved students ranging across the grade span of first grade through college. He concluded that, overall, research findings support a combination of incidental learning and direct instruction to be most beneficial. Scott (2000) reviewed research on three methods of spelling instruction—memorization of lists, word analysis, and indirect instruction via authentic reading and writing activities—as these apply to poor spellers. She concluded that poor spellers must be provided with intense, systematic, and individualized instruction. The poorest spellers, regardless of age, require basic work in phonological awareness and the alphabetic principle to support their learning of spelling strategies.

By way of a compromise between direct instruction in specific skills out of context and reliance on modeling and immersion in literacy activities to support acquisition of reading and spelling, Strickland (1998) proposes a balanced approach to instruction. A balanced approach brings together aspects of skills instruction including letter–sound knowledge, visual memory (how a word looks), and knowledge of word parts such as common suffixes and spelling patterns that might support spelling by analogy (p. 21). Strickland recommends providing opportunities to acquire these skills through formal and incidental (spontaneous, context-based) instruction.

Conclusion.   Research over the past 20 years has addressed the question of how we learn to spell from a variety of theoretical perspectives, resulting in two theories that attempt to explain the underlying mental processes involved in spelling and two that attempt to explain how people learn to spell. Arising out of this body of research are a few common conclusions that have relevance for adult literacy instruction:

- Both visual and auditory systems play important roles in learning to spell.

- Learning to spell proceeds in a predictable, developmental sequence.
- Phonological processing abilities are essential for growth in spelling.
- Reading experience supports spelling development.
- Pronunciation of words affects spelling accuracy.
- Analysis of spelling errors is useful for assessing spelling status and differentiating instruction for clusters of students having similar skill needs.
- Direct instruction involving letter–sound associations, syllable structures, spelling patterns, and derivational forms is essential and is most effective when coupled with reading and writing activities that are personally meaningful.

THE STATUS OF SPELLING
IN ABE CLASSES

A View of Public Policy

To discover how spelling instruction is addressed in ABE programs, in Spring 2003 we informally surveyed, via an e-mail inquiry, state directors of literacy programs in all 50 states and the District of Columbia. We wanted to learn the extent to which there was explicit reference to spelling instruction in either a formal statement of policy or in recommended curricula, or if licensure requirements might be used to infer professional preparation to teach spelling, at some level. We asked the following questions: In your state, is there a policy statement or suggested curriculum having to do with teaching spelling in ABE classes? Does your state have standards for teacher licensure in adult education? Directors in 22 states and the District of Columbia responded. Responses indicated that, in these states, no policy or specific curriculum for spelling instruction is in place at the state level. However, the District of Columbia is currently field-testing a general ABE curriculum that does not now address spelling although the respondent indicated that this curriculum could possibly incorporate "new suggestions" for curriculum content. South Carolina reported that a general ABE curriculum is now being developed but did not indicate how, if at all, spelling will be addressed in the curriculum.

In all states responding, curriculum is reportedly the responsibility of local programs. The state director in Arkansas asked regional program directors to also respond to our questions. Seven replied and provided this picture of spelling curriculum at the local level: One reported that there is no local spelling curriculum but that some staff development "touches on spelling"; two reported using a computer program; four reported using a variety of text sources including reading programs that incorporate spelling, phonics, and whole-word workbooks, and individual planning wherein spelling is incidental to vocabulary development. Comments described spelling instruction as involving "printing," "visualizing," "hearing correct pronunciations of sounds," "memorizing rules," and "studying patterns." We conclude that spelling instruction in ABE classes may have little guidance or structure beyond that provided by published materials that might be available in the classroom. A coherent view of spelling as a process that involves orthographic and phonological systems appears to be lacking.

Responses to our second question revealed that only 5 of the 22 respondents have specific adult education certification available. Only Arkansas requires this endorsement for full-time adult education teachers. Most require a teaching certificate in elementary or secondary education. However, no teaching certificate of any type is required for employment in adult education in Alaska, in some programs in Michigan (related to funding source), or in North Carolina. Three states indicated that professional development through state-sponsored workshops (about 20 hours) was required of teachers in adult education; two states indicated they are just beginning to consider standards for teacher competencies. It is not possible to infer from responses to our survey that ABE teachers have generally had some level of formal preparation for teaching spelling.

To consider how the results of our survey meshed with practice in all 50 states, we turned to the Survey of Professional Development for Adult Education Instructors (Tolbert, 2001). The survey found that 22 states require teacher certification in elementary, secondary, or adult education; 15 states apply sets of instructor competencies. An important finding of this survey is that more than two thirds of state adult education systems employ predominantly part-time instructors. Perhaps even more important, ". . . a majority of states reported . . . that they do not require preservice training of full-time, part-time, or volunteer instructors" (p. 9). Nine states require 10 to 20 hours of preservice training for volunteers.

Drawing on the results of our survey and the survey sponsored by the National Institute for Literacy, we infer that, at the state level, there may be little explicit consideration of spelling as an essential component in the education of ABE students. Not surprisingly, perhaps, we found that state policy reflects national guidelines. In documents containing statements of national literacy goals, we found either no mention of spelling as an outcome goal (U.S. Department of Education, 2002) or only a reference to spelling embedded in the broader goal of attention to conventions of English usage (Stein, 2000). We must conclude that, in the absence of specific policy objectives, curriculum goals, and staff development, spelling may well be a neglected skill in adult basic literacy programs today. Some support for this conclusion was obtained from those "in the trenches" at a recent conference sponsored by Pro-Literacy Worldwide (Washington, DC, November, 2003). In a session presented by Sawyer and attended by about 60 literacy tutors, teachers, trainers, and program site directors from across the country, conferees were asked if they taught spelling directly and, if so, what degree of emphasis they placed on the skill. Without exception, responses indicated that spelling, when taught, was incidental to reading instruction and was not routinely addressed in any formal way. One teacher's emphatic comment aptly summed up the comments in the room—"These students need to learn to read! They probably can spell well enough to get by!" It seems that current practice, in the case of spelling instruction in ABE classes, may well adhere to that of current policy, or the lack thereof.

A Perspective on Practice

A large proportion of ABE teachers have experience teaching in K–12 settings (Sabatini et al., 2000; Smith, Hofer, Gillespie, Solomon, & Rowe, 2003). Their approach to teaching spelling to adults may well be influenced by practices in their K–12 classes. Traynelis-Yurek and Strong (1999) surveyed 670 school districts in 41 states to gather information on spelling instruction practices. They concluded that the status of spelling in the United States is unclear. Fifty-three percent of the school districts were using a published series of spelling texts in the elementary grades. Some districts combined individualized spelling (incidental to the writing activities of each student) with direct instruction (whole class lessons specific to a particular pattern or rule), or with the sequential lessons in published spelling texts, or with developmental spelling (perhaps associated with a particular stage of development appropriate for subgroups within the class). In an Internet search of the 37 state departments of education that publish curriculum guides, Traynelis-Yurek and Strong (1999) found only four documents that mentioned a spelling guideline consistent with its use as a language convention, rooted in language process. In this context, we must assume that even those adult literacy teachers with K–6 teaching credentials may have limited experience in assessing spelling status or tailoring instruction to the special needs of adults in basic education classes. We conducted a similar search of ERIC documents to find materials prepared by state agencies that address spelling instruction in adult basic education. The Massachusetts Career Development Institute (1998) published an ABE curriculum that specifically addresses spelling. The approach is rule-governed phonics instruction. The Port of Baltimore (Janiszewski, 1994) published a workplace skills program for reading and spelling development that is a word-structure approach, supplemented with some rules for letter–sound correspondence. The Colorado State Department of Education (1991) published a handbook to prepare volunteers who tutor adults in basic skills. The spelling section advocates a "neurolinguistic" approach for students on reading levels 5–12. This approach seems to be based on the assumption that good spellers use a remembered visual image of a word followed by a kinesthetic check to see if it "feels" right. Developing visual memory is a dominant focus in this training document and, thus, it would seem to relate to a uniprocess theory suggesting that spelling is rooted in word-specific knowledge. This may be similar to the conclusions reported by Burt and Fury (2000) and Cunningham and Stanovich (1990), as discussed earlier in this chapter.

Our sampling of curricula tends to confirm, in the field of adult literacy, the findings of Traynelis-Yurek and Strong (1999) in K–12 education: Approaches to spelling instruction are mixed. Implicit in these curricula are commitments to various theories of what is required in order to spell — access to the lexicon (visual route), establishing graphophonic relationships (phonological route), or understanding the orthographic structure of words as these relate to pronunciation and meaning (morphophonemic route).

Two additional documents we reviewed were prepared by literacy providers and bring the reality of teacher–learner interactions to bear on spelling instruction. *If Only I Could Read, Write, Spell* is the product of an action research project sponsored by the Tennessee Literacy Resource Center (1994).[2] The teachers involved in this project recommended that instructional strategies begin with assessment of phonological awareness, followed by lists of words relevant to the learner as well as word sorts to strengthen letter–sound correspondences and to recognize spelling patterns as these relate to sound and meaning.

The second document, by Hager (2001), describes techniques for teaching beginning level (0 through Grade 2) adults. Drawing on 8 years of

---

[2] The study was conducted at the Center for Literacy Studies at Knoxville.

experience teaching ABE classes, Hager recommends an integrated approach wherein word analysis (visual/auditory) and spelling (auditory/visual) instruction complement each other, and the multisensory approach (seeing, saying, and tracing or writing) supports learning phonetically irregular words. This is the only source we found where a specific amount of time (20 minutes of a 3-hour session) is suggested for spelling instruction during each class meeting.

We also examined some guides for teachers that specifically address spelling instruction. We reasoned that these materials might have been used in K–12 teacher preparation programs or graduate classes, or as resources in professional development programs. Chall and Popp (1996) advocate a phonics approach. The importance of prerequisite skills— rhyming, segmenting, and blending—is noted, along with the necessity of learning a few whole words to form the foundation for learning initial consonants and spelling by analogy, then sound-to-letter spelling, and learning rules or generalizations. In contrast, Rosencrans (1998) recommends an approach that combines whole language with phonics through word sorts and other attention-focusing strategies such as word webs (showing how the meaning of different words relate). These activities bring visual, phonological, and semantic abilities to bear on the process. This approach is probably best described as balanced.

The Texas Education Agency (1996) produced a teacher's guide to spelling for Grades K–12. This guide defines spelling as a critical literacy skill acquired within a framework of five developmental stages. The importance of linking learning to read with learning to spell and write is underscored.

The Utah Outcome Based Curriculum Development Project (Utah State Office of Education, 1985) developed materials for preliteracy (refugees) and literacy (beginning and nonreader) adults. The spelling component of the literacy curriculum appears to be consistent with dual-route models of learning. Instruction is designed to develop skills for committing whole words to memory, as well as using rules to support grapheme–phoneme correspondences.

We leave this survey of current practice with two impressions: (a) Spelling instruction in ABE classes—what to teach and how to teach—is most likely left to the discretion of the teacher, and (b) Teachers are given little opportunity to specifically learn about spelling as a subject to be taught and a process to be learned. It appears that neither public policy nor practice substantially address a foundational literacy skill that has value in society.

ABE STUDENTS
WITH SPECIAL NEEDS

Adults With Learning Disabilities

The U.S. Employment and Training Administration (1991) estimated that 50% to 80% of all ABE students reading below the seventh-grade level have learning disabilities. The incidence in the entire U.S. population is estimated at 15% to 30%. The national adult literacy survey (Kirsch, Jungleblut, Jenkins, & Kolstad, 1993) reported that whereas 21% of the general population functions at the lowest literacy level (Level 1), 58% of individuals who claim a learning disability demonstrate skills at Level 1. Clearly, it is important for educators in ABE programs to recognize the special learning needs of their students with learning disabilities.

A learning disability is commonly defined as significant difficulty with learning, despite adequate opportunity to learn, in the absence of intellectual, sensory, environmental, or emotional factors that might impede learning. In K–12 programs, a significant point difference in score (referred to as the discrepancy) between intelligence and achievement has historically been used to determine if a learning disability may be present. Students in ABE classes who left the K–12 system in the United States after about 1979 might report that they were identified with a learning disability. However, information obtained at intake for ABE services can be compiled to draw inferences about a possible learning disability. For example, a student who left school in ninth or tenth grade (thus having had ample opportunity to learn), who appears to have a good oral vocabulary (which reflects an adequate level of intelligence to have profited from instruction), reports no history of significant vision, hearing, or adjustment difficulties, but reports that very poor reading or spelling ability interferes with getting a job or advancing on the job, should raise the suspicion of a possible learning disability.

Low literacy may be the product of a learning disability, which is generally understood to be a consequence of biology—the way the brain works. Dyslexia, a specific learning disability, refers to a learning difficulty that affects reading, writing, and spelling. A specific learning disability is our focus in this section. We refer readers to Corley and Taymans (2002) for a complete review of research on learning disabilities in adult education.

The National Institute for Literacy (NIFL) convened a national focus group in 1997 to consider services for all students with disabilities in

ABE programs. Several important points were made: (a) A large subset of the ABE population has one or more disabilities that can affect literacy acquisition; (b) ABE administrators and service providers lack the training necessary to meet the needs of these clients; (c) Students with learning disabilities are the most problematic with respect to the provision of appropriate educational services; and (d) Services to learning-disabled adults vary greatly from state to state (NIFL, 1997, pp. 9–10).

In a needs-assessment survey of 381 adults with learning disabilities, Hoffman et al. (1987) found that the most significant learning problems students reported involved spelling and reading. Sixty-five percent reported problems with spelling and 63% with reading. The authors noted that these two academic areas continue to inhibit adults in vocational rehabilitation programs. In this same study, memory difficulties were reported by 30% of adults with learning disabilities.

Spelling ability among students with learning disabilities is generally poorer than that of low-achieving peers who are not learning disabled (Deshler, Schumaker, Alley, Warner, & Clark, 1982). Furthermore, the magnitude of the spelling deficits increases as students move from elementary to secondary school (Poplin, Gray, Larsen, Banikowski, & Mehring, 1980). Among students with learning disabilities, spelling strategies change little over time. Bruck (1993) found that among college students with a childhood diagnosis of dyslexia, poor spelling was primarily due to failure to acquire letter–sound mappings. Furthermore, the students' use of orthographic (visual) and morphologic (word root/meaning) information was related to the level of reading and spelling skill they possessed. She concluded that extensive reading—exposure to print—was important in developing the component skills of spelling. Davis, Gregg, Coleman, Habiger, and Stennett (2002) found that college students with a childhood diagnosis of a learning disability (LD) were more dependent on phonological (auditory) coding for spelling words than non-LD peers. The LD group primarily used a letter–sound strategy. However, those with stronger orthographic knowledge were relatively more successful (Gregg, Knight, Hoy, Stennett, & Mather, 2002). As noted in our earlier consideration of normal acquisition, reading facilitates spelling, through interaction of the phonological and orthographic routes.

A specific learning disability is presumed to be the result of a core deficit that limits the ability to process phonological information (Lyon, 1995). A strong relationship has been established between phonological abilities and reading and spelling (Lundberg, Frost, & Peterson, 1988; Rhol & Tunmer, 1988; Stuart & Masterson, 1992; Treiman, 1991; Wagner

& Torgesen, 1987; Wimmer, Magringer, & Lander, 1998). The deficit in phonological processing abilities occurs in families and may be genetically transmitted. Pennington et al. (1986) examined the spelling errors of 24 adults with dyslexia, 17 of their unaffected relatives, and 17 control subjects matched by spelling age to the dyslexics. The unaffected relatives were significantly better on reading and spelling tasks but similar to those with dyslexia in terms of IQ, age, and education. Analysis of spelling errors made by each of the three groups showed that the dyslexics performed more like the younger age controls when complex phonological skills were considered, but like the unaffected adults when complex orthographic skills were considered. The researchers concluded that, among the families in this study, an inherited cognitive deficit in phonological processing was the root source of dyslexia. However, the reader is urged to heed the fact that spelling ability is learned, not inherited. In their study of spelling among more than 1,000 adults, Green and Schroeder (1992) concluded that although specific aptitudes or dispositions may affect spelling, spelling is a learned skill, not an inherent aptitude.

Learning disabilities are heterogeneous. They may affect learning differently from person to person and may vary in severity as well. For these reasons, assessment undertaken in order to detect a learning disability, as well as to estimate its specific impact on the learner, is critical for planning effective educational intervention. With such a large concentration of individuals with learning disabilities in ABE classes, it seems reasonable to use assessment of spelling ability to also infer if, and in what way, a learning disability might be limiting growth in spelling.

Kamhi and Hinton (2000), as discussed earlier, noted that poor spellers seem to follow a different developmental route than good spellers, relying primarily on visual strategies—on how a word looks —rather than on how it sounds. The authors suggested that this overreliance on only one input system might be due to limited phonological knowledge. Research cited throughout this chapter supports the importance of both the phonological (auditory) route and the orthographic (visual) route, in consort, for achieving efficient and accurate spelling.

Convincing evidence has accumulated to suggest that activities that develop phonological awareness among adults with low literacy skills result in improvement in reading and spelling (Durgunoglu, Nagy, & Hancin-Bhatt, 1993; Durgunoglu & Oney, 2002). For students who show a phonological processing deficit, whether due to biology or previous educational experiences, or lack thereof, this is a critical entry point for intervention. Phoneme discrimination, segmentation, sequencing, and blending are critical foundational skills on which phoneme–grapheme knowledge is built. The important influence of accurate pronunciation on spelling was discussed earlier. Moats (1995) carefully documented the relation between errors in the perception of sounds and errors in spelling. Sawyer, Lipa-Wade, and Kim (1999) documented these relationships as pivotal in understanding spelling performance among dyslexic students having the greatest number of grapheme–phoneme coding errors.

A review of 38 published studies of spelling interventions designed primarily for elementary school students with LD (Fulk & Stormont-Spurgin, 1995) revealed that a variety of approaches can yield positive results. The significant caveat was that the instruction be systematic (carefully sequenced). Fulk and Stormont-Spurgin make two other points: (a) The underlying cognitive issues related to poor spelling—phonological awareness, language, memory, visual-motor processes, or inefficient study strategies—must be addressed along with instruction that adheres to a developmental sequence, and (b) Students with LD are not likely to spontaneously acquire spelling skill from exposure to literature or invented spelling approaches in the naturalistic framework of whole-language instruction (p. 509). A similar review of 27 published studies led to the conclusion that structured intervention was essential for growth in spelling (McNaughton, Hughes, & Clark, 1994).

Graham (1999) conducted an extensive review of research on handwriting and spelling instruction for students with LD. He approached this review from the position that both explicit, systematic instruction and incidental learning approaches are essential in order to maximize the development of spelling in students with LD. Studies of spelling instruction were discussed within 10 categories related to word selection, instruction and practice, knowledge of the spelling system, and application and use of technology. Although Graham found support for this balanced approach in the research, he also stressed the need for further empirical research.

Use of computer-assisted spelling programs is growing in ABE settings. Fulk and Stormont-Spurgin (1995) reviewed nine studies that addressed this approach with LD students. Only three studies reported effects on spelling achievement, and only one of these reported significant achievement gains. However, it was suggested that these gains might be attributed to the novelty of using computers. Eight studies reported the positive effects of these programs on developing positive attitudes and increasing on-task practice rates. The programs provided models of correct spelling when errors were made and opportunities to imitate such models (p. 499). Fulk and Stormont-Spurgin note that the time teachers need to spend learning how these programs work, organizing them for delivery, and monitoring student progress is an important consideration in selecting computer-assisted spelling instruction. This poses a significant limitation in ABE programs staffed primarily by part-time teachers.

MacArthur (1999) reviewed research on the utility of computer tools (i.e., spell checkers in word-processing programs) in supporting the mechanics of writing. He cautions that all methods involved with getting words into print tap working memory capacity and, for some, using a computer tool may be more burdensome than writing by hand. In his review of research on spell checkers, MacArthur identifies two major problems of spell checkers for students with LD: failure to flag a misspelling if it is another real word, and failure to reliably suggest the correct spelling. In a comparison of 10 spell checkers, correct spellings were suggested for only 44% to 66% of misspelled words identified. For severely misspelled words, the rate of correct suggestions dropped to 16% to 41%. Although computer-assisted instruction and computer tools for writing are useful, there are significant limitations that bear on their potential in ABE classes with LD students.

Adults With Hearing Impairments

The National Adult Literacy Survey (Kirsch et al., 1993) found that 36% of adults who claim hearing difficulties function at the lowest level of literacy skill (Level 1). We found no statistics on the percentage of adults with hearing impairments attending ABE classes. Although it is likely that the majority of adults in these classes are not completely deaf, we believe that it will be useful for adult literacy providers to recognize the special challenges to spelling that hearing impairments pose.

Recent reports indicate that less than half of 18-year-old deaf students leaving high school have reached a fifth-grade level of reading and writing competence, and more than 30% of those leaving school are functionally illiterate (skills equal to NALS literacy Levels 1 or 2; Marschark, 2001). Establishing the link between spoken and written language is not easy for those who cannot readily access spoken language. Auditory discrimination of some or many sounds will be difficult for those students in ABE with hearing impairments and will affect their ability to establish letter–sound correspondences.

Phonological abilities among the deaf develop out of a combination of articulation cues, speech reading, finger spelling, residual hearing, and exposure to writing, but no one of these, independent of the others, is sufficient (Marschark, 2001). This suggests that working on spelling with the hard-of-hearing in ABE classes requires focused attention to the visual-motor aspects of speech—to feel in the mouth and see in a mirror or on the mouth of another how confusing or indistinguishable sounds are formed and how each relates to a letter or a spelling pattern. Burt and Shrubsole (2000) found that, among college students, the most significant difference between good and poor spellers was their ability to accurately pronounce unfamiliar words. Poor spellers produced inaccurate pronunciations for printed nonsense words, suggesting weakness in phonological coding.

The deaf rely heavily on visual language. American Sign Language, which involves a kind of logographic representation for concepts and words, is reportedly easier for deaf children to learn and to use than any other form of English (Baker & Baker, 1997; Caccamise, Ayres, Finch, & Mitchell, 1997; Finnegan, 1992). Similarly, young deaf children focus on the meaning of whole words in text to the detriment of the meaning of phrases and sentences (Marschark, 2001). However, Gaustad, Kelly, Payne, and Lylak (2002) found that deaf college students do apply a visual segmentation of whole words that reflects knowledge of the morphological structure at a skill level that is about equal to that of hearing middle-school students. These students had learned to use the orthographic system to support comprehension. Aaron, Wilczynski, and Keetay (1998), in their investigations of spelling among deaf students, also found evidence of visual segmentation. In their study, deaf students' spelling of non-words projected briefly onto a screen showed dependence on memory for commonly appearing intraword letter patterns (letter strings that appear frequently in English words, e.g., *"kram"*), rather than on pure visual memory for any letter string presented (letter combinations not found in real English words, e.g., *"rmka"*). More errors were made in reproducing nonwords built from strings of letters not found in English.

For teachers of hard-of-hearing adults, the studies we have referenced suggest the need to approach literacy instruction that addresses, simultaneously, the learning of whole words, letter–sound correspondences, spelling patterns, and structural units of meaning. In a 4-year study of how deaf children learn to spell, in a language-rich environment that applied a process approach to writing, Mayer and Moskos (1998) found that the children progressed through the same sequence of stages as hearing children—scribble, random strings of letters, invented spelling, conventional spelling. We might expect hard-of-hearing adults to also move through stages as they acquire knowledge of the graphophonic and orthographic systems and learn to apply this knowledge in personally meaningful written communication. Critical to supporting this process, however, will be individual assessment to identify what is already known and is available to serve as a beginning point for instruction.

English for Speakers of Other Languages

The number of adults enrolled in ESOL classes is large and growing rapidly (M. Burt, Peyton, & Adams, 2002). In 2001, 42% of adults enrolled in state-administered, federally funded programs were enrolled in ESOL classes. In addition, English-language learners are served in a variety of other programs, including ABE, adult secondary education, community-based, and volunteer programs for which enrollment rates were not available. In their review of available research over 20 years, Burt et al. (2002) summarized findings as follows: (a) The degree of literacy in the first language (L1) significantly affects ability to acquire a second (L2); and (b) Age; motivation; educational and sociocultural background; home, work, instructional environment; and presence or absence of a learning disability also affect success. Younger, more advantaged students, who are motivated to achieve at work or in the community and have some level of literacy in L1, acquire L2 literacy skills with greater ease. M. Burt et al. (2002) list five types of L1 literacy that describe the L2 English learner: preliterate, nonliterate, semiliterate, non-Roman alphabet literate, and literate in another Roman alphabet. The greater the degree of L1 literacy (last two types), the greater the potential to transfer literacy concepts and skills to L2 task demands (M. Burt et al., 2002, pp. 2–4).

Meschyan and Hernandez (2002) studied Spanish-speaking college students who were learning English. They found that decoding ability in L1 predicted decoding skill in L2 (U.S. Department of Human Services, 1985, in National Center for ESL Literacy Education, 2003). ESOL learners with skills classed within the first three types of L1 literacy mentioned earlier pose the greatest challenge to spelling instruction in ABE classes because they have little knowledge about any writing system to draw on.

It is possible that proficient L2 users could offer informative insights into the processes they apply when spelling, and these insights might inform literacy instruction. Cook (1997) compared the spelling of 375 adult L2 users of English (in the United Kingdom) with 1,492 L1 native speakers, both children and adults, in order to determine if L2 users applied both direct access (visual) and letter–sound (phonological) strategies, or if they would show a preference for the prominent route associated with L1 (e.g., Japanese = characters that represent syllables or words but not speech sounds; Spanish = letters that map directly onto speech sounds). Cook found that the phonological route was dominant, regardless of L1. A preponderance of L2 errors involved inappropriate letter–sound correspondences, some of which could be attributed to variation in pronunciation. For example, a native speaker of Japanese, which does not contain the spoken representation for /l/ might, initially, code that sound with a /w/ when spelling English words. Accurate pronunciation does play a role in achieving accurate L2 spelling.

Durgunoglu et al. (1993) found a cross-language transfer (Spanish to English) of phonological awareness that affected word reading in L2, as well as evidence of the impact of phonological awareness among very low-literacy adults learning to read and spell in their native (Turkish) language (Durgunoglu & Oney, 2002). These studies provide additional support for the idea that phonological awareness is a foundational skill that supports learning to decode and spell in alphabetic languages and this awareness is facilitative for children and adult learners.

Tompkins, Abramson, and Pritchard (1999) studied the acquisition of spelling among ESOL students in Grades 3 and 4, as compared to native English-speaking peers. Students in the study came from five linguistic backgrounds and attended school in two different neighborhoods—low income, ethnically diverse; affluent, upper-middle class. The researchers took spelling productions from classroom journals and classified them according to five developmental stages. They then analyzed and described the errors. Results showed that these L2 students progressed through the same sequence of developmental stages as L1 users and that no difference in development could be attributed to native language influences except that English learners tended to omit inflectional endings. (Such omissions are often apparent in the oral language of L2 users.) Additionally, this study identified significant differences in development that distinguished students in the low-income school from those in the affluent school, where spellings were found to be more conventional. This was true for L1 and L2 students. The authors cite the body of literature on the relationship between socioeconomic status and literacy development as a possible explanation.

It is important to remember that adults with learning disabilities are also enrolled in ESOL classes. A language-based learning disability affects learning in all languages but may be less apparent in languages where letter–sound associations are regular (Paulesu et al., 2001). Among Japanese children, for example, teachers report that literacy learning disabilities first become apparent when students begin to learn English, at about fifth grade (Sawyer, 1995, consulting in Fukushima, Japan). Researchers who work with learning disabled L2 learners suggest that multisensory learning strategies (Sparks, Ganshow, Kenneweg, & Miller, 1991) and structure (Schwarz & Burt, 1995) are critical. The need for targeted assessment to determine the appropriate entry point is also emphasized (Holt, 1995).

IMPLICATIONS FOR PRACTICE

In our informal survey of state program directors, discussed earlier, one response to our question regarding the existence of a state policy or suggested curriculum for the teaching of spelling in ABE classes was, "No, we have no policy regarding teaching spelling to adults and we have no curriculum. I found your request interesting, however, because I guess I never thought much about spelling."

The work discussed in this chapter suggests that spelling should be a specific component of instruction in ABE classes and that this instruction will be most effective if:

• Spelling acquisition is understood as a developmental process that relies on the integration of visual and auditory systems for learning.

• Reading and spelling skill are understood as supportive of each other; decoding and spelling are taught in ways that reveal the morphophonemic nature of the English orthography.

• Phonological awareness is recognized as essential for internalizing the alphabetic principle (i.e., letters map onto speech sounds).

• Formal and informal assessment of students' knowledge and skills— phonological awareness, letter–sound correspondences, spelling patterns—precedes and informs instructional planning.

• Students are taught strategies that support learning whole-word units, letter–sound mappings, and spelling patterns as these relate to pronunciation and meaning.

• The focus of instruction is matched to the concepts about spelling that each student has sufficient background knowledge to learn (i.e., it is matched to the zone of proximal development).

In the special case of adults with a specific learning disability, effective instruction must be explicit, structured, sequential, and systematic. Multisensory techniques can focus attention, support memory, and facilitate accuracy.

In the case of ESOL adults, in order to be effective, instruction should begin at whatever stage the student is currently in. This requires determining the student's level of L1 literacy, assessing what the student knows about the English alphabet and print conventions, and providing instruction that is structured, sequential, and repetitive.

Although direct instruction is crucial when working with adults, learning is likely to be most efficient when the tasks are personally meaningful and instruction encourages students to apply emerging skills and concepts to activities that are integral to their daily lives—writing a get-well message, a note to a child's teacher, or notes related to job demands. Fagan (1988) engaged 50 low-literate adults in structured interviews to ascertain their understanding about reading and writing. On the whole, "writing" was understood as handwriting, not as communication. The adults' past experiences with instruction instilled an expectation that improvement in writing would require working on ". . . all the big and small letters, apostrophes, dots, and all that" (Fagan, 1988, p. 56) and sounding out words for reading. Fagan interpreted the perceptions of these adults as counterproductive to goals for becoming readers and writers. Word reading and spelling will be more successful if instruction is closely aligned with literacy tasks that the students recognize as relevant to their own lives.

IMPLICATIONS FOR FURTHER RESEARCH

Insights into the acquisition of spelling in the ABE population rest primarily on studies comparing the errors of adults to those of normally developing children. Knowing that relatively poor adult spellers exhibit about the same degree of knowledge, or lack thereof, as students in the elementary grades does not help us determine how they will respond to instruction or what approach to instruction will be most effective. Our review of research suggests the need for longitudinal studies of spelling among the ABE population, as well as carefully designed experimental studies that assess the efficacy of different instructional methods with adults at varying literacy levels. In addition, our review of current practice suggests the need to survey ABE administrators at the local level, across the country, to gain a better understanding of how the need for spelling instruction is being addressed.

IMPLICATIONS FOR PUBLIC POLICY

Our survey of state directors, our review of documents related to statements of national literacy goals (U.S. Department of Education, 2002), and our review of the *Survey of Professional Development for Adult Literacy Instructors,* State Policy Update (Tolbert, 2001) suggests that spelling is a neglected component in guidelines for ABE programs, for training literacy providers, and for the allocation of dollars for instructional resources in ABE programs. In preparing this chapter, we have concluded that state guidelines for developing spelling instruction are needed in order to enhance educational outcomes for this population. Furthermore, states need to provide high-quality professional development to ensure that ABE teachers have the knowledge and skills necessary to provide effective spelling instruction.

Finally, it appears that national policy for literacy development has also neglected the role of spelling within the complex arena of literacy skill acquisition. Spelling is given only passing reference in *Equipped for the Future, Content Standards* (National Institute for ESL Literacy Education, 2003) and in *Bridges to Practice* (National Institute for Literacy, 1999). Whether this is the result of a conscious decision or an oversight is not immediately apparent. However, we have documented, through this review of research, that competent spelling influences an individual's potential to get and keep a job and to participate fully in one's family and community. Poor spelling reflects negatively on the speller—people question his or her attitude and even intelligence. Adult poor spellers recognize that this limitation is a barrier to full, effective participation in various aspects of life. Gaining spelling skill is no less important to students in ABE classes than acquiring skill in reading and math. It is vitally important that policymakers, program directors, and ABE teachers give immediate and careful consideration to providing specific and planned, as opposed to incidental, instruction in spelling. Discussion and clarification of the issues associated with spelling in adult basic education, led by those who interpret and shape national literacy policy, would benefit the field and offer much needed leadership for the states.

REFERENCES

Aaron, P. G., Wilczynski, S., & Keetay, V. (1998). The anatomy of word-specific memory. In C. Hulme & R. M. Joshi (Eds.), *Reading and spelling development and disorders* (pp. 405–419). Mahwah, NJ: Lawrence Erlbaum Associates.

Baker, S., & Baker, K. (1997). Educating children who are deaf or hard of hearing: Bi-lingual, bi-cultural education. Reston, VA: ERIC Clearinghouse on Disabilities and Gifted Education. (ERIC Document Reproduction Service No. ED414671)

Balmuth, M. (1982). *The roots of phonics: A historical perspective.* Baltimore, MD: York Press.

Bear, D. R., Templeton, S., Invernizzi, M., & Johnston, F. (2000). *Words their way: Word study for phonics, vocabulary, and spelling instruction* (2nd ed.). Upper Saddle River, NJ: Prentice-Hall.

Bear, D. R., Truex, P., & Barone, D. (1989). In search of meaningful diagnosis: Spelling-by-stage assessment of literacy proficiency. *Adult Literacy and Basic Education, 13*(3), 165–185.

Bourassa, D. C., & Treiman, R. (2001). Spelling development and disability: The importance of linguistic factors. *Language, Speech, and Hearing Services in Schools, 32,* 172–181.

Bruck, M. (1993, Summer). Component spelling skills of college students with childhood diagnosis of dyslexia. *Learning Disability Quarterly, 16,* 171–184.

Burt, J. S., & Fury, M. B. (2000). Spelling in adults: The role of reading skills and experience. *Reading & Writing: An Interdisciplinary Journal, 13,* 1–30.

Burt, J. S., & Shrubsole, C. S. (2000). Processing of phonological representations and adult spelling proficiency. *American Journal of Psychology, 52*(2), 100–109.

Burt, M., Peyton, J. K., & Adams, R. (2002). *Reading and adult English language learners: A review of the research.* Washington, DC: National Center for ESL Literacy Education & Center for Applied Linguistics.

Butyniec-Thomas, J., & Woloshyn, V. E. (1997). The effects of explicit-strategy and whole language instruction on students' spelling ability. *The Journal of Experimental Education, 65*(4), 293–302.

Caccamise, F., Ayres, R., Finch, K., & Mitchell, M. (1997). Signs and manual communication systems. *American Annuals of the Deaf, 142*(3), 90–105.

Chall, J. S., & Popp, H. M. (1996). *Teaching and accessing phonics, a guide for teachers.* Cambridge, MA: Educators Publishing Service, Inc.

Chomsky, N. (1968). *Language and mind.* New York: Harcourt, Brace, Jovanovich.

Chomsky, N., & Halle, M. (1968). *The sound pattern of English.* New York: Harper & Row.

Colorado State Department of Education (1991). *Training the trainer: Helping tutors teach adults to read and write.* Denver, CO: Office of Adult Education. (ERIC Document Reproduction Service ED353460)

Coltheart, M. (1978). Lexical access in simple reading tasks. In G. Underwood (Ed.), *Strategies of information processing* (pp. 151–216). New York: Academic Press.

Cook, V. J. (1997). L2 users and English spelling. *Journal of Multilingual and Multicultural Development, 18*(6), 474–488.

Corley, M. A., & Taymans, J. M. (2002). Adults with learning disabilities: A review of the literature. In J. Comings, B. Garner, & C. Smith (Eds.), *Annual review of adult learning and literacy* (Vol. 3, pp. 44–83). San Francisco, CA: Jossey-Bass.

Crowder, R. G., & Wagner, R. K. (1992). *The psychology of reading: An introduction* (2nd ed.). New York: Oxford University Press.

Cunningham, A., & Stanovich, K. (1990). Assessing print exposure and orthographic processing skill in children: A quick measure of reading. *Journal of Educational Psychology, 82* (4), 733–740.

Davis, J. M., Gregg, N., Coleman, C., Habiger, M., & Stennett, R. (2002, November). *Diagnostic dilemmas in assessing older adolescents and young adults for learning disabilities: Changes in the discrepancy between I.Q., and achievement.* Paper presented at the annual meeting of the International Dyslexia Association, Atlanta, GA.

Deshler, D. D., Schumaker, J. B., Alley, G. R., Warner, M. M., & Clark, F. L. (1982). Learning disabilities in adolescent and young adult populations: Research implications. *Focus on Exceptional Children, 15,* 1–12.

Dietrich, J. A., & Brady, S. A. (2001). Phonological representations of adult poor readers: An investigation of specificity and stability. *Applied Psycholinguistics, 22,* 383–418.

Durgunoglu, A. Y., Nagy, W. E., & Hancin-Bhatt, B. J. (1993). Cross-language transfer of phonological awareness. *Journal of Educational Psychology, 85,* 453–465.

Durgunoglu, A. Y., & Oney, B. (2002). Phonological awareness in literacy acquisition: It's not only for children. *Scientific Studies of Reading, 6*(3), 245–266.

Ehri, L. (1991). Development of the ability to read words. In R. Barr, M. Kamil, P. Mosenthal, & P. D. Pearson (Eds.), *The handbook of reading research* (Vol. 2, pp. 383–417). New York: Longman.

Ehri, L. (1994). Development of the ability to read words: Update. In R. Ruddell, M. Ruddell, & H. Singer (Eds.), *Theoretical models and processes of reading* (4th ed., pp. 323–358). Newark, DE: International Reading Association.

Ehri, L. (2000). Learning to read and learning to spell: Two sides of a coin. *Topics on Language Disorders, 20*(3), 19–36.

Ehri, L. C., & Wilce, L. (1987). Does learning to spell help beginners learn to read words? *Reading Research Quarterly, 22,* 47–65.

Fagan, W. T. (1988). Concepts of reading and writing among low-literate adults. *Reading, Research, and Instruction, 27*(4), 47–60.

Finnegan, M. (1992). Bilingual, bicultural education. *The Endeavor, 3,* 1–8, American Society for Deaf Children.

Fischer, F. W., Shankweiler, D., & Liberman, I. Y. (1985). Spelling proficiency and sensitivity to word structure. *Journal of Memory & Language, 24,* 423–441.

Fresch, M. J. (2001). Journal entries as a window on spelling knowledge. *The Reading Teacher, 54*(5), 500–513.

Frith, U. (1980). Unexpected spelling problems. In U. Frith (Ed.), *Cognitive processes in spelling* (pp. 495–516). London: Academic Press.

Frith, U. (1985). Beneath the surface of developmental dyslexia. In K. Patterson, J. Marshall, & M. Colthart (Eds.), *Surface Dyslexia* (pp. 301–330). London: Lawrence Erlbaum Associates.

Fulk, B. M, & Stormont-Spurgin, M. (1995). Spelling interventions for students with disabilities: A review. *The Journal of Special Education, 28*(4), 488–513.

Ganske, K. (2000). *Word journeys: Assessment-guided phonics, spelling, and vocabulary instruction.* New York: Guilford Press.

Gaustad, M. G., Kelly, R. R., Payne, J. A., & Lylak, E. (Winter, 2002). Comparing the morphological knowledge of hearing and deaf students. *NTID Research Bulletin, 7*(1), 1–5.

Gentry, J. R. (1981). Learning to spell developmentally. *The Reading Teacher, 34*(4), 378–381.

Gerber, M. M., & Hall, R. J. (1987). Information processing approaches to studying spelling deficiencies. *Journal of Learning Disabilities, 20,* 34–42.

Goswami, U. (1988). Orthographic analogies and reading development. *Quarterly Journal of Experimental Psychology, 40A,* 239–268.

Graham, S. (1999, Spring). Handwriting and spelling instruction for students with learning disabilities: A review. *Learning Disability Quarterly, 22,* 78–97.

Graham, S. (2000). Should the natural learning approach replace spelling instruction? *Journal of Educational Psychology, 92*(2), 235–247.

Green, K. E., & Schroeder, D. H. (1992). *The spelling project technical report.* Chicago, IL: Johnson O'Connor Research Foundation. (ERIC Document Reproduction Service No. 360362)

Greenberg, D., Ehri, L., & Perin, D. (1997). Are word-reading processes the same or different in adult literacy students and third–fifth graders matched for reading level? *Journal of Educational Psychology, 89*(2), 262–275.

Gregg, N., Knight, D., Hoy, S., Stennett, R., & Mather, N. (2002, November). *Phonological and orthographic coding in the decoding & spelling of college students with and without learning disabilities.* Paper presented at the annual meeting of the International Dyslexia Association, Atlanta, GA.

Hager, A. (2001, August). Techniques for teaching beginning-level reading to adults. *Focus on Basics, 5* (A). Retrieved June 3, 2003, from http://www.ncsall.net/?id=280.

Henderson, E. (1985). *Teaching spelling.* Boston: Houghton Mifflin.

Hodges, R. E. (1977). In Adam's fall: A brief history of spelling instruction in the United States. In H. A. Robinson (Ed.), *Reading and writing instruction in the United States: Historical trends* (pp. 1–16). Newark, DE: International Reading Association.

Hoffman, J. F., Sheldon, K. L., Minskoff, E. H., Sautter, S. W., Steidle, E. F., Baker, D. P. et al. (1987). Needs of learning disabled adults. *Journal of Learning Disabilities, 20*(1), 43–52.

Holmes, V. M., & Carruthers, J. (1998). The relation between reading and spelling in skilled adult readers. *Journal of Memory and Language, 39,* 264–289.

Holmes, V. M., & Ng, E. (1993). Word-specific knowledge, word-recognition strategies, and spelling ability. *Journal of Memory and Language, 32,* 230–257.

Holt, G. M. (1995). *Teaching low-level adult ESL learners.* Washington, DC: ERIC Clearinghouse for ESL Literacy Education. (ERIC Document Reproduction Service No. ED379965)

International Multisensory Structured Language Education Council. (1995). *Clinical studies of multisensory structured language education.* Salem, OR: Author.

Janiszewski, K. (1994). *Spelling & vocabulary improvement: The Port of Baltimore workplace skills development project.* Washington, DC: Office of Vocational and Adult Education. (ERIC Document Reproduction Service ED 381656)

Kamhi, A. G., & Hinton, L. N. (2000). Explaining individual differences in spelling ability. *Topics on Language Disorders, 20*(3), 37–49.

Kirsch, I., Jungeblut, A., Jenkins, L., & Kolstad, A. (1993). *Adult literacy in America.* National Center for Education Statistics. Washington, DC: U.S. Department of Education.

Kitz, W. R., & Nash, R. T. (1992). Testing the effectiveness of the project success summer program for adult dyslexics. *Annals of Dyslexia, 42,* 3–24.

Kriener, D. S., Schnakenberg, S. D., Green, A. G., Costello, M. J., & McClin, A. F. (2002). Effects of spelling errors on the perception of writers. *Journal of General Psychology, 129,* 5–18.

Lennox, C., & Siegel, L. S. (1996). The development of phonological rules and visual strategies in average and poor spellers. *Journal of Experimental Child Psychology, 62,* 60–83.

Leong, C. K. (1998). Strategies used by 9-to-12-year-old children in written spelling. In

C. Hulme & R. M. Joshi (Eds.), *Reading and spelling: Development and disorders* (pp. 421–432). Mahwah, NJ: Lawrence Erlbaum Associates.

Lundberg, I., Frost, J., & Petersen, O. P. (1988). Effects of an extensive program for stimulating phonological awareness in school children. *Reading Research Quarterly, 23,* 263–284.

Lyon, G. R. (1995). Toward a definition of dyslexia. *Annals of Dyslexia, 45,* 3–27.

MacArthur, C. A. (1999). Overcoming barriers to writing: Computer support for basic writing skills. *Reading & Writing Quarterly, 15,* 169–192.

Marschark, M. (2001). *Language development in children who are deaf: A research synthesis.* Alexandria, VA: National Association of State Directors of Special Education.

Massachusetts Career Development Institute. (1998). *Adult basic education curriculum.* Washington, DC: National Workplace Literacy Program. (ERIC Document Reproduction Service No. ED424434)

Mayer, C., & Moskos, E. (1998). Deaf children learning to spell. *Research in the Teaching of English, 33,* 158–180.

McNaughton, D., Hughes, C. A., & Clark, K. (1994, Summer). Spelling instruction for students with learning disabilities: Implications for research and practice. *Learning Disability Quarterly, 17,* 169–185.

Meschyan, G., & Hernandez, A. (2002). Is native-language decoding skill related to second-language learning? *Journal of Educational Psychology, 94*(1), 14–22.

Moats, L. C. (1995). *Spelling: Development, disabilities, and instruction.* Baltimore, MD: York Press.

Nation, K., & Hulme, C. (1998). The role of analogy in early spelling development. In C. Hulme & R. M. Joshi (Eds.), *Reading and spelling development and disorders* (pp. 433–445). Mahwah, NJ: Lawrence Erlbaum Associates.

National Center for ESL Literacy Education (2003). *Adult English language instruction in the 21st century.* Washington, DC: Center for Applied Linguistics.

National Institute for Literacy. (1997). *Disability and literacy: How disabilities are addressed in adult basic education: Findings of a national focus group.* Washington, DC: Office of Adult and Vocational Education.

National Institute for Literacy. (1999). *Bridges to practice.* Washington, DC: National Adult Literacy and Learning Disabilities Center.

National Reading Panel Report. (1998). *Teaching children to read.* Washington, DC: National Academy Press.

Paulesu, E., Demonet, J. F., Fazio, F., McCrory, E., Chanoine, V., & Brunswick, N. (2001). Dyslexia: Cultural diversity and biological unity. *Science, 291,* 2165–2167.

Pennington, B. F., McCabe, L. L., Smith, S. D., Lefly, D. L., Bookman, M. O., Kimberling, W. et al. (1986). Spelling errors in adults with a form of familial dyslexia. *Child Development, 57,* 1001–1013.

Perfetti, C. A., & Marron, M.A. (1995). *Learning to read: Literacy acquisition by children and adults.* Philadelphia, PA: National Center on Adult Literacy.

Poplin, M. S., Gray, R., Larsen, S., Banikowski, A., & Mehring, T. (1980). A comparison of components of written expression abilities in learning disabled and non-learning disabled students at three grade levels. *Learning Disability Quarterly, 3,* 46–55.

Post, Y. (2000). *Patterns of global, vowel, and consonant spelling development in adult literacy students.* Houston, TX: Neuhaus Education Center. Retrieved June 3, 2003, from http://www.neuhaus.org/research.htm.

Read, C. (1975). *Children's categorization of speech sounds in English.* Urbana, IL: National Council of Teachers of English. (NCTE Research Report No. 17)

Read, C., & Ruyter, L. (1985). Reading and spelling skills in adults of low literacy. *Reading and Special Education, 6*(6), 43–52.

Rhol, M., & Tunmer, W. E. (1988). Phonemic segmentation skill and spelling acquisition. *Applied Linguistics, 9,* 335–350.

Rosencrans, G. (1998). *Teaching children how to spell, not what to spell.* Newark, DE: International Reading Association.

Sabatini, J. P., Daniels, M., Ginsburg, L., Limeul, K., Russell, M., & Stites, R. (2000). *Teacher perspectives on the adult education profession: National survey findings about an emerging profession* (Technical Report 00-02). Philadelphia: National Center on Adult Literacy.

Sawyer, D. J. (1991). Whole language in context: Insights into the current great debate. *Topics on Language Disorders, 11*(3), 1–13.

Sawyer, D. J., Lipa-Wade, S., & Kim, J. K. (1999). Spelling errors as a window on variations in phonological deficits among students with dyslexia. *Annals of Dyslexia, 49,* 137–159.

Schramm, R. M., & Dortch, R. N. (1991, Sept.). An analysis of effective resume content, format, and appearance based on college recruiter perceptions. *The Bulletin,* 18–23.

Schwarz, R., & Burt, M. (1995). *ESL instruction for learning disabled adults.* Washington, DC: ERIC Clearinghouse for ESL Literacy Education. (ERIC Document Reproduction Service No. ED379966)

Scott, C. M. (2000). Principles and methods of spelling instruction: Applications for poor spellers. *Topics on Language Disorders, 20*(3), 66–82.

Seidenberg, M. S., & McClelland, J. L. (1989). A distributed developmental model of word recognition and naming. *Psychological Review, 96,* 523–568.

Share, D. L., Jorm, A. F., MacLean, R., & Matthews, R. (1984). Sources of individual differences in reading acquisition. *Journal of Educational Psychology, 76,* 1309–1324.

Simpson, S. B., Swanson, J. M., & Kunkel, K. (1992). The impact of an intensive multisensory reading program on a population of learning-disabled delinquents. *Annals of Dyslexia 42,* 54–66.

Smith, C., Hofer, J., Gillespie, M., Solomon, M., & Rowe, K. (2003). *How teachers change: A study of professional development in adult education.* Report 25. Boston, MA: National Center for the Study of Adult Learning and Literacy.

Sparks, R., Ganshow, L., Kenneweg, S., & Miller, K. N. (1991). Use of an Orton-Gillingham approach to teach a foreign language to dyslexic/learning-disabled students: Explicit teaching of phonology in a second language. *Annals of Dyslexia, 41,* 96–118.

Sparks, R., Ganshow, L., Pholman, J., Skinner, S., & Artzer, M. (1992). The effects of multisensory structured language instruction on native language and foreign language aptitude skills of at-risk high school foreign language learners. *Annals of Dyslexia, 42,* 25–53.

Stein, S. (2000). *Equipped for the future, content standards.* Washington, DC: National Institute for Literacy.

Strickland, D. (1998). *Teaching phonics today: A primer for educators.* Newark, DE: International Reading Association.

Stuart, M., & Masterson, J. (1992). Patterns of reading and spelling in 10-year-old children related to prereading phonological abilities. *Academic Press, 54,* 168–187.

Templeton, S. (2002). Spelling, logical, learnable—and critical. *ASHA Leader, 7*(3), 4–7.

Templeton, S., & Morris, D. (2000). Spelling. In M. L. Kamil, P. B. Mosenthal, P. D. Pearson, & R. Barr (Eds.), *Handbook of reading research* (Vol. 3, pp. 525–543). Mahwah, NJ: Lawrence Erlbaum Associates.

Tennessee Literacy Resource Center. (1994). *If only I could read, write, spell.* Knoxville, TN: University of Tennessee Center for Literacy.

Texas Education Agency. (1996). *How do you spell . . . ? A teacher's guide to spelling instruction.* Austin, TX: ERIC Clearinghouse on Disabilities and Gifted Education. (ERIC Document Reproduction Service No. ED395296)

Tolbert, M. (2001). *Professional development for adult education instructors: State policy update.* Washington, DC: National Institute for Literacy.

Tompkins, G. E. (2002). Struggling readers are struggling writers, too. *Reading & Writing Quarterly, 18,* 175–193.

Tompkins, G., E., Abramson, S., & Pritchard, R. H. (1999). A multilingual perspective on spelling development in third and fourth grades. *Multicultural Education, 6*(3), 12–18.

Traynelis-Yurek, E., & Strong, M. W. (1999). Spelling practices in school districts and regions across the United States and state spelling standards. *Reading Horizons, 39*(4), 279–294.

Treiman, R. (1991). Phonological awareness and its roles in learning to read and spell. In D. J. Sawyer & B. Fox (Eds.), *Phonological awareness in reading: The evolution of current perspectives* (pp. 159–190). New York: Springer-Verlag.

U.S. Department of Education. (2002). *Strategic Plan for 2002–2007.* Washington, DC: U.S. Government Printing Office.

U.S. Employment and Training Administration. (1991). *The learning disabled in employment and training programs* (Research and Evaluation Series 91-E). Washington, DC: U.S. Department of Labor.

Utah State Office of Education. (1985). *Outcome-based curriculum development project.* Provo, Utah: ERIC Clearinghouse. (ERIC Document Reproduction Service No. ED2900000)

Van Orden, G. C., Bosman, A. M. T., Goldinger, S. D., & Farrar, W. T. (1997). A recurrent network account of reading, spelling, and dyslexia. In J. W. Donahoe & V. P. Dorsel (Eds.), *Neural-networks models of cognition* (pp. 522–538). Amsterdam: Elsevier Science.

Viise, N. M. (1995). A study of the spelling development of adult literacy learners compared with that of classroom children. *Journal of Literacy Research, 28,* 561–587.

Vygotsky, L. S. (1962). *Thought and language.* Cambridge, MA: MIT Press.

Wagner, R. K., & Barker, T. A. (1994). The development of orthographic processing ability. In V. Berninger (Ed.), *The varieties of orthographic knowledge* (Vol. I, pp. 243–276). Dordrecht, The Netherlands: Kluwer Academic Publishers.

Wagner, R., & Torgesen, J. (1987). The nature of phonological processing and its causal role in the acquisition of reading skills. *Psychological Bulletin, 101,* 192–212.

Weekes, B. S. (1994). Spelling skills of lexical readers. *British Journal of Psychology, 85*(2), 245–258.

Wilson, B. A. (1998). Matching student needs to instruction. In S. A. Vogel & S. Reder (Eds.), *Learning disabilities, literacy, and adult education* (pp. 213–235). Baltimore, MD: Paul H. Brookes.

Wimmer, H., Magringer, H., & Lander, K. (1998). Poor reading: A deficit in skill automati-
zation or a phonological deficit? *Scientific Studies of Reading, 2*(4), 321–340.
Worthy, J., & Viise, N. M. (1996). Morphological, phonological, and orthographic differences between the spelling of normally achieving children and basic literacy adults.
Reading and Writing, 8, 139–159.

5

Issues in Teaching Speaking Skills to Adult ESOL Learners

Kathleen M. Bailey

Teaching ESL to adults means being awed every day as we witness the tenacity and perseverance of immigrants carving out better lives for themselves and their families.

—Spelleri, 2002

INTRODUCTION

The immigrants Spelleri is referring to in that quote need to acquire a wide range of skills and knowledge to achieve a better life. Chief among those skills is the ability to speak English well. This chapter addresses speaking instruction for nonacademic adult ESOL (English for speakers of other languages) learners in the United States. By nonacademic ESOL learners I mean people who are learning English, but not primarily to obtain a postsecondary degree at a college or university. Adult learners of English in the United States include refugees, documented and undocumented immigrants, and permanent residents.[1] Such learners may be found in adult schools, community college programs, community-based programs (e.g., at libraries and churches), on-the-job training courses, and some university extension programs.

These adult ESOL learners may reside in the United States permanently, or in some cases for indefinite but long periods of time (in contrast to international university students who are typically expected to return to their home countries). Also included here are the adult children of these immigrants and refugees—children who arrived in the United States late enough in life that their own spoken English is noticeably nonnative and not their dominant language.[2]

The vast majority of second-language acquisition research has been done with elementary and secondary school children or with university-based adult learners with generally high levels of proficiency and academic goals for improving their English. These groups are quite different from adult ESOL learners (e.g., in their use of English on a daily basis, or in terms of types and amount of exposure to English), so findings about their learning cannot readily be generalized to the population of interest here. However, the existing studies must serve as a foundation until research specifically related to nonacademic adult ESOL learners is available.

It is important that four key groups understand the issues related to and challenges faced by adults lacking English-speaking skills. These groups include (a) policymakers who influence the design, funding, and evaluation of adult ESOL programs; (b) researchers who investigate the success of adult education programs; (c) educators who prepare teachers to work with adult ESOL learners; and (d) the teachers themselves.

In this chapter, we first review the demographics of this population and their needs. The components of spoken language and communicative competence are discussed, followed by a consideration of how speaking

---

[1] This report does not deal with international students who enroll in U.S. universities or 4- or 2-year colleges to pursue academic degrees. Instead, it focuses on adults who are learning English for other purposes, including basic education, vocational ESOL, and literacy skills. It also intentionally excludes international students who have come from other countries to attend proprietary programs that teach EAP (English for academic purposes) to prepare them for college or university studies.

[2] A *foreign language (FL) context* is one where the language being learned is not the society's main language of communication (e.g., learning English as a secondary school student in Korea). A *second language (SL) context* is one where the language is the language of wider communication in the society (such as English in the United Kingdom, Australia, or the United States). Teaching ESOL internationally includes both EFL and ESL.

skills are taught and assessed. Educational standards related to the teaching of speaking and promising curricular developments are reviewed. The chapter ends with a discussion of implications for practice, research, and policy related to teaching speaking skills to adult ESOL learners.

ADULT ESOL LEARNERS

Adult ESOL learners are a subset of, but not analogous to, the adult basic education (ABE) population in the United States. The latter's proficiency in the English language separates the two groups:

> The focus of the majority of ABE students is acquisition of base skills in reading, writing and math, whereas for many adult [English-language learners] who have already mastered those basic skills in their native language, the focus is on the acquisition of a new language, including listening and speaking skills. (TESOL, 2000, p. 10)

The key distinction is that in the United States, ABE students use their mother tongue—English—to improve basic skills, gain knowledge, and handle learning tasks. ABE students communicate easily with their instructors, whereas many adult ESOL learners must struggle "constantly to cope with both oral and written directions, understand conversations laced with idiomatic language, and master not just the language of educational materials but also the culture on which they are based" (TESOL, 2000, p. 10).

Demographics of the Adult ESOL Learner Population

What do we know about the demographics of this diverse population? In 1990, Buchanan estimated that there were approximately 30 million people in the United States whose native language was not English. In 1998, Cheng said that there were 8 million immigrants from Southeast Asia alone. The 2000 United States census (U.S. Bureau of the Census, 2003) reports a total of more than 31 million foreign-born individuals. More than half (51.7%) are from Latin America and more than one fourth (26.4%) are from Asia. The rest were born in Europe (15.8%), Africa (2.8%), Oceania (0.5%), and Northern America (2.7%). These figures represent the total foreign-born population, however, including individuals who have not yet reached adulthood, and some who speak English with varying degrees of proficiency.

The 2000 census also documents the languages spoken at home by members of the population who were 5 years old and older. Whereas 82.1% (more than 215 million people) report speaking only English at home, 17.9% (nearly 47 million people) report speaking a language other than English at home. Of these, more than 21 million people (8.1% of the total U.S. population over the age of 5) report that they "speak English less than 'very well'" (U.S. Bureau of the Census, 2003).

It is difficult to estimate the number of adult ESOL students in the United States because many are highly mobile and some are undocumented. According to the National Center for ESL Literacy Education, "The most recent statistics from the U.S. Department of Education, Office of Vocational and Adult Education, show that 1,119,589 learners were enrolled in federally funded, state-administered adult ESL classes. This represents 42% of the enrollment in federally funded, state-administered adult education classes" (Florez, personal communication, 2001). Florez adds, however, that this number does not address the many students who are enrolled in programs that are not federally funded. She says, for example, "Laubach Literacy,[3] in a 1999–2000 report on their programs nationwide, indicated that approximately 77% of their member programs provided ESL instruction to 67,547 adult English language learners. This is just one segment of the non-federally funded services provided" (personal communication, 2001).

Fitzgerald (1995) describes the adult ESOL learner population as "primarily Hispanic (69%) and Asian (19%), with the vast majority (85%) living in major metropolitan areas and residing primarily (72%) in the Western region of the United States" (ESL Profile section, ¶ 1). Fitzgerald notes that:

> Adult education clients in ESL programs are overwhelmingly (98%) foreign born, with most (72%) speaking Spanish in the home. While most all ESL clients (92%) reported that they read well or very well in their native language, few (13%) reported that they could speak English well at the time of enrollment, and most (73%) were initially placed at the beginning level of ESL instruction. Thirty-six percent of the ESL clients were employed at the time of enrollment in adult education, and 11% had been public assistance recipients during the preceding year. (ESL Profile section, ¶ 1)

Fitzgerald adds that, in general, ESOL learners have more formal education than their ABE counterparts: "Half of the ESL clients had completed

---

[3] Laubach Literacy merged with Literacy Volunteers of America in 2002 to form a new organization: ProLiteracy.

at least high school compared to only 17% of the ABE . . . group" (ibid., ¶ 1).

According to TESOL (2000), the adult learner population has a wide range of educational backgrounds. Some have no education, whereas others arrive in the United States with doctoral degrees. The introduction to these standards, citing data from Wrigley (1993), states that in federally funded programs:

> . . . 32% had fewer than nine years of education, and of those, 9% had fewer than five years of schooling (Fitzgerald, 1995; NCLE, 1999). Another study, focusing specifically on participants in adult ESOL literacy programs, found that most of these ESOL literacy learners had only a few years of schooling, whether they came from literate societies, such as Mexico and El Salvador, or from preliterate societies, as in the case of the Hmong. (TESOL, 2000, p. 11)

Thus, adult ESOL learners in the United States are linguistically and culturally heterogeneous.

The Oral Communication Needs of Adult ESOL Learners

Given the diversity of the adult ESOL population, these learners clearly have varying needs for English language use (Weddel & Van Duzer, 1997), specifically in terms of their oral communication. The Equipped for the Future (EFF) initiative asked adult learners across the United States to respond to Goal 6 of the National Education Goals: "By the year 2000, every adult American will be literate and will possess the knowledge and skills necessary to compete in a global economy and exercise the rights and responsibilities of citizenship" (Merrifield, 2000, p. 4). More than 1,000 adult learners, some of whom were ESOL students, responded to an essay prompt about what this goal meant to them. EFF staff members analyzed this corpus and derived four macro goals, which they called "Four Purposes for Learning":

1. ACCESS: To gain access to information and resources so that adults can orient themselves in the world.
2. VOICE: To express ideas and opinions with the confidence they will be heard and taken into account.

3. ACTION: To solve problems and make decisions without having to rely on others to mediate the world for them.

4. BRIDGE TO THE FUTURE: Learning to learn so that adults can be prepared to keep up with the world as it changes. (Merrifield, 2000)

These four purposes provide a framework for describing the oral communication needs of adult ESOL learners. First, adult ESOL learners need *access* to information and resources. For example, the needs of newly arrived immigrants and refugees include obtaining housing, medical care, and sustenance. They must also develop the speaking skills to find work and subsequently to carry out the responsibilities of their employment. All of these access-oriented needs require spoken English.

Numerous social needs for spoken English are related to the EFF categories of *voice* and *action*. These include adult ESOL learners being able to communicate with their employers and neighbors in mixed-language environments, deal with their children's teachers and other school authorities, obtain ongoing social services and medical care, advocate for their own rights and those of their children, and participate in political and recreational activities in the community.

Adult ESOL learners also need ongoing education to build a *bridge to the future*. They may wish to participate in English-based vocational training or literacy programs. They may want to complete their secondary education or may aspire to receive higher education in the United States (Ignash, 1995). Whatever their goals, adults whose spoken English is inadequate have few opportunities for educational advancement in this country.

Challenges Facing Adult ESOL Learners

Immigrants and refugees who do not speak English well face obvious challenges. First, the lack of interactive language skills sustains a pattern of *high enclosure* (i.e., the tendency to live in neighborhoods with people from one's home culture and to interact almost exclusively in the native language). Early second-language acquisition research (Schumann, 1976) suggests that high enclosure contributes to social distance between the language learners (in this case, adult ESOL learners) and the host culture. This isolation—whether intentional (to maintain the home culture and mother tongue) or as the result of economic pressures—limits access to opportunities to practice English in meaningful communicative situations, and thus leads to a poor environment for learning English.

Research on an analogous population in Canada—adult immigrants learning French as a second language in Quebec—studied the communicative skills of two cohorts of learners at the end of a 900-hour instructional program and again 6 months later (d'Anglejan, Painchaud, & Renaud, 1986). The first cohort consisted of 36 Southeast Asian immigrants whose average age was 27 years, and the second included 45 Polish and Latin American immigrants (average age, 34 years). Using the Foreign Service Institute (FSI) Oral Proficiency Interview as the criterion measure, these authors found that after 30 weeks of instruction, half of Cohort 1 placed at FSI Level 2, which means they had "acquired the minimal knowledge of French necessary for limited functions in a workplace setting" (d'Anglejan et al., 1986, p. 191). The remaining half of Cohort 1 was rated at FSI Level 1, indicating that their French was "barely adequate to fulfill their personal needs . . . [and was] not considered adequate for the workplace" (d'Anglejan et al., 1986). Cohort 2 fared somewhat better, with 20% scoring at Level 1, 64.4% rated at Level 2, and 15.6% at Level 3 after the instructional phase. When the two groups were tested again 6 months later, "results for both cohorts improved significantly over the six-month period" (d'Anglejan, 1986, p. 192). The authors conclude that these immigrants "are not equipped with the language skills necessary to enter into competition with native speakers in the job market—other than in low-status jobs with little language" (d'Anglejan et al., 1986, p. 199).

These authors summarized earlier Canadian research by Mastai (1979, in d'Anglejan et al., 1986), which showed that "while finding suitable employment ranked as the most critical task facing the newcomer, success in doing so was largely contingent upon second language skills" (d'Anglejan et al., 1986, p. 185). In the United States, employment opportunities for adult ESOL learners who lack speaking proficiency may be limited to those that entail no public contact and thus do not require spoken English skills, such as assembly line work, construction, or manual labor in agriculture. Other adult ESOL learners find jobs in dishwashing, janitorial services, and housekeeping—positions that Burt (1995) called "back-of-the-house jobs" (p. 2) in the public service sector.

Even immigrants who have had professional or vocational training in their own countries may be seen as lacking employability skills if their spoken English is weak. *Employability skills* are defined as "transferable core skill groups that represent essential functional and enabling knowledge, skills, and attitudes required by the 21st century workplace" (Overtoom, 2000, p. 1). The ability to speak English is certainly one such enabling skill in the United States.

Finally, there is a less obvious but perhaps more pervasive result of adult ESOL learners' limited English-speaking abilities. Initial perceptions of individuals are often based on very brief speech samples. For the past four decades, sociolinguistic research has consistently shown that people's accents and speech patterns influence others' perceptions of the speakers' intelligence, trustworthiness, and social status. For instance, Zuengler (1988) found that the pronunciation of English vowels by Mexican speakers of Spanish led to stereotypical evaluations of those speakers by Americans. (See Fasold, 1984, for a cogent review of the early literature on this topic.)

A landmark study in Canada established the matched guise technique as a viable procedure for eliciting stereotypical responses based on speech (Lambert, Hodgson, Gardner, & Fillenbaum, 1960). In the matched guise, one bilingual speaker is presented to respondents as two different people, speaking different languages or varieties of a language. Respondents then evaluate the speech samples on different personal attributes, and the same speaker is evaluated lower when he or she speaks the less prestigious language or variety (including an accented version of the standard variety). The Canadian research influenced research on accentedness in the United States. For example, in California, Ford (1984) had 40 teachers respond to the speech samples of children whose academic ability had been pre-determined to be equivalent to one another. She found that "the Spanish-influenced speakers were rated lower than the non-Spanish-influenced speakers in intelligence, effectiveness of communication, confidence, ambition, pleasantness, and relative quality as students" (p. 33). Based on her review of the literature, Pennington (1994) concludes that "teachers should train early and most intensively those features of the nonnative's phonology that cause the most negative reactions in the relevant native-speaker population" (p. 104).

WHAT IS SPOKEN LANGUAGE?

This section examines the components of spoken English, drawing on a model proposed by van Lier (1995). It is not necessary for learners to have metalinguistic awareness of these components in order to use them effectively. However, it is necessary for teachers to understand fully these inter-related components in order to help adult learners improve their speaking skills. The components of spoken English are discussed here to illustrate the complexity of the adult ESOL learners' task.

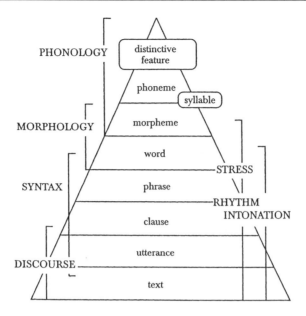

FIG. 5.1.   Units of spoken language (van Lier, 1995, p. 15).
Adapted with the permission of the author.

The Components of Spoken English

Speaking is perhaps the most fundamental of human skills, and because we do it constantly, we do not often stop to examine the processes involved. Yet having a simple conversation is anything but a simple process—particularly if someone is speaking a new language.

Figure 5.1 depicts the many elements involved in teaching speaking to adult ESOL learners. The left column lists four traditional areas of linguistic analysis (which teachers must understand), and the center column labels the units of spoken language (which learners must master). All of these units, or levels of language, must function together when adult ESOL learners speak English.

Beginning at the pyramid's base, *text* refers to stretches of language of an undetermined length. Texts can be either written or spoken, but here the focus is exclusively on spoken discourse. Spoken texts are composed of *utterances:* what someone says. An utterance may not always be a full sentence, as it would be if written. For example, if two friends are talking about what to eat, one might ask, "Would you like to have pizza for supper?" This utterance is a fully formed grammatical sentence, but such sentences are not typical of casual conversation. If it is clear that the topic of the conversation is what to eat, one person might simply ask the other, "Pizza?" Although this is not a grammatical sentence, it is an utterance that would certainly be understood in context.

A *clause* is two or more words that contain a verb marked for tense and a grammatical subject. *Independent clauses* are complete sentences that can stand alone ("Juan went to work"), whereas *dependent clauses* cannot ("While Juan was going to work . . ."). In contrast, a *phrase* is two or more words that function as a unit but do not have a subject or a verb marked for tense. These include prepositional phrases ("in the hospital" or "after school") and infinitive phrases ("to drive" or "to move up"). Clauses and phrases do not usually appear alone in formal writing, but they are quite common in speech. Both clauses and phrases can be utterances, as can individual words, the next level in the pyramid.

A word is called a *free morpheme*—a unit of language that can stand on its own and convey meaning (*bus, apply, often*). In contrast, *bound morphemes* are always connected to words. These include prefixes, such as *un-* or *pre-*, as well as suffixes, such as *-tion* or *-s* or *-ed*. Often, during the pressure of speaking, it is difficult for English learners to use the expected suffixes—especially if their native language does not utilize these kinds of morphemes as grammatical markers.

A *phoneme* is a unit of sound that distinguishes meaning. Phonemes can be either consonants (like /p/ or /b/ in the words *pat* and *bat*) or vowels (like /I/ and /æ/ in *bit* and *bat*). Phonemes differ from one language to another. Some of the sounds that are common in English are quite unusual in other languages and are therefore difficult for adult ESOL learners to pronounce. For example, the "th" sounds in *think* and *the* are relatively rare in the phonemic inventory of the world's languages, even though they are pervasive in English. Adult ESOL learners often approximate or replace the "th" sounds with "s" or "z" or "d" or "t," which contributes to a notably foreign accent.

In the top levels of Fig. 5.1, the word *syllable* overlaps the levels of morphemes and phonemes because a syllable can consist of a morpheme or simply one or more phonemes. The structure of syllables is referred to as being either open (ending with a vowel) or closed (ending with a consonant). Many languages use the open syllable structure, in which a syllable consists of just a vowel (V), or of a consonant (C) followed by a vowel. Spoken English, in contrast, allows both open syllables (C-V, or just V) and closed syllables (C-V-C, or simply V-C), as well as consonant clusters, where two or more consonants occur in sequence (as in the words *stretched* or *jumped*). For this reason, the spoken English of adult

ESOL learners often sounds ungrammatical to native speakers. Learners whose native language is Vietnamese, for instance, may omit word-final consonants, thereby eliminating the sounds that convey important linguistic information, such as plurality, possession, or tense.

Consonants and vowels are called *segmental phonemes.* Sometimes a spoken syllable consists of one phoneme (/o/ in *okay*). Syllables also consist of combined sounds (the second syllable of *okay*), and of both free and bound morphemes. For instance, the free morpheme *hat* consists of three phonemes but only one syllable. The word *disheartened* has three syllables, four morphemes (*dis* + *heart* + *en* + *ed*), and nine phonemes.

A smaller unit, the *distinctive feature,* relates to how and where in the mouth a sound is produced when we speak. These minute contrasts contribute to adult ESOL learners' accents. For example, the distinctive feature that makes /b/ and /p/ separate phonemes in English is *voicing.* When /b/ is pronounced the vocal cords are vibrating, but when /p/ is pronounced, they are not. For adult learners whose language does not have this contrast (Arabic, for example), failure to master this distinction can lead to being misunderstood.

The three other labels in Fig. 5.1—stress, rhythm, and intonation— represent the *suprasegmental phonemes.* When we speak, these phonemes carry meaning differences "above" the segmental phonemes. For instance, the sentence "I am going now" can convey at least four different meanings, depending on where the stress is placed. The differences are related to the context where the utterances occur. Consider these interpretations:

I am going now. (You may be staying here, but I choose to leave.)
I *am* going now. (You may assert that I'm staying, but I insist that I am leaving.)
I am *going* now. (I insist that I am leaving, rather than staying.)
I am going *now.* (I am not waiting any longer.)

Sociolinguistic research has demonstrated that adult second-language speakers can be misunderstood and even receive poor job evaluations because of their misuse of the English suprasegmentals (see, e.g., Gumperz & Tannen, 1987).

How do these levels of spoken language relate to the speaking skills of nonnative-speaking adult immigrants? Two key points derive from a substantial review of the research on foreign accent by Major (2001). First, he says that really learning the sound system of a language entails mastering (a) the individual segments (the vowel and consonant phonemes), (b) the combinations of segments, (c) prosody (stress, intonation, rhythm, etc.), and (d) "global accent, or the overall accent of a speaker" (p. 12). He adds that a global foreign accent is the result of a nonnative combination of (a), (b), and (c).

Second, Major (2001) notes that "both the learner's age of arrival (AOA, to the country as a resident) and the age of learning (AOL, when the learner was first exposed to the language) have been found to be important variables in governing whether and to what degree a learner can acquire a nativelike accent" (pp. 6–7). He concludes that "the vast majority of the research indicates that the younger the learner the more nativelike the pronunciation" (p. 11).

Adult ESOL learners must make themselves understood by the people they are speaking with, and this is not an easy task, especially at the beginning and intermediate levels. For less-than-proficient speakers, managing the multiple components of language that must work together as they speak is very demanding indeed, as shown by the numerous and complex components in Fig. 5.1. The ability to use these components to produce and understand language is known as *linguistic competence.*

An important element of successful speaking that is not addressed in this model is fluency—the extent to which a speaker interacts with others with normal speed, apparent confidence, and freedom from excessive pauses or vocabulary searches. Hammerly (1991) notes that laypersons use fluency to mean "speaking rapidly and well" (p. 12), but in this chapter fluency is used with its specialist meaning: "speaking rapidly and smoothly, not necessarily grammatically" (p. 12).

Contrasting Spoken and Written Language

We describe the four traditional skills of language use (speaking, listening, reading, and writing) in terms of their *direction* and *modality.* Language generated by the learner (in speech or writing) is *productive,* and language directed at the learner (in reading or listening) is *receptive* (Savignon, 1991). *Modality* refers to the medium of the message (aural/oral or written). Thus, *speaking* is the productive aural/oral skill. It consists of producing systematic verbal utterances to convey meaning. Speaking is "an interactive process of constructing meaning that involves producing and receiving and processing information" (Florez, 1999, p. 1). It is "often spontaneous, open-ended, and evolving" (p. 1), but it is not completely unpredictable.

Spoken language and written language differ in many important ways (van Lier, 1995). Spoken language is received auditorially, whereas written language is received visually. As a result, the spoken message is temporary and its reception by the learner is usually immediate. In contrast, written language is permanent, and reception by the learner typically occurs some time after the text was generated (sometimes even centuries later). Meaning in spoken language is conveyed in part through the supra-segmental phonemes (including rhythm, stress, and intonation), whereas punctuation marks and type fonts convey such information in writing.

For adult ESOL learners, speaking English can be particularly difficult because, unlike reading or writing, speaking happens in "real time." That is, the person we are talking to (the *interlocutor*) is listening and waiting to take his or her own turn to speak. Spoken English "is almost always accomplished via interaction with at least one other speaker. This means that a variety of demands are in place at once: monitoring and understanding the other speaker(s), thinking about one's own contribution, producing its effect, and so on" (Lazaraton, 2001, p. 103). In addition, except in recorded speech, verbal interaction typically involves immediate feedback from one's interlocutor, whereas feedback to the authors of written texts may be delayed or nonexistent. Finally, because spoken communication occurs in real time, the opportunities to plan and edit output are limited, whereas in most written communication, the message originator has time for planning, editing, and revision. Except when audiotaping a letter or dictating a memo, when we speak we cannot edit and revise what we wish to say, as we usually can in writing.

Being able to speak English is clearly important for adult ESOL learners in order to get their needs met. However, speaking is also significant in terms of ongoing language acquisition. By communicating orally with others in English, adult ESOL learners can experience *modified interaction*—"that interaction which is altered in some way (either linguistically or conversationally) to facilitate comprehension of the intended message" (Doughty & Pica, 1986). Such modifications occur through repetition of the spoken message as well as through three types of conversational moves: (a) *clarification requests,* "when one interlocutor does not entirely comprehend the meaning and asks for clarification," (b) *confirmation checks,* when "the listener believes he or she has understood, but would like to make sure," and (c) *comprehension checks,* in which "the speaker wants to be certain that the listener has understood." These modifications are important because in both research and theory, "such modified interaction is claimed to make input comprehensible to learners and to lead ultimately to successful classroom second language acquisition" (p. 322).

In discussing current second-language acquisition research, Swain (2000) states that generating output (i.e., speaking or writing) "pushes learners to process language more deeply—with more mental effort—

than does input" (via listening and reading; p. 99). Swain suggests that output promotes noticing: "Learners may notice that they do not know how to express precisely the meaning they wish to convey *at the very moment of attempting to produce it*" (p. 100; italics in the original). It is through interaction that learners confront the gaps in their knowledge and skills. Speaking is thus both the product and the process of second language acquisition.

This brief discussion of spoken language has not even begun to address cross-cultural differences in discourse patterns, such as the rules for taking turns in English and how they differ from those of other languages. As Florez (1999) notes, "Speaking requires that learners not only know how to produce specific points of language such as grammar, pronunciation, or vocabulary . . . but also that they understand when, why, and in what ways to produce language" (pp. 1–2). Knowing how to use the linguistic components of English is part of an adult ESOL learner's communicative competence, the topic of the next section.

COMMUNICATIVE COMPETENCE AND ADULT ESOL LEARNERS

For many years, teaching language was viewed as developing *linguistic competence*—that is, providing students with the phonemes, morphemes, words, and grammar patterns—so that students could eventually put them all together and communicate. In the 1970s and 1980s, however, language teaching in the United States underwent a significant shift in focus, influenced by developments in linguistics and pedagogy from Canada, Australia, and the United Kingdom, by sociolinguistic research in the United States and elsewhere, and by the social pressures of refugees and immigrants resettling from Southeast Asia, Latin American, Africa, and Eastern Europe.

In particular, many refugees from Southeast Asia were semiliterate or had only rudimentary literacy skills in their home language. Others came from cultures whose languages lacked written systems. Like all immigrants, these new Americans had immediate needs for housing, food, employment, medical care, social services, and education where they relocated. With large numbers of semiliterate or nonliterate adult ESOL students in their classrooms—students with immediate survival needs for interactive English skills—teachers could no longer rely on written tests or textbook exercises. They had to get right to the heart of the matter: spoken communication in English.

The Components of Communicative Competence

In the mid-1970s the notion of linguistic competence came to be viewed as part of the broader construct of *communicative competence*—"the ability of language learners to interact with other speakers, to make meaning, as distinct from their ability to perform on discrete-point tests of grammatical knowledge" (Savignon, 1991, p. 264). Being communicatively competent "requires an understanding of sociocultural contexts of language use" (p. 267).

There are various models of communicative competence (see especially Canale & Swain, 1980), but in addition to *linguistic competence,* communicative competence includes *sociolinguistic competence,* or the ability to use language appropriately in various contexts. Sociolinguistic competence entails register (degrees of formality and informality), appropriate lexical choice, style shifting, and politeness strategies. Another component of communicative competence is *strategic competence*—the ability to use language strategies (such as circumlocution and approximation) to compensate for gaps in one's second-language skills. A fourth component is *discourse competence,* which includes "rules of both cohesion—how sentence elements are tied together via reference, repetition, synonymy, etc.—and coherence—how texts are constructed" (Lazaraton, 2001, p.104; see also Bachman, 1990; Douglas, 2000).

These four components of communicative competence have several practical implications for teaching adult ESOL speakers. For example, given their significance, they were selected to be the guiding framework in determining goals of workplace ESOL instruction for adult learners (Friedenburg, Kennedy, Lomperis, Martin, & Westerfield, 2003). Because communicative competence is a multifaceted construct, it is important that curriculum planners, materials writers, teacher educators, researchers, test developers, and teachers working with adult ESOL learners understand the complexity involved in speaking English.

Transactional Versus Interactional Communication

For adult learners in particular (as opposed to school-aged children), being able to use both transactional and interactional speech is important, as is the ability to negotiate English speech acts in a variety of speech events. Outside of language classrooms, people usually use speech for interactional or transactional purposes (Brown & Yule, 1983; Pridham, 2001). Broadly speaking, *interactional speech* is communicating with someone for social purposes. It includes both establishing and maintaining social relationships. *Transactional speech* involves communicating to accomplish something, including the exchange of goods and services.

Most spoken interactions "can be placed on a continuum from relatively predictable to relatively unpredictable" (Nunan, 1991, p. 42). Interactional conversations are relatively unpredictable and can range over many topics, with the participants taking turns and commenting freely. In contrast, Nunan states that "transactional encounters of a fairly restricted kind will usually contain highly predictable patterns" (p. 42). So for example, the communication between a customer and an adult immigrant working in a fast-food restaurant would be more restricted and predictable than would a casual conversation among friends.

According to Nunan (1991), interactional speech is more fluid and unpredictable than transactional speech (such as telephoning for a taxi cab), which is shaped in part by the needs of the parties involved to successfully accomplish the exchange of information, goods, or services. Teaching materials and speaking activities in the classroom must address both interactional and transactional purposes, because adult ESOL learners will have to accomplish both.

Speech Acts and Speech Events

As the contrast between transactional and interactional speech indicates, people speak to accomplish specific purposes. The linguistic means for accomplishing those purposes are called *speech acts.* These utterances include seeking information, asking for help, ordering people to do things, complimenting, complaining, apologizing, inviting, refusing, warning, and so on.

Adult ESOL learners must be able to accomplish these and other speech acts effectively in order to function successfully in an English-speaking society. "A good speaker synthesizes [an] array of skills and knowledge to succeed in a given speech act" (Florez, 1999, p. 2). Language teachers, curriculum designers, and materials developers, therefore, must understand speech acts and how they work.

Communication typically occurs in recognizable discourse contexts called *speech events.* Examples include sermons, lectures, job interviews, eulogies, dinner-table conversations, and so on. As these examples suggest, speech events are typically associated with particular social purposes and places. For instance, we would expect a job interview to occur in a place of business rather than a church. Speech events can involve very few speech acts (such as ordering food in a fast-food restaurant), but more complex speech events can consist of many different speech acts. A lecture might include defining, describing, exemplifying, telling a joke, encouraging, apologizing, and so on. In order to participate in complex speech events, adult ESOL learners must understand and be able to use a wide array of speech acts.

Successfully executing speech acts involves both sociocultural choices and sociolinguistic forms (Cohen, 1996). The term *sociocultural choices* refers to "the speaker's ability to determine whether it is acceptable to perform the speech act at all in the given situation" (p. 254). This decision requires the speaker to be familiar with a wide range of contexts and power relationships. The speaker must select among the various *sociolinguistic forms* available—that is, "the actual language forms used to realize the speech act (e.g., *sorry* vs. *excuse me, really sorry* vs. *very sorry*)" (pp. 254–255). Selecting appropriate strategies is complicated because "speech acts are conditioned by a host of social, cultural, situational, and personal factors" (p. 255). Adult ESOL learners, particularly those living in high-enclosure areas where their native language predominates, may have little opportunity to encounter these forms used in context, except in English classes.

In classroom settings learners are exposed to the grammatical structures (the forms) of English, but they also need to learn the functions. For example, learners may be taught the modal auxiliaries (*can, could, shall, should, will, would, may, might* and *must*) and may quickly master the forms. However, it takes time and a great deal of exposure to contextualized interaction to learn when and how to use these forms appropriately to make and deny requests, issue warnings, give advice, and so on. For many adult ESOL learners, opportunities for interaction with native or proficient speakers of English can be rare, so learning the function can lag behind learning the form. As a result, the spoken English of adult ESOL learners can sound inappropriately (and unintentionally) aggressive or tentative (Gumperz & Tannen, 1987).

For all these reasons, it is important that adult ESOL programs provide learners with instruction and opportunities to develop their communicative competence. The next section provides a brief historical overview of how speaking traditionally has been taught.

HOW SPEAKING SKILLS HAVE BEEN TAUGHT TO ADULT ESOL LEARNERS

Although several language-teaching methods have been used to teach speaking in a second or foreign language (see Murphy, 1991, for a review), three methods have dominated language teaching in the United States in the past 60 years. This section first briefly reviews each method, focusing specifically on how the method treats the speaking skills of adult ESOL learners, then addresses language awareness and the issue of *intelligibility*—the extent to which others can easily understand a person's speech.

The Grammar-Translation Method

In the grammar-translation method, students are taught to analyze grammar and to translate (usually in writing) from one language to another. The key instructional goal is to read the literature of a particular culture. According to Richards and Rodgers (1986), the main characteristics of the grammar-translation method are that (a) reading and writing are the major focus; (b) the vocabulary studied is determined by the reading texts; (c) "the sentence is the basic unit of teaching and language practice" (p. 4); (d) the primary emphasis is on accuracy; (e) teaching is deductive (i.e., grammar rules are presented and then practiced through translating); and (f) the medium of instruction is typically the students' native language. Richards and Rodgers note that although the "grammar translation method is still widely practiced, it has no advocates; it is a method for which there is no theory" (p. 5).

The grammar-translation method does not prepare students to speak English, so it is not appropriate for nonacademic adult ESOL students who want to improve their speaking skills. The method is not consistent with the goals of increasing fluency, oral production, or communicative competence of adult ESOL learners. In grammar-translation lessons, speaking consists largely of reading translations aloud or doing grammar exercises orally. There are few opportunities for expressing original thoughts or personal needs and feelings in English.

The Audiolingual Method

For many years, the audiolingual method dominated English-language instruction in the United States. In this method, speaking skills are taught by having students repeat sentences and recite memorized textbook dialogues. Repetition drills, a hallmark of the audiolingual method, are designed to familiarize students with the sounds and structural patterns of the language. The theory behind the audiolingual method is that students learn to speak by practicing grammatical structures until producing those structures has become automatic. Then, it is thought, the learners would be able to engage in conversation. As a result, "teaching oral language was thought to require no more than engineering the repeated oral production of structures . . . concentrating on the development of grammatical and phonological accuracy combined with fluency" (Bygate, 2001, p. 15).

The behaviorist concept of good habit formation is the theoretical basis of the audiolingual method. This theory proposes that for learners to form good habits, language lessons must involve frequent repetition and correction. Teachers address spoken errors quickly, in hopes of preventing students from forming bad habits. If errors are left untreated, both the speaker and the other students in class might internalize those erroneous forms. There is little or no explanation of vocabulary or grammar rules in audiolingual lessons. Instead, intense repetition and practice are used to establish good speaking habits to the point that they are fluent and automatic—that is, the adult ESOL learner would not have to stop and think about how to form an utterance before speaking.

The language laboratory is the central technological component of the audiolingual method. In addition to attending classroom lessons and doing homework, students are expected to spend time in the lab, listening to audiotapes of native speakers talking in rehearsed dialogues, which embody the structures and vocabulary items currently being studied in the curriculum. The taped speech samples students hear in the lab are carefully articulated and highly sanitized. They typically present neither realistic samples of the English that learners would hear on the street nor accurate models of how adult learners should try to speak in order to be understood and sound natural. In addition, when learners do speak in the lab, it is often to repeat after the tape-recorded voice, with no opportunity for constructing their ideas in English or expressing their own intended meaning. "While audiolingualism stressed oral skills (evidenced by the amount of time spent in the language laboratory practicing drills), speech production was tightly controlled in order to reinforce correct habit formation of linguistic rules" (Lazaraton, 2001, p. 103). This sort of tightly controlled practice does not necessarily prepare learners for the spontaneous, fluid interaction that occurs outside the classroom.

Audiolingualism "rapidly lost popularity in the United States, partly as a result of the strong theoretical arguments that were advanced against it, but also because the results obtained from classroom practice were disappointing" in several ways (Ellis, 1990, p. 29). Many learners lost interest in language learning because the pattern practice and audiolingual drills were boring. Adult learners often felt hampered because the method downplayed the explicit teaching of grammar rules. In addition, the memorization of patterns "did not lead to fluent and effective communication in real-life situations" (p. 30).

Communicative Language Teaching

During the 1970s and 1980s, language acquisition research (and dissatisfaction with the audiolingual method) made TESOL professionals reconsider some long-standing beliefs about how people learn languages. People do not learn the pieces of the language and then put them together to make conversations. Instead, infants acquiring their first language and people acquiring second languages learn the components of language through interaction with other people. (For summaries of research on interaction and language learning, see Ellis, 1990; Gass, 1997; and Larsen-Freeman & Long, 1991.) This realization has several interesting implications, the most central of which is that if people learn languages by interacting, then learners should interact during lessons. As a result, communicative language teaching arose.

In some language teaching methods, such as Total Physical Response (Asher, Kusodo, & de la Torre, 1993), beginning learners undergo a period of listening to English before they begin to speak it. In these methods, the focus is on input-based activities. For instance, in Total Physical Response, learners initially respond to spoken commands from the teacher, rather than speaking themselves.

In contrast, communicative language teaching methods, particularly from the high beginner to more advanced levels, feature more interaction-based activities, such as role-plays and *information gap tasks* (activities in which learners must use English to convey information known to them but not to their classmates). Curricular choices, such as task-based and project-based activities (see Moss & Van Duzer, 1998), also promote interaction. Pair work and group work are typical organizational features of interaction-based lessons in communicative language teaching.

In this method teachers often downplay accuracy and emphasize students' ability to convey their messages (Hammerly, 1991). Accuracy is the extent to which the adult ESOL learners' speech matches the (local) native speaker norms (in terms of their speech being free of notable errors). Fluency is the speed, ease, and naturalness with which ESOL learners communicate orally. Proficient speakers are both fluent and accurate, but at the lower levels, fluency and accuracy often work against one another. That is, to be accurate and apply learned rules, adult ESOL learners may speak hesitantly or haltingly. To be fluent in conversation, they may overlook the time-consuming application of rules. The instructional implications are that teachers should not focus only on accuracy, but should use both form-focused and fluency building activities in adult ESOL classes.

Intelligibility, Pronunciation, and the Language-Awareness Movement

As already noted, producing accurate speech in a second language is demanding because there is limited time to plan and edit speech during conversations. However, some attention to accuracy is needed in order to communicate effectively. One important aspect of intelligibility is pronunciation (see Florez, 1998). Historically, the teaching of pronunciation has changed with the dominant teaching method. Florez (1998) reviewed the literature on improving adult ESOL learners' pronunciation and reported:

> In the grammar-translation method of the past, pronunciation was almost irrelevant and therefore seldom taught. In the audio-lingual method, learners spent hours in the language lab listening to and repeating sounds and sound combinations. With the emergence of more holistic, communicative methods . . . pronunciation is addressed within the context of real communication. (p. 1)

Unfortunately for adult immigrants to the United States, studies have shown that the earlier a person arrives in a new country, the more likely it is that he or she will develop native-like pronunciation (see, e.g., Piper & Cansin, 1988). However, intelligibility and nativeness are two separate constructs. (For further information, see Celce-Murcia, Brinton, & Goodwin, 1996; Goodwin, 2001; and Morley, 1991.)

Morley (1991) identified five groups of learners "whose pronunciation difficulties may place them at a professional or social disadvantage" (p. 490). Three of those groups are among the adult ESOL learner population addressed in this chapter. These are:

(1) adult and teenage refugees in vocational and language training programs;
. . . (2) immigrant residents who have passed through the educational system

and graduated into the workplace only to find that their spoken language and particularly their intelligibility prohibits them from taking advantage of employment opportunities or from advancing educationally; [and] (3) a growing population of nonnative speakers of English in technology, business, industry and the professions. (pp. 490–491)

(See Morley, 1991, p. 502, for an example of an intelligibility scale that can be used with adult ESOL learners.)

The language-awareness movement is a pedagogical development that began in the United Kingdom in the early 1980s (van Lier, 2001, p. 161). *Language awareness* has been defined as "a person's sensitivity to and conscious awareness of the nature of language and its role in human life" (Donmall, 1985). It consists of "an understanding of the human faculty of language and its role in thinking, learning and social life" (van Lier, 1995, p. xi; however, see Stainton, 1992, for a discussion of the problems in defining language awareness).

Language awareness is not a method of language teaching per se; rather it is a focus that transcends methods and can be used in the teaching of any language skill. The language awareness movement recognizes the importance of learners' metacognitive knowledge and processing. It represents another pendulum swing in the focus of language teaching—the field moved away from the highly form-focused days of grammar-translation and audiolingualism to an emphasis on communication (sometimes at the expense of accuracy), but now attention to form is being emphasized once more. The language-awareness movement offers adult ESOL teachers procedures with which to build meaningful attention to form into language courses based on adults' communicative needs and goals. In university ESOL programs and teacher education contexts, language learners and teacher trainees systematically collect speech data and analyze the way native speakers express their ideas. Lazaraton (2001) notes, "One of the more recent trends in oral skills pedagogy is the emphasis on having students analyze and evaluate the language that they or others produce" (p. 108). For instance, in a unit on the speech act of complaining, a student might record and analyze examples of how people complain when they return items to a department store. (See van Lier, 1992, 1997.)

Although communicative language teaching often downplays explicit attention to form, in the language-awareness approach, attention to form (and to the meaning it conveys) is very important. Citing research by Sharwood-Smith (1981, 1994), van Lier (1995) states, "Many researchers and teachers argue that awareness, attention and noticing particular features of language adds to learning" (p. 161). The instructional emphasis is on noticing and understanding speech as much as it is on accuracy of production. The key characteristics of teaching driven by language awareness are that it "must be *experiential* (based on teachers' [and learners'] knowledge and expertise), *task-based* (based on real-life concerns and projects), and *critical* (examining the roles of language in life)" (van Lier, 1992, p. 91).

One potentially important application of language awareness lies in the use of technology to help improve the pronunciation of adult ESOL learners. Although research by Moholt (1988) involved a different population, his results are promising. Moholt used two different forms of computer display to help U.S.-based university students (native speakers of Chinese) to see the differences between their own English pronunciation patterns and those produced by native speakers. Moholt notes:

> With a computer display of pronunciation comparing a native speaker's model with [the learner's] attempt to match it, we can instantly show students objective information about the location, extent, type and significance of the error, as well as the progress made in correcting the error. (p. 92)

Computer-generated feedback may be useful in helping adult ESOL learners become aware of their pronunciation patterns and improve their intelligibility. (See also Pennington, 1989.)

It is not clear whether the language-awareness movement has influenced the teaching of speaking to nonacademic adult ESOL learners yet, although Graham (1994) has discussed four procedures she used to raise language awareness in a course for professional adult ESOL learners:

> (1) give brief, targeted explanations of language patterns, accompanied by examples; (2) teach students to mark written texts for various suprasegmentals such as intonation, emphasis and pauses; (3) provide listening activities that focus on form rather than on meaning; [and] (4) teach students to analyze their own recorded voices. (pp. 27–28)

To summarize, ESOL teaching methods have evolved over the years to encompass the broad goal of communicative competence. Both accuracy and fluency are important, and adult ESOL learners' speech must be intelligible to their interlocutors. Procedures for assessing learners' spoken English are the topic of the next section.

ASSESSING THE SPEAKING SKILLS
OF ADULT ESOL LEARNERS

The evaluation of speaking skills is an important concern in adult ESOL programs (Van Duzer, 2002). In addition, the concept of communicative competence presents interesting challenges for evaluating speaking skills. When linguistic competence was the primary focus of instruction, tests could focus on learners' abilities to apply grammar rules, produce and recognize vocabulary, and interpret spoken or written texts. When the focus shifts to communicative competence, however, testing speaking skills is a much more complex undertaking.

First, it is important to recognize the distinction between formal testing and other forms of assessment. A test can be defined as a "measurement instrument designed to elicit a specific sample of an individual's behavior" (Bachman, 1990). In instructional settings, adult learners' spoken English may or may not be formally tested, and there is little research on assessing the spoken English of this population. Adult classes tend to be rather large, which makes it difficult for teachers to utilize oral interviews or other speaking tests that require one-on-one administration. This practical issue is embodied in the distinctions among *direct, semidirect,* and *indirect* tests of speaking.

Direct, Semidirect, and Indirect Tests of Speaking

The testing of speaking skills is normally thought of as direct, semidirect, or indirect (Clark, 1979). In a *direct test,* a learner interacts with the test administrator and actually produces spoken utterances. The oral component of the Basic English Skills Test (BEST), which was designed by the Center for Applied Linguistics (1982) specifically for nonnative-speaking adult refugees and immigrants to the United States, is an example of a direct test of speaking. The oral interview portion is administered to one person at a time, and the administrator evaluates the learner's speaking skills on a three-point scale by rating the learner's communication, pronunciation, and fluency, as well as by estimating his or her listening ability (Center for Applied Linguistics, 1982; see also Eakin & Ilyin, 1987).

In a *semidirect test,* the evaluation of learners' spoken English is based on tape recordings of their speech in response to tape-recorded stimulus materials. Semidirect speaking tests are very practical because several students can be tested at once and the evaluator does not need to be present to score the tape-recorded speech samples. However, sometimes test takers find it awkward to carry on a conversation with a tape recorder. Semidirect tests of speaking can be criticized for generating unnatural language samples.

An *indirect test* of speaking is one in which the learners do not speak. Instead, they perform nonspeaking tasks that are statistically related to scores on actual speaking tasks. For example, a *conversational cloze test* is a written passage based on a transcript of a conversation. Words are systematically deleted (e.g., every ninth word of a text is replaced by a blank line) and the student's task is to fill in each blank with an appropriate and grammatically correct word. Scores on conversational cloze tests have strong correlations with scores on direct speaking tests (see Hughes, 1981), even though the learners do not speak at all while completing the assessment tasks.

There is typically an inverse relationship between the directness of a speaking test and its practicality. Although several hundred students conceivably could take a conversational cloze test at one sitting, only one person can take the oral interview portion of the BEST at any given administration. Some direct tests of speaking involve small groups of learners (e.g., the British Cambridge Advanced Examination has two examinees talk with a test administrator and with each other), but this procedure is not commonplace in the United States. Semidirect tests are more practical than direct tests in terms of time efficiency and number of students tested, but less practical than indirect tests. In addition, the semidirect tests have the added disadvantage that learners have to speak into a tape recorder to a disembodied interlocutor, a process that many native speakers find artificial. Although indirect tests are highly practical, their face validity is always in question. Underhill (1987) explains this notion:

> On the face of it, does it look like a reasonable test? Do the people who use the test think it's a good test? If either the testers or the learners are unhappy with it, then it won't yield good results. Clearly the best way of researching this form of validity is to question the different people who come into contact with the test. (pp. 105–106)

Learners may feel that their speaking has not been adequately or fairly tested if they do not actually speak during the test.

Validity Issues in Testing the Spoken English of Adult ESOL Learners

Although test practicality is certainly a legitimate concern, validity concerns are equally important. There are many types of validity (see Cumming, 1996), but the basic issue is whether or not a test measures what it claims to measure. Another concern is *washback,* or the influence of a test on teaching and learning (Hughes, 1989). As Buck (1988) explains:

There is a natural tendency for both teachers and students to tailor their classroom activities to the demands of the test, especially when the test is very important to the future of the students, and pass rates are used as a measure of teacher success. This influence of the test on the classroom (referred to as *washback* by language testers) is, of course, very important; this washback effect can be either beneficial or harmful. (pp. 257–258)

Although the washback effect of several tests has been studied in many different countries (see Alderson & Wall, 1993 for a review), the wash-back effect of tests used with adult ESOL learners in the United States is not clearly understood.

The two main standardized tests used with adult ESOL learners in the United States are the BEST and the Comprehensive Adult Student Assessment System, or CASAS (Burt & Keenan, 1995; Van Duzer & Berdan, 2000; Weinstein, 2001). Other standardized tests[4] are used with adult ESOL learners, but if they were not written for and normed on this population, they can be problematic in a variety of ways (Van Duzer & Berdan, 2000).

Given the number of adult ESOL learners and the open-enrollment policies prevalent in many programs, it is not surprising that the speaking skills of adult learners in such programs are seldom formally tested. Funding requirements for accountability do mandate the use of some testing mechanisms, such as CASAS. However, although it claims to test a "student's ability to speak and understand English" (CASAS, 1993, p. 6), the CASAS item bank consists of more than 5,000 multiple-choice items and "does not test oral skills" (Burt & Keenan, 1995, p. 1). At best, the CASAS provides an indirect test of speaking. An important question remains: "Can we bridge the gap between what we teach and test in the classroom and what the state tests with CASAS?" (Price-Machado, 2000, p. 1).

An interesting new development that will soon influence the formal testing of adult ESOL learners' speaking skills is computer-adaptive testing. In fact, a computerized version of the BEST is currently under development (Center for Applied Linguistics, 2000). In this system "the prompt and response are both oral, [so] the examinee is not required to read any items or type any answers" (p. 5). This is an important consideration in evaluating the speaking skills of ESOL adults, whose literacy level may lag

---

[4] Here the term *standardized test* refers to codified, systematically developed examinations that are consistently administered. In addition, their scoring procedures and score reporting are standardized across locations and testing occasions.

behind their speech development in English. It is hoped that the computer-adaptive BEST will maintain its validity as an actual speaking test (albeit a semidirect one), with increased practicality of administration.

Alternative Assessment and Adult ESOL Learners

Formal tests such as the BEST and the CASAS are typically used for *general assessment,* which "allow comparisons across programs" (Weinstein, 2001, p. 182). In contrast, *program-based assessments* "reflect the approach of the program and the content of the curriculum" (p. 182). Such procedures may include formal tests or more informal types of assessment, which are often seen as alternatives to formal tests.

Alternative assessment is a catchall phrase that covers a range of procedures. Brown and Hudson (1998) identify "checklists, journals, logs, videotapes and audiotapes, self-evaluation, and teacher observations [as well as] portfolios, conferences, diaries, self-assessments, and peer-assessments" (p. 653) as examples. Bailey (1998) juxtaposes traditional and alternative assessments in language learning along nine dimensions: (a) one-shot tests versus continuous, longitudinal assessment; (b) indirect versus direct tests; (c) inauthentic versus authentic tests; (d) individual projects versus group projects; (e) absence or presence of detailed feedback provided to the learners; (f) speeded exams versus untimed exams or tasks; (g) decontextualized versus contextualized tasks; (h) norm-referenced versus criterion-referenced score interpretation; and (i) standardized tests versus classroom-based tests.

Some types of alternative assessment (such as checklists, surveys, teacher observation forms, and learners' logs) hold promise as program-based means for validly assessing the speaking skills of adult ESOL learners (Weinstein, 2001). However, as Weinstein (2001) notes, "Unfortunately, without guidelines and rigorous procedures, until a system is agreed upon, alternative assessments do not yet produce reliable hard data and are difficult to compare across programs" (p. 182). She adds, "This is a serious drawback for funders" (p. 182). On one hand, there is an apparent need for large-scale standardized but indirect testing procedures, such as the CASAS, which allow comparisons across programs (for both evaluation and research). On the other hand, it is desirable to promote speaking skills through direct testing and locally appropriate program and course assessment procedures.

EFFECTIVE PRACTICES AND STANDARDS FOR TEACHING SPEAKING TO ADULT ESOL LEARNERS

This section briefly reviews what is known about successful teaching of speaking skills and the development of standards related to the teaching of speaking to adult ESOL learners, before turning to issues related to the preparation of adult ESOL teachers. Although a number of studies have been done on literacy instruction for adult ESOL learners, there is little research on the effectiveness of teaching of oral skills in the adult ESOL context. Although ESOL programs are "the fastest growing component in federally funded adult education efforts . . . there is a dearth of empirical research about what works for whom and under what circumstances" (Weinstein, 2001, p. 181). (However, see Banke et al., 2002, for research conducted at Portland State University's lab school.)

One national study (Condelli, Wrigley, Yoon, Cronen, & Sebum, 2003) of literacy development reported some findings regarding documented gains in low-level adult ESOL learners' speaking skills. Data were collected in 38 classes across 13 different programs in Arizona, California, Illinois, Minnesota, New York, Texas, and Washington. The total sample involved 495 students, more than half of whom were Spanish speakers. Other participants spoke Hmong, Somali, or any of 30 other home languages.

Using the oral component of the BEST as the criterion measure, Condelli et al. (2003) determined that instructional variables, class variables, and student variables were related to growth in oral language skills. First, with regard to instructional variables, "students in classes where teachers used the students' native language as an aid to instruction had faster development" (p. 4). Likewise, where the teacher "used a varied practice and interaction strategy" and "emphasized oral English communication" (p. 4), the learners had faster growth. Second, "classes that had more scheduled instruction time (hours per week) had more student growth" (p. 4). Finally, three student variables were significant: Younger students, students that attended at a higher rate, and students with higher initial basic reading skills had faster growth in their speaking skills.[5] This research is promis-

---

[5] The Condelli et al. study has not yet been formally published, so these comments are based on the summary. The results are related to the BEST test, and the report summary does not specify the relationship of speaking and listening scores in the research findings. Nor does it state whether "rate" represents frequency or intensity.

ing, but because the main focus of the study was on literacy, more detailed information is needed about teaching speaking to adult ESOL learners.

Standards Promoting Effective Practices

In the United States, the standards movement has begun to influence adult ESOL programs. Standards are codified, official, agreed-upon outcome statements that embody expectations about learning and performance. As Brindley (1998) notes, "Variously known . . . as *standards, benchmarks, attainment targets, bandscales, profiles* and *competencies,* outcome statements are, broadly speaking, standards of performance against which learners' progress and achievement can be compared" (p. 48; italics in the original).

Teachers of English to Speakers of Other Languages, Inc. (TESOL), an international professional association, has spearheaded the development of standards for adult ESOL learners in the United States. TESOL has offered workshops and produced guidelines (see, e.g., TESOL, 2000) to help adult educators better meet the needs of nonnative-speaking refugees and immigrants. These standards were developed by recognized leaders in adult ESOL with the input of concerned educators and other stakeholders throughout the country. (See Florez, 2002, and Short, 2000.)

Another promising development is the National Reporting System (NRS), an accountability system for federally funded adult education programs. According to its Web site (http://www.nrsweb.org), the NRS includes the following components:

- A set of student measures to allow assessment of the impact of adult education instruction,
- Methodologies for collecting the measures,
- Reporting forms and procedures,
- Training and technical assistance activities to assist states in collecting the measures.

On entering a program, students are assessed to determine their educational functioning level. After a given amount of instruction or time, a follow-up assessment takes place, and the results of the initial and follow-up assessments are compared. The change in educational functioning level determines students' educational gains.

There are six levels each for adult basic education and ESOL students in the NRS. Each level describes what students entering at a particular level can do in the areas of reading, writing, numeracy, speaking, listening, functional and workplace skills, and competencies. The six "functioning levels" for adult ESOL learners are Beginning ESL Literacy, Beginning ESL, Low Intermediate ESL, High Intermediate ESL, Low Advanced ESL, and High Advanced ESL. The appendix provides a copy of only those skills and competencies related to speaking. (This information was downloaded January 30, 2004, from http://www.nrsweb.org.)

Using these descriptors, programs determine the appropriate initial placement level for adult ESOL learners based on a standardized assessment procedure. In fact, each level is connected to benchmarks from the BEST and CASAS. For example, the NRS Level 2, "Beginning ESL," skills are connected to scores between 16 and 41 on the oral section of the BEST, and those for NRS Level 4, "High Intermediate ESL," relate to BEST oral section scores between 51 and 57. In comparison, "High Advanced" skills listed at NRS Level 6 are related to BEST oral scores of 65 or higher. The program staff determines the skill areas in which to assess the student, based on the individual's instructional needs and goals.

ESOL Speaking Standards in Other Countries

In Canada, the standards movement has also influenced the education of adult ESOL learners. *The Canadian Language Benchmarks 2000* for adult ESOL learners (Pawlikowska-Smith, 2000) are organized in terms of basic, intermediate, and advanced proficiency. For each stage, the document contains global performance descriptions. The accompanying "benchmark" explains what learners at this level can do, gives examples of tasks and texts they can work with, and also lists performance indicators. (See Holt, 1995, for further discussion of low-level adult ESOL learners.)

In Australia, national standards have been written for several facets of education, but those most closely related to concerns about the adult ESOL population in the United States are from Australia's Adult Migrant English Program (AMEP; see Brindley, 1998, and Lipa, 1993). For example, the core competencies at Stage 1 for adult ESOL learners in the AMEP program say such learners "can exchange highly familiar information in spoken language; can negotiate a simple oral transaction to obtain specific goods and services; can recount a short familiar event; [and] can open and respond appropriately in short casual conversation exchanges" (Lipa, 1993, p. 40). By Stage 2 in the AMEP core competencies, adult ESOL learners "can understand and give spoken instructions in a range of contexts; can exchange familiar information in spoken language; can negotiate oral transactions for goods and services in a range of contexts; [and] can initiate and participate in short casual conversations" (p. 41). (For more about the teaching of speaking in Australia, see Burns & Joyce, 1997.)

Such national standards provide one means for defining goals, systematizing instruction, and evaluating adult ESOL learners' progress, both within and across programs. The next decade will provide many opportunities for investigating the impact of such standards on instructional programs, but the widespread standards initiative does raise some concerns. Brindley (1998) has written an extensive review of assessment in the context of standards projects in Australia, Canada, the United Kingdom, and the United States. He cautions that "a constant preoccupation with targets and 'terminal behaviour' brings with it a number of potential pitfalls, not the least of which is the tendency for assessment to dominate teaching and learning" (p. 52). Brindley also reminds us that "the quality of the information provided on outcomes will only be as good as the assessments on which the reporting is based" (p. 76).

Professional Preparation for Adult ESOL Teachers

In some states, "there is still no requirement beyond a college degree to teach adult ESL" (Florez, 1997, p. 1). Kutner (1992) notes that "because of the lack of state certification requirements and the lack of training opportunities in institutions of higher education, most adult education staff development takes place through voluntary inservice offerings (e.g., workshops and conferences) rather than in preservice training" (Staff Development Formats section, ¶ 1). Unfortunately, "many ABE and ESL teachers and volunteer instructors receive little or no training, either in subject matter content or in the process of teaching English to adults" (Kutner, 1992, Staff Development section, ¶ 1).

A report from the National Institute for Literacy (2000) reviewed state certification requirements for adult education instructors in general, and only mentioned ESOL instructors in a few places. The report states that a "large majority of adult education teachers are part-time (87% in 1993), and often receive little training and experience high turnover" (p. 4). It also says that 24 states require certification for adult educators (see p. 8), but does not specify which of these states require special certification for adult ESOL teachers. The report does say, however, that "roughly 80 to 90 percent of [adult] ESOL instructors are part-time, without benefits or contracts, and are often volunteers" (p. 11). In addition, many states "include ESOL teachers in their adult education certification requirements but in several states there is no requirement beyond a college degree to teach ESOL" (p. 11).[6]

There is evidence that, in the absence of effective preservice education and inservice development, teachers typically teach as they have been taught, whether or not such methods are appropriate for their students. Kennedy (1990) noted that "teachers acquire seemingly indelible imprints from their own experiences as students, and these imprints are tremendously difficult to shake" (p. 17). Lortie (1975) referred to this phenomenon as the *13,000-hour apprenticeship of observation*—that is, the many thousands of hours teachers spend as students observing the implicit models provided by their own teachers.

After conducting a longitudinal study of language teachers, Freeman (1992) concluded that "the memories gained through their 'apprenticeship of observation' function as de facto guides for teachers as they approach what they do" (p. 3). This early imprinting might affect the quality of instruction if teachers who wish to teach communicatively were taught languages with the grammar-translation method or the audiolingual method. If teachers themselves did not "observe" communicative language teaching skills as learners, they could acquire these skills through inservice or preservice training, individual readings, and observation of communicative lessons.

Whether the working conditions of adult ESOL teachers support high-quality instruction for adults who want to improve their speaking skills is also unknown. Citing the work of Willett and Jeannot (1993), Florez (2002) says professionals who teach adult ESOL learners "work in the margins" (p.1): "They work in left-over spaces, with inappropriate materials, under unpleasant conditions, for little money or professional status, with students who are ignored and excluded by the dominant society" (Willett & Jeannot, 1993, p. 477). According to Florez (2002), many teachers who work with adult learners are part-time, hourly employees teaching in more than one program: "Turnover rates are high, and burn-out is common. . . . Adult ESL professionals often feel that recognition and compensation are

---

[6]Joy Kreeft Peyton of the Center for Applied Linguistics says, "Where structured programs have been established to meet the demand, you may see very clearly defined certification requirements. However, if you are in an area of low demand, or where programs are very informally structured, the requirements may be different" (personal communication, February 4, 2004).

less than adequate and that their programs are given a low status relative to other adult education components" (p. 1).

It is worrisome, therefore, that ESOL speaking classes for adults may be taught by untrained teachers without the appropriate linguistic knowledge and pedagogic background for helping ESOL learners improve their speaking skills (Florez, 1997; Kutner, 1992). One wonders whether teachers who do not receive specific and ongoing ESOL training in how to teach adult learners can really provide the type of effective instruction necessary for learning the complex skill of speaking English fluently and accurately in everyday settings.

Although it is unclear the extent to which ESOL teachers are trained to teach speaking skills, there are efforts in the field to provide resources to teachers. For example, TESOL has produced resources for teachers of adult ESOL learners, such as the books *New Ways in Teaching Adults* (Lewis, 1997) and *New Ways in Teaching Speaking* (Bailey & Savage, 1994). TESOL has also published guidelines for people teaching English in workplace contexts (Friedenberg, Kennedy, Lomperis, Martin & Westerfield, 2003). Such associations also offer short-term training opportunities for teachers, including workshops and conferences at the regional, state, and national level.

CURRICULAR ISSUES IN TEACHING SPEAKING TO ADULT ESOL LEARNERS

Curriculum refers to what is taught in educational programs and the sequence in which that subject matter is presented. In order for adult ESOL learners to benefit from the curriculum of speaking courses (or the speaking component of general courses), they must first have access to the content. In other words, instruction must be scheduled at convenient times and classes must meet in accessible places, at a tuition rate that does not prohibit ESOL learners from enrolling. Second, the course content must be relevant to the adult ESOL learners' needs. That is, the topics and skills covered should be directly related to issues that adult ESOL learners deal with as they speak English in their daily lives.

I did not find any research that specifically addresses whether one curricular model is more effective than another in fostering adult ESOL speaking skills. However, it is worthwhile to consider innovative curricular models and program structures that might better meet the speaking needs of adult ESOL learners in terms of access and relevance than do traditional grammar-based syllabuses. This section considers content-based instruction, use of authentic materials, and English for specific purposes—particularly workplace ESOL, in which work-related language classes are offered at the jobsite.

Content-Based Curricula

Research suggests, "Adults learn best when learning is contextualized, emphasizing communication of meaning and use of English in real situations" (TESOL, 2000, p. 15). In addition, "By drawing on learners' background knowledge and thus ratifying the value of experiences that adult learners bring into the classroom, adult education ESOL programs can make instruction more relevant to the learners, who have limited time to devote to formal learning" (p. 15).

Central to content-based instruction is the concept that students learn the language by using it to study some particular content area. Brinton, Snow, and Wesche (1989) define content-based instruction (CBI) as "the integration of particular content with language teaching aims" and "the concurrent teaching of academic subject matter and second language skills" (p. 2). The CBI curricular model appears especially promising for teaching speaking (as well as other skills) in adult ESOL programs, given the limited time working adults have for studying. In effective content-based instruction, learners can gain subject-matter knowledge and language skills at the same time.

Reilly (1988) reviews combining the teaching of English with math, science, and social studies and explains that CBI integrates ESOL instruction with subject-matter coverage. Thus, this curricular model promotes dual goals: the learning of the subject matter and the development of English skills. English is the vehicle for teaching and learning (see Crandall, 1994), and the students' English-language development is also a learning outcome. Shaw (1996) says CBI is beneficial "in terms of practicality (the experience would facilitate future professional performance) and motivation (students would be more interested in language classes which are a vehicle for content relevant to their professional interests)" (p. 319).

Practicality and student motivation are directly related to curricular decisions affecting adult ESOL learners. Content courses (i.e., those built around a content rather than around language structures) can relate to adult ESOL students' professional and social needs for spoken English. One such content area for developing students' speaking skills is citizenship. As Nixon and Keenan (1997) note:

> Speaking English has been a requirement for citizenship since the turn of the last century . . . [i.e., 1900]. An INS examiner evaluates the applicants' knowledge of U.S. history and government by asking selected questions. . . . However, the ability to speak and understand English must still be demonstrated in an oral interview. (p. 1)

Other likely CBI foci for adult ESOL learners include the U.S. education system, local community resources, and health care.

In fact, substantial work has been done on the topic of health care in the development of literacy skills for ESOL learners (see, e.g., Adkins, Sample, & Birman, 1999; Rudd, Moeykens, & Colton, 2000). Research by Cathcart (1989) on spoken doctor–patient interactions could provide the basis for adult ESOL speaking lessons in a course with health-related content.

To offer content-based curricula, ESOL teaching professionals must have the skills to conduct needs assessments, interpret the resulting data, and design appropriate curricula to meet adult ESOL learners' needs. This approach to curriculum design may be particularly important for new arrivals who must meet their day-to-day needs in a new country, because, as Kuo (2000) noted, "Successful ESL curricular designs attempt to address these student needs to ensure proper acclimation to the new environment" (The ESL Curriculum section, ¶ 2).

English for Special Purposes (ESP)

Content-based instruction is related to (but different from) English for specific purposes (ESP) curricula. ESP is an approach to curriculum design that analyzes the linguistic needs of a particular group of learners defined by a common setting or goal (see Castaldi, 1991). In content-based instruction, the learners' focus is the actual subject matter rather than the language in which they are learning that content. In contrast, in ESP curricula, the focus is on the language as it is used in a particular context (such as business English or Spanish for nursing purposes), rather than on the subject matter per se (e.g., the business or the nursing curricula).

With the development of the ESP movement in the 1970s, universities, adult schools, and community colleges began to develop special-purpose courses for ESOL students. At first the topics of ESP courses were related to postsecondary academic disciplines, such as English for science and technology, and English for business courses. For nonacademic adult learners, the ESP movement at that time resulted in two types of curricula: vocational ESOL (VESL) and survival English.

One promising model of curriculum delivery connects the educational program with the adult ESOL learners' employers. For some time, VESL programs have been offered through adult schools, community colleges, and vocational–technical schools (see Buchanan, 1990). More recently, however, some adult ESOL programs have been offered at the learners' actual work sites. The phrase *workplace ESOL* refers to both the linguistic content of the language lessons and to the venue where the courses are offered.

In this context, the language instruction is typically sponsored by the employer and housed at the learners' place of employment. An example from agriculture is a California vineyard that offers a summer ESOL course for field workers. Every April the company designates 20 senior workers to take the class. Those who choose to participate are released from work for 2 hours, 4 days per week. (The company pays their normal wage for the first hour, and they are expected to put in their own time for the second hour.) A 12-week ESOL course begins in early May, concentrating on basic literacy and oral communication skills with a focus on the language needed in their work (Sherry Baildon, personal communication).

Workplace ESOL lessons focus on the vocabulary, grammar, and speech acts needed by employees in their work context. For instance, a community college in Washington State has agreements with several businesses to provide ESOL instruction for employees with limited English-speaking abilities. Room attendants, laundry workers, and kitchen stewards receive ESOL training at some major hotels. Classes are also housed in vocational programs at the college, such as the wood-construction program and culinary program. Adult ESOL learners develop their speaking skills while learning workplace basics and then are placed in entry-level jobs in their field. Employers are very supportive of these programs (Daphne Cuizon, personal communication).

Discussions of workplace ESOL programs (e.g., Martin & Lomperis, 2002; McGroarty & Scott, 1993) suggest that because such programs are located at the learners' job sites and are tailored specifically to their on-the-job communication needs, workplace ESOL is an efficient vehicle for the delivery of instruction. However, Burt and Saccomano (1995) caution, "It is unlikely that a workplace ESL class of 40–60 hours will turn participants with low-level English skills into fluent speakers of English" (p. 3).

Authentic Materials in Teaching Speaking for Adult ESOL Learners

ESP curricula are typically based on the close examination of naturally occurring texts (both spoken and written) and involve the use of authentic materials for teaching speaking and listening. *Authentic materials* are based on naturally occurring conversations and other spoken (or written) samples, such as announcements and radio broadcasts, that are relevant to the learners' lives. Spelleri (2002) defines authentic materials as "any items created for the general community and not specifically for the ESL community" (p. 16). They are contrasted with intentionally pedagogical texts, such as written dialogues and simplified listening passages constructed for teaching purposes.

When examining textbooks, videotapes, audiotapes, or computer-delivered lessons for authenticity, one must consider at least three issues. First, there is the *authenticity of the text* (how natural the language sample is). Second, there is *authenticity of the task* (what adult ESOL learners are supposed to do with that language for learning or practice opportunities; Nunan, 1989). Third, there is *authenticity of response*—that is, how natural, contextualized, and uncontrived the speech required of the learners may be (e.g., in a testing situation; see McNamara, 2000, pp. 27–29, for further discussion.) Thus, authentic materials must be relevant to the learners' lives.

Cathcart (1989) argued for curricula based on authentic rather than contrived language and noted the "mismatch between grammar structures in natural conversation and those in ESL texts" (p. 107). To analyze the characteristics of conversations, Cathcart collected naturally occurring speech data in a pediatrician's office and two women's clinics. The use of authentic materials based on such data for teaching speaking is important because "simulated excerpts may serve to mislead students about the nature of everyday interactions" (p. 105).

Teachers of adult ESOL learners "may, or may not, be given textbooks or materials for teaching the oral skills class" (Lazaraton, 2001, p 105). Where there are prepared texts available, they may be lacking in terms of their authenticity. Lazaraton and Skuder (1997) analyzed ESOL speaking texts published between 1976 and 1995, and found that "even the most recent texts fell short on the authenticity criteria used (formality, turn-taking, quantity of talk, etc.)" (Lazaraton, 2001, p.105).

IMPLICATIONS FOR TEACHING SPEAKING TO ADULT ESOL LEARNERS

All of the foregoing information has implications for the teaching of speaking to adult ESOL students in the United States. These implications are discussed next in terms of practice, research, and policy. They raise a number of important questions to be addressed by researchers and policy-makers with regard to educational opportunities for adult ESOL learners in the United States.

Implications for Practice

As previously noted, the grammar-translation method teaches primarily reading and writing skills, and "the shortcomings of audiolingual methodology are widely acknowledged" (Savignon, 1991, p. 262). In helping nonacademic adult ESOL learners meet the demands of speaking English in everyday life, courses based on interactive communicative-language teaching combined with language-awareness activities seem to be a promising instructional approach for adult ESOL learners to improve their speaking skills (Graham, 1994; Swain, 2000). Communicative language teaching emphasizes speaking and listening rather than reading and writing. Although communicative language teaching has traditionally emphasized fluency, accuracy can also be developed, particularly if a language-awareness component is central to the instruction. I have found no convincing research on adult ESOL learners that demonstrates the superiority of any particular method; however, the activities associated with communicative-language teaching and language awareness seem, by their nature, more likely to be helpful to nonacademic ESOL learners who really want to speak naturally.

As discussed throughout this chapter, the complexity of spoken language means that teachers need solid knowledge and understanding about the nature of speech and strong methodological skills for helping adult ESOL learners develop their speaking skills. It should be clear that teaching adult ESOL speaking classes (or working on speaking in four-skills courses) does not simply involve having conversations with the students. Thus, preservice training programs should prepare novice teachers specifically to work with adult ESOL learners, whose needs differ dramatically from those of elementary or secondary school ESOL pupils and from those of academic adult ESOL learners. Student teaching or internships should take place in actual adult school and community college courses that serve adult ESOL learners (even if that is less convenient for faculty members than placing trainees in their own university's ESOL program). (See Rymes, 2002, for a description of an adult ESOL course at a neighborhood center that served as the practicum site for teachers in training.)

The findings of Condelli et al. (2003) have implications for teacher education as well. They found that when teachers were able to use the students' first language, the students experienced faster development. Also, where the teacher "used a varied practice and interaction strategy" and "emphasized oral English communication," the learners had faster growth (p. 4). The skills for teaching oral communication using varied, interactive activities should thus be part of the preservice training for adult ESOL teachers.

Implications for Research

The population of adult ESOL learners has not been studied as widely as either international students at colleges and universities, or linguistic minority children in K–12 public school contexts in this country. The research that does exist has focused more on adult ESOL learners' literacy skills than their speaking skills. Yet "immigration to the United States is approaching an all-time high" (Kurzet, 1997, p. 69). In spite of the current numbers of ESOL learners and the predicted increase in their numbers, we have relatively little research about the most effective ways to teach speaking skills to nonacademic adult ESOL learners for effective and efficient development. Answering these specific research questions, among others, would help ESOL programs and practitioners better serve adult ESOL learners:

1. What specific in-class activities selected by teachers promote the development of adult ESOL learners' oral skills most effectively and efficiently? (The research by Condelli et al. [2003] is promising but it focused primarily on literacy development, using data from fewer than 500 low-level learners in five states. Replications and extensions of this research are needed.)

2. What teaching activities and curricula lead to gains reported in the NRS?

3. Given the time pressures on adult ESOL learners, what combination of class time and out-of-class opportunities help them achieve the levels of speaking proficiency (including both accuracy and fluency) to which they aspire?

4. To what extent do patterns of high enclosure and social isolation inhibit the development of adult ESOL learners' English speaking skills? Where patterns of high enclosure exist, what community resources can be used to increase opportunities for English interaction?

5. What roles can technology play in the teaching of speaking to adult ESOL learners? Can software programs comparing the learners' output to

that of native or proficient speakers of English demonstrably improve the learners' pronunciation? Can technology increase adult ESOL learners' access to English in ways that affect their speaking skills?

6. As pronunciation problems have been shown to influence others' perceptions of adult ESOL learners, what are the most effective and efficient means for improving learners' pronunciation?

7. Do standards influence how speaking skills are taught to adult ESOL learners in the United States? What impact do the standards for adult ESOL learners (TESOL, 2000) have on teacher preparation programs?

8. Regarding assessment, to what extent do scores on the BEST and CASAS tests accurately predict adult ESOL learners' success in speaking English in social and work-related contexts? What, if any, is the washback effect generated by the widespread use of the multiple-choice CASAS exam in teaching speaking to adult ESOL learners? What is the washback effect of the BEST, a direct test of speaking? What, if any, will be the washback effect of the newly developed computerized version of the BEST in teaching speaking to ESOL learners?

There are also general contexts that need to be studied. For instance, it is felt that partnerships with learners' employers (or potential employers) offer time-effective opportunities for adults who might otherwise not be able to do so to attend classes. Fitzgerald (1995) reported that 36% of adult ESOL learners "were employed at the time of [their] enrollment in adult education" (ESL Profile section, ¶ 1), and Condelli et al. (2003) found that greater instructional time led to greater student gains on the oral component of the BEST. Given time pressures on working adults, the combination of the workplace site as a venue and financial support from employers is a promising combination for promoting class attendance and subsequently language acquisition by adult learners. (See, e.g., Burt & Saccomano, 1995; Martin & Lomperis, 2002; McGroarty & Scott, 1993.) Research is needed to determine which features of workplace ESOL programs (e.g., accessible sites, financial support, situated relevance of the curriculum, etc.) lead to greater attendance and improvement of the adult learners' speaking skills.

The preservice and inservice training of adult ESOL instructors is also a broad topic for further investigation. A national survey of preparation practices of adult ESOL instructors would be useful for determining whether adult ESOL teachers have the knowledge and skills they need to teach the complex skill of speaking English. Observational studies of effective adult ESOL teachers (those whose students make notable gains, attend regularly, show increased willingness to try to use English outside of class, etc.) could inform teacher-preparation programs.

Funding should be devoted to research on the development of adult ESOL learners' speaking skills, as has been done for their literacy development. With support from the public and the private sectors, organizations such as the TESOL International Research Foundation (TIRF; see http://www.tirfonline.org) could encourage and adjudicate proposals for research on the language development of adult ESOL learners.

Implications for Policy

Policymakers at local, state, and national levels should be aware of the needs of adult ESOL learners in the United States. They should also be conversant with the educational issues and choices we face as a nation with regard to maximizing educational opportunities for new Americans. These issues include the following concerns.

Partnerships in support of adult ESOL programs have become very important as public funding for adult education decreases. In Massachusetts, for instance, Fish (2002) notes that 82% of the growth in the workforce in the 1980s and 1990s resulted from immigration. He estimates that immigrants who are proficient in English are likely to earn about 20% more than those who lack English proficiency. Fish adds that many Massachusetts organizations, such as the Boston Foundation, Citizens Bank, Fleet Bank, Verizon, the State Street Foundation, and the New England Regional Council of Carpenters, have been providing English-language instruction for their employees and, in some cases, for the surrounding community. Fish also states, however, that there are more than 15,000 people on the waiting list for government-funded ESOL courses. He calls for communication among government officials, the private sector, labor unions, and nonprofit organizations to determine how best to meet the need for ESOL courses. Unfortunately, a national survey of 12,000 businesses by the Bureau of Labor Statistics in 1994 revealed that only 3% of those businesses offered basic skills or ESL training for employees (Burt, 1995; see also Spence, 1999, for a discussion of worker-centered learning).

TESOL and other U.S.-based organizations (such as the Center for Applied Linguistics) have participated in the development of standards for adult ESOL learners (Short, 2000; TESOL, 2000). There are also models of standards available from other English-speaking countries (see, e.g., Pawlikowska-Smith, 2000). Policymakers should devote resources to the implementation of these standards (e.g., for designing curricula, developing materials, and guiding assessment), and researchers should investigate the standards' impact on instruction and assessment (Brindley, 1998).

Funding policies are influenced by demonstrable results, often scores from standardized tests. As policymakers demand educational accountability, however, they should be aware that assessment instruments—including inappropriate tests—can drive instruction and shape the curriculum.

Implications for policy should have an effect on resource distribution. Writing about professionalism in adult ESOL literacy instruction, Crandall (1993) stated:

> Large multi-level classes, limited resources, substandard facilities, intermittent funding, limited contracts with few benefits: This is the context in which adult ESL literacy practitioners work. Adult education is a stepchild of K–12 education and an afterthought in U.S. educational policy. (p. 497)

These comments are still true today and apply just as well to speaking instruction for adult ESOL learners as to literacy training contexts.

The number of adult ESOL learners in this country is growing, and their importance in the workforce and in communities should not be underestimated. Given the complexity of speaking in a new language and the importance of spoken interaction to promote language acquisition, there is a great need for further research on how best to help this significant group of learners acquire the English speaking skills they need.

APPENDIX: NRS SPEAKING SKILLS AND COMPETENCIES FOR ADULT ESOL LEARNERS

Level 1: Beginning ESL Literacy

Speaking and Listening

- Individual cannot speak or understand English, or understands only isolated words or phrases.

Functional and Workplace Skills

- Individual functions minimally or not at all in English and can communicate only through gestures or a few isolated words, such as name and other personal information.
- May recognize only common signs or symbols (e.g., stop sign, product logos).

- Can handle only very routine entry-level jobs that do not require oral or written communication in English.
- Has no knowledge of computers or technology.

Level 2: Beginning ESL

Speaking and Listening

- Individual can understand frequently used words in context and very simple phrases spoken slowly and with some repetition.
- There is little communicative output and only in the most routine situations.
- There is little or no control over basic grammar.
- Communicates survival needs simply, and there is some understanding of simple questions.

Functional and Workplace Skills

- Individual functions with difficulty in situations related to immediate needs and in limited social situations.
- Has some simple oral communication abilities using simple learned and repeated phrases.
- May need frequent repetition.
- Can handle routine entry-level jobs that require only the most basic written or oral English communication and in which job tasks can be demonstrated.

Level 3: Low Intermediate ESL

Speaking and Listening

- Individual can understand simple learned phrases and limited new phrases containing familiar vocabulary spoken slowly with frequent repetition.
- Can ask and respond to questions using such phrases.
- Can express basic survival needs and participate in some routine social conversations, although with some difficulty.
- Has some control of basic grammar.

Functional and Workplace Skills

- Individual can interpret simple directions and schedules, signs and maps.

- Can fill out simple forms but needs support on some documents that are not simplified.
- Can handle routine entry-level jobs that involve some written or oral English communication, but in which job tasks can be demonstrated.
- Can use simple computer programs and can perform a sequence of routine tasks given directions using technology (e.g., fax machine, computer).

Level 4: High Intermediate ESL

Speaking and Listening

- Individual can understand learned phrases and short new phrases containing familiar vocabulary spoken slowly and with some repetition.
- Can communicate basic survival needs with some help.
- Can participate in conversation in limited social situations and use new phrases with hesitation.
- Relies on description and concrete terms.
- Has inconsistent control of more complex grammar.

Functional and Workplace Skills

- Individual can meet basic survival and social needs, can follow some simple oral and written instruction, and has some ability to communicate on the telephone on familiar subjects.

Level 5: Low Advanced ESL

Speaking and Listening

- Individual can converse on many everyday subjects and some subject with unfamiliar vocabulary, but may need repetition, rewording, or slower speech.
- Can speak creatively but with hesitation.
- Can clarify general meaning by rewording and has control of basic grammar.
- Understands descriptive and spoken narrative and can comprehend abstract concepts in familiar contexts.

Functional and Workplace Skills

- Individual can function independently to meet most survival needs and can communicate on the telephone on familiar topics.

- Can interpret simple charts and graphics.
- Can handle jobs that require simple oral and written instructions, multistep diagrams, and limited public interaction.
- Can use all basic software applications, understand the impact of technology, and select the correct technology in a new situation.

Level 6: High Advanced ESL

Speaking and Listening

- Individual can understand and participate effectively in face-to-face conversations on everyday subjects spoken at normal speed.
- Can converse and understand independently in survival, work, and social situations.
- Can expand on basic ideas in conversation, but with some hesitation.
- Can clarify general meaning and control basic grammar, although still lacks total control over complex structures.

Functional and Workplace Skills

- Individual has a general ability to use English effectively to meet most routine social and work situations.
- Can interpret routine charts, graphs, and tables and complete forms.
- Has high ability to communicate on the telephone and understand radio and television.
- Can meet work demands that require reading and writing and can interact with the public.
- Can use common software and learn new applications.
- Can define the purpose of software and select new applications appropriately.
- Can instruct others in the use of software and technology.

ACKNOWLEDGMENTS

I wish to thank Sarah Springer and Anne Kiel at the Monterey Institute of International Studies for their help with library research, word-processing, and locating online resources. At the Center for Applied Linguistics, Miriam Burt, Stephanie Stauffer, Carol Van Duzer, and Sarah Young helped me locate resources, as did Larry Condelli at the American Institute for Research. Earlier versions of the manuscript benefited from helpful comments by Brian Lynch, Gail Weinstein, and the staff of the National Center for the Study of Adult Learning and Literacy—particularly Cristine Smith. Of course, remaining oversights or errors in reporting are my own responsibility.

REFERENCES

Adkins, M. A., Sample, B., & Birman, D. (1999). *Mental health and the adult refugee: The role of the ESL teacher.* Washington, DC: National Center for ESL Literacy Education. (ERIC Document Reproduction Service No. ED439625)

Alderson, J. C., & Wall, D. (1993). Does washback exist? *Applied Linguistics, 14,* 115–129.

Asher, J. J., Kusodo, J. A., & de la Torre, R. (1993). Learning a second language through commands: The second field test. In J. W. Oller, Jr. (Ed.), *Methods that work: Ideas for literacy and language teachers* (3rd ed., pp. 13–21). Boston: Heinle & Heinle.

Bachman, L. (1990). *Fundamental considerations in language testing.* Oxford: Oxford University Press.

Bailey, K. M. (1998). *Learning about language assessment: Dilemmas, decisions and directions.* Boston: Heinle & Heinle.

Bailey, K. M., & Savage, L. (Eds.). (1994). *New ways in teaching speaking.* Alexandria, VA: Teachers of English to Speakers of Other Languages, Inc.

Banke, S., Brillanceau, D., Harris, K., Kurzet, R., Lynch, B., Reder, S., & Setzler, K. (2002, October). Research at Portland State University's adult ESOL lab school. *TESOL Research Interest Section Newsletter, 9*(2), 4–6.

Brindley, G. (1998). Outcomes-based assessment and reporting in language learning programmes: A review of the issues. *Language Testing, 15*(1), 45–85.

Brinton, D., Snow, M. A., & Wesche, M. (1989). *Content-based second language instruction.* Boston: Heinle & Heinle.

Brown, G., & Yule, G. (1983). *Teaching the spoken language: An approach based on the analysis of conversational English.* Cambridge: Cambridge University Press.

Brown, J. D., & Hudson, T. (1998). The alternatives in language assessment. *TESOL Quarterly, 32*(4), 653–675.

Buchanan, K. (1990). *Vocational English-as-a-second-language programs.* Washington, DC: ERIC Clearinghouse on Languages and Linguistics. (ERIC Document Reproduction Service No. ED321551)

Buck, G. (1988). Testing listening comprehension in Japanese university entrance examinations. *JALT Journal,* 10, 15–42.

Burns, A., & Joyce, H. (1997). *Focus on speaking.* Sydney: National Center for English Language Teaching and Research.

Burt, M. (1995). *Selling workplace ESL instructional programs.* Washington, DC: National Clearinghouse for ESL Literacy Education. (ERIC Document Reproduction Service No. ED392315)

Burt, M., & Keenan, F. (1995). *Adult ESL learner assessment: Purposes and tools.* Washington, DC: National Clearinghouse for ESL Literacy Education. (ERIC Document Reproduction Service No. ED0-LE-95-08)

Burt, M., & Saccomano, M. (1995). *Evaluating workplace ESL instructional programs.* Washington, DC: National Clearinghouse for ESL Literacy Education. (ERIC Document Reproduction Service No. ED386961)

Bygate, M. (2001). Speaking. In R. Carter & D. Nunan (Eds.), *The Cambridge guide to teaching English to speakers of other languages* (pp. 14–20). Cambridge: Cambridge University Press.

Canale, M., & Swain, M. (1980). Theoretical bases of communicative approaches to second language testing and teaching. *Applied Linguistics, 1*(1), 1–47.

Castaldi, T. (1991). *Ethnography and adult workplace literacy program design.* Washington, DC: National Clearinghouse for ESL Literacy Education. (ERIC Document Reproduction Service No. ED334867)

Cathcart, R. L. (1989). Authentic discourse and the survival English curriculum. *TESOL Quarterly, 23*(1), 105–126.

Celce-Murcia, M., Brinton, D., & Goodwin, J. (1996). *Teaching pronunciation: Reference for teachers of English to speakers of other languages.* Cambridge: Cambridge University Press.

Center for Applied Linguistics. (1982). *Basic English Skills Test: Core section scoring booklet.* Washington, DC: Author.

Center for Applied Linguistics. (2000). BEST evolves to meet new needs. *CAL Reporter, 14,* 1 & 5.

Cheng, L. L. (1998). *Enhancing the communication skills of newly-arrived Asian American students.* Washington, DC: ERIC Clearinghouse on Urban Education. (ERIC Document Reproduction Service No. ED420726)

Clark, J. L. D. (1979). Direct and semi-direct tests of speaking ability. In E. J. Briere & F. B. Hinofotis (Eds.), *Concepts in language testing* (35–49). Washington, DC: Teachers of English to Speakers of Other Languages, Inc.

Cohen, A. (1996). Developing the ability to perform speech acts. *Studies in Second Language Acquisition, 18,* 253–267.

Comprehensive Adult Student Assessment System. (1993). *CASAS technical manual.* San Diego: Author.

Condelli, L., Wrigley, H., Yoon, K., Cronen, S., & Sebum, M. (2003). *What works study for adult ESL literacy students: Study summary.* Washington, DC: U.S. Department of Education.

Crandall, J. (1993). Professionalism and professionalization of adult ESL literacy. *TESOL Quarterly, 27*(3), 497–515.

Crandall, J. (1994). *Content-centered language learning.* Washington, DC: ERIC Clearinghouse on Languages and Linguistics. (ERIC Document Reproduction Service No. ED367142)

Cumming, A. (1996). The concept of validation in language testing. In A. Cumming & R. Berwick (Eds.), *Validation in language testing* (pp. 1–14). Clevedon, Avon, UK: Multilingual Matters, Ltd.

d'Anglejan, A., Painchaud, G., & Renaud, C. (1986). Beyond the language classroom: A study of communicative abilities in adult immigrants following intensive instruction. *TESOL Quarterly, 20*(2), 185–205.

Donmall, B. G. (Ed.). (1985). *Language awareness. NCLE Papers and Reports 6.* London: Centre for Information on Language Teaching and Research.

Doughty, C., & Pica, T. (1986). "Information gap" tasks: Do they facilitate second language acquisition? *TESOL Quarterly, 20*(2), 305–325.

Douglas, D. (2000). *Assessing languages for specific purposes.* Cambridge: Cambridge University Press.

Eakin, E., & Ilyin, D. (1987). Review of the *Basic English Skills Test.* In J. C. Alderson, K. J. Krahnke, & C. W. Stansfield (Eds.), *Reviews of English language proficiency tests* (pp. 9–10). Alexandria, VA: Teachers of English to Speakers of Other Languages, Inc.

Ellis, R. (1990). *Instructed second language acquisition.* Oxford: Basil Blackwell.

Fasold, R. (1984). *The sociolinguistics of society.* Oxford: Blackwell.

Fish, L. K. (2002, November 23). Mastering English for economic reasons. *The Boston Globe,* p. A15.

Fitzgerald, N. B. (1995). *ESL instruction in adult education: Findings from a national evaluation.* Washington, DC: ERIC Clearinghouse for ESL Literacy Education. (ERIC Document Reproduction Service No. ED385171)

Florez, M. A. C. (1997). *The adult ESL teaching profession.* Washington, DC: ERIC Clearinghouse for ESL Literacy Education. (ERIC Document Reproduction Service No. ED413794)

Florez, M. A. C. (1998). *Improving adult ESL learners' pronunciation skills.* Washington, DC: ERIC Clearinghouse for ESL Literacy Education. (ERIC Document Reproduction Service No. ED-LE-98-04)

Florez, M. A. C. (1999). *Improving adult English language learners' speaking skills.* Washington, DC: Clearinghouse for ESL Literacy Education. (ERIC Document Reproduction Service No. EDO-LE-99-01)

Florez, M. A. C. (2002). *Content standards of adult ESL: NCLE annotated bibliography.* Washington, DC: National Center for ESL Literacy Education.

Ford, C. (1984). The influence of speech variety on teachers' evaluation of students with comparable academic ability. *TESOL Quarterly, 18*(1), 25–40.

Freeman, D. (1992). Language teacher education, emerging discourse, and change in classroom practice. In J. Flowerdew, M. Brock, & S. Hsia (Eds.), *Perspectives on language teacher education* (pp. 27–45). Hong Kong: City Polytechnic of Hong Kong.

Friedenberg, J., Kennedy, D., Lomperis, A., Martin, W., & Westerfield, K. (2003). *Effective practices in workplace language training: Guidelines for providers of workplace English language training services.* Alexandria, VA: Teachers of English to Speakers of Other Languages, Inc.

Gass, S. M. (1997). *Input, interaction, and the second language learner.* Mahwah, NJ: Lawrence Erlbaum Associates.

Goodwin, J. (2001). Teaching pronunciation. In M. Celce-Murcia (Ed.) *Teaching English as a second or foreign language* (3rd ed., pp. 117–138). Boston: Heinle & Heinle.

Graham, J. G. (1994). Four strategies to improve the speech of adult learners. *TESOL Journal, 3*(3), 26–28.

Gumperz, J. J., & Tannen, D. (1987). Individual and social differences in language use. In W. Wang & C. Fillmore (Eds.), *Individual differences in language ability and language behavior* (pp. 305–325). New York: Academic Press.

Hammerly, H. (1991). *Fluency and accuracy: Toward balance in language teaching and learning.* Clevedon, UK: Multilingual Matters.

Holt, G. M. (1995). *Teaching low-level adult ESL learners.* Washington, DC: ERIC Clearinghouse for ESL Literacy Education. (ERIC Document Reproduction Service No. ED379965)

Hughes, A. (1981). Conversational cloze as a measure of oral ability. *ELT Journal, 35*(2), 161–168.

Hughes, A. (1989). *Testing for language teachers.* Cambridge, UK: Cambridge University Press.

Ignash, J. M. (1995). Encouraging ESL students' persistence: The influence of policy on curricular design. *Community College Review, 23*(3), 17–34.

Kennedy, M. (1990). *Policy issues in teacher education.* East Lansing, MI: National Center for Research on Teacher Learning.

Kuo, E. W. (2000). *English as a second language: Program approaches at community colleges.* Washington, DC: ERIC Clearinghouse for Community Colleges. (ERIC Document Reproduction Service No. ED47859)

Kurzet, R. (1997, Winter). Quality versus quantity in the delivery of developmental programs for ESL students. *New Directions for Community Colleges, 100,* 53–62.

Kutner, M. (1992). *Staff development for ABE and ESL teachers and volunteers.* Washington, DC: National Clearinghouse for ESL Literacy Education. (ERIC Document Reproduction Service No. ED353862)

Lambert, W. E., Hodgson, R. C., Gardner, R. C., & Fillenbaum, S. (1960). Evaluational reactions to spoken language. *Journal of Abnormal and Social Psychology, 60*(1), 40–51.

Larsen-Freeman, D., & Long, M. H. (1991). *An introduction to second language acquisition research.* London: Longman.

Lazaraton, A. (2001). Teaching oral skills. In M. Celce-Murcia (Ed.) *Teaching English as a second or foreign language* (3rd ed., pp. 103–115). Boston: Heinle & Heinle.

Lazaraton, A., & Skuder, P. F. (1997). *Evaluating dialogue authenticity in ESL speaking texts.* Paper presented at the 31st Annual TESOL Convention, Orlando, Florida.

Lewis, M. (1997). *New ways in teaching adults.* Alexandria, VA: Teachers of English to Speakers of Other Languages, Inc.

Lipa, L. (1993). *Learner pathways in the Adult Migrant English Program.* Sydney, Australia: Macquarie University.

Lortie, D. (1975). *Schoolteacher: A sociological study.* Chicago: University of Chicago Press.

Major, R. C. (2001). *Foreign accent: The ontogeny and phylogeny of second language phonology.* Mahwah, NJ: Lawrence Erlbaum Associates.

Martin, W. M., & Lomperis, A. F. (2002). Determining the cost benefits, the return on investment, and the intangible impacts of language programs for development. *TESOL Quarterly, 36*(3), 399–429.

McGroarty, M., & Scott, S. (1993). *Workplace ESL instruction: Varieties and constraints.* Washington, DC: ERIC Clearinghouse for ESL Literacy Education. (ERIC Document Reproduction Service No. ED367190)

McNamara, T. (2000). *Language testing.* Oxford: Oxford University Press.

Merrifield, J. (2000). *Equipped for the future research report: Building the framework, 1993–1997.* Washington, DC: National Institute for Literacy.

Moholt, G. (1988). Computer-assisted instruction in pronunciation for Chinese speakers of American English. *TESOL Quarterly, 22*(1), 91–111.

Morley, J. (1991). The pronunciation component in teaching English to speakers of other languages. *TESOL Quarterly, 25*(3), 481–520.

Moss, D., & Van Duzer, C. (1998). *Project-based learning for adult English language learners.* Washington, DC: National Clearinghouse for ESL Literacy Education. (ERIC Document Reproduction Service No. ED427556)

Murphy, J. M. (1991). Oral communication in TESOL: Integrating speaking, listening and pronunciation. *TESOL Quarterly, 25*(1), 51–75.

National Institute for Literacy. (2000). *State policy update: The professionalization of adult education: Can state certification of adult educators contribute to a more professional workforce?* Washington, DC: Author.

Nixon, T., & Keenan, F. (1997). *Citizenship preparation for adult ESL learners.* Washington, DC: ERIC Clearinghouse for ESL Literacy Education. (ERIC Document Reproduction Service No. ED409747)

Nunan, D. (1989). *Designing tasks for the communicative classroom.* Cambridge: Cambridge University Press.

Nunan, D. (1991). *Language teaching methodology: A textbook for teachers.* New York: Prentice Hall.

Overtoom, C. (2000). *Employability skills: An update.* Columbus, OH: Center on Education and Training for Employment. (ERIC Document Reproduction Service No. ED445236)

Pawlikowska-Smith, J. (2000). *Canadian language benchmarks 2000.* Ottawa: Citizenship and Immigration Canada.

Pennington, M. C. (1989). Applications of computers in the development of speaking/listening proficiency. In M. C. Pennington (Ed.), *Teaching languages with computers: The state of the art* (pp. 99–121). La Jolla, CA: Athelstan.

Pennington, M. C. (1994). Recent research in L2 phonology: Implications for practice. In J. Morley (Ed.), *Pronunciation pedagogy and theory: New views, new directions* (pp. 92–108). Alexandria, VA: TESOL.

Piper, T., & Cansin, D. (1988). Factors influencing the foreign accent. *The Canadian Modern Language Review, 44*(2), 334–342.

Price-Machado, D. (2000). Can we bridge the gap between what we teach and test in the classroom and what the state tests with CASAS? *CATESOL News, 32*(1), 20, 21, 23.

Pridham, F. (2001). *The language of conversation.* London: Routledge.

Reilly, T. (1988). *ESL through content area instruction.* Washington, DC: ERIC Clearinghouse on Languages and Linguisitcs. (ERIC Document Reproduction Service No. ED296572)

Richards, J. C., & Rodgers, T. (1986). *Approaches and methods in language teaching: A descriptive analysis.* Cambridge: Cambridge University Press.

Rudd, R. E., Moeykens, B. A., & Colton, T. C. (2000). Health and literacy: A review of medical and public health literature. In J. Comings, B. Garner, & C. Smith (Eds.), *Annual review of adult learning and literacy* (Vol. 1, pp. 158–199). San Francisco: Jossey-Bass.

Rymes, B. (2002). Language development in the United States: Supervising adult ESOL preservice teachers in an immigrant community. *TESOL Quarterly, 36*(3), 431–452.

Savignon, S. J. (1991). Communicative language teaching: The state of the art. *TESOL Quarterly, 25*(2), 261–277.

Schumann, J. H. (1976). Social distance as a factor in second language acquisition. *Language Learning, 26*(1), 135–143.

Sharwood-Smith, M. (1981). Consciousness-raising and the second language learner. *Applied Linguistics, 2,* 159–168.

Sharwood-Smith, M. (1994). *Second language learning: Theoretical foundations.* London: Longman.

Shaw, P. A. (1996). Voices for improved learning: The ethnographer as co-agent of pedagogic change. In K. M. Bailey & D. Nunan (Eds.), *Voices from the language classroom: Qualitative research on language education* (pp. 318–338). New York: Cambridge University Press.

Short, D. J. (2000). *The ESL standards: Bridging the academic gap for English language learners.* Washington, DC: ERIC Clearinghouse on Languages and Linguistics. (ERIC Document Reproduction Service No. ED447728)

Spelleri, M. (2002). From lessons to life: Authentic materials bridge the gap. *ESL Magazine,* March/April, 16–18.

Spence, J. G. (1999). *Worker-centered learning: Labor's role.* Columbus, OH: ERIC Clearinghouse on Adult Career and Vocational Education. (ERIC Document Reproduction Service No. ED434247)

Stainton, C. (1992). Language awareness: Genre awareness—a focused review of the literature. *Language Awareness, 1*(2), 109–121.

Swain, M. (2000). The output hypothesis and beyond: Mediating acquisition through collaborative dialogue. In J. P. Lantolf (Ed.), *Sociocultural theory and second language learning* (pp. 97–114). Oxford: Oxford University Press.

Teachers of English to Speakers of Other Languages, Inc. (2000). *Program standards for adult education ESOL standards.* Alexandria, VA: Author.

Underhill, N. (1987). *Testing spoken language: A handbook of oral testing techniques.* Cambridge, UK: Cambridge University Press.

U.S. Bureau of the Census. (2003). *The foreign-born population: 2000.* Washington, DC: Author.

Van Duzer, C. (2002). *Issues in accountability and assessment for adult ESL instruction.* National Center for ESL Literacy Education. Washington, DC: Center for Applied Linguistics.

Van Duzer, C. H., & Berdan, R. (2000). Perspectives on assessment in adult ESOL instruction. In J. Comings, B. Garner, & C. Smith (Eds.), *Annual review of adult learning and literacy* (Vol. 1, pp. 200–242). San Francisco: Jossey-Bass.

van Lier, L. (1992). Not the nine o'clock linguistics class: Investigating contingency grammar. *Language Awareness, 1*(2), 91–108.

van Lier, L. (1995). *Introducing language awareness.* London: Penguin English.

van Lier, L. (1997). Language awareness. In L. van Lier & D. Corson (Eds.), *Knowledge about language. Encyclopedia of language and education* (Vol. 6, pp. 217–227). Dordrecht, Holland: Kluwer Academic.

van Lier, L. (2001). Language awareness. In R. Carter & D. Nunan (Eds.), *The Cambridge guide to teaching English to speakers of other languages* (pp. 160–165). Cambridge: Cambridge University Press.

Weddel, K. S., & Van Duzer, C. (1997). *Needs assessment for adult ESL learners.* Washington, DC: ERIC Clearinghouse for ESL Literacy Education. (ERIC Document Reproduction Service No. ED407882)

Weinstein, G. (2001). Developing adult literacies. In M. Celce-Murcia (Ed.), *Teaching English as a second or foreign language* (3rd ed., pp. 170–186). Boston: Heinle & Heinle.

Willett, J., & Jeannot, M. (1993). Resistance to taking a critical stance. *TESOL Quarterly, 27*(3), 477–495.

Wrigley, H. S. (1993). *Adult ESL literacy: Findings from a national study.* Washington, DC: National Clearinghouse for Adult ESL Literacy Education.

Zuengler, J. (1988). Identity markers and L2 pronunciation. *Studies in Second Language Acquisition, 10,* 33–49.

6

The Preparation and Stability of the ABE Teaching Workforce: Current Conditions and Future Prospects

M Cecil Smith

During an era of heightened accountability for education programs, teachers, and students, and with the connection between teacher preparation and student outcomes well established in K–12, the adult basic education (ABE) field should be able to demonstrate that the ABE teacher workforce is qualified, competent, and able to meet the learning needs of a diverse group of adult learners. The field must achieve a consensus on strategies for creating such a workforce. We must also determine what factors will help keep ABE teachers working in the field. First, however, leaders in adult basic education must define an ideal teacher workforce.

I address five questions in this chapter:

- What should the ABE teacher workforce look like?
- What does the ABE teacher workforce look like now?

- What conditions contribute to the current makeup of the ABE teacher workforce?
- What could help ABE move toward a qualified teacher workforce?
- What are the implications for research, policy, and practice that will address the issues regarding the ABE teacher workforce?

In order to answer these questions, I examined the literature in K–12 teacher education, teacher certification, and teacher quality. I also reviewed surveys of ABE teachers for their data on teacher characteristics. In addition, to gather information on ABE teacher characteristics, I interviewed 10 program administrators responsible for hiring and supervising ABE teachers. The administrators were solicited via a request for assistance posted to the National Literacy Advocacy listserv. At the time of the interviews, in July 2001, the administrators I interviewed were the directors of:

- a career center in northwestern Indiana.
- a public school district's ABE center in a university community in central Illinois.
- an ABE program within a community college in the western Illinois Quad Cities area.
- a school district's ABE program in a midsized Louisiana city.
- an ABE program in a southeastern Texas community college.
- a community-based adult education organization in Seattle.
- a technical college basic skills program in western Washington state.
- an ABE center in Vermont.
- an adult literacy center in Philadelphia.
- a private, nonprofit adult literacy agency in western Pennsylvania.

I conducted 45- to 60-minute phone interviews with each director and asked for comments on:

1. The characteristics of the individuals they hire to teach ABE, including the individuals' skills (e.g., educational credentials, prior teaching experience), knowledge of adult learning, and competencies.
2. The administrators' ability to hire and retain ABE staff despite reported teacher shortages in the K–12 system in some areas of the country.
3. The administrators' perceptions of the costs of developing and maintaining a qualified ABE teacher workforce.

WHAT *SHOULD* THE ABE TEACHER WORKFORCE LOOK LIKE?

In this section, I discuss what is known about the characteristics of teachers' background and preparation that research has identified as being associated with student achievement. As the studies cited have shown, teachers indisputably have important effects on their students' learning. However, the ABE field has never answered the question: How much and what type of preparation is appropriate to teach adults? The ABE field must also address the stability of the teacher workforce. I suggest that qualified teachers should have an adequate understanding of instructional methods, classroom management procedures, and adult learner assessment procedures. They also should be prepared in the skills they are teaching, have knowledge of learning and disabilities, possess an appreciation of adult learner diversity, and be committed to adult education.

Teacher Preparation: How Much?

Formal Education.   An examination of the literature on K–12 teacher quality and qualifications suggests that two factors are critically important to student outcomes: specific preparation within a teacher training program and holding a teaching license (certification). Darling-Hammond (1999) defines those teachers who are trained in such programs and have a teaching certificate as "well-qualified," or highly qualified teachers. Evidence from one recent review of the empirical literature demonstrates a positive relationship between teacher education and teacher effectiveness (Wilson, Floden, & Ferrini-Mundy, 2001), suggesting that those who embark on a teaching career should first participate in a teacher-training program (Laczko-Kerr & Berliner, 2002). Darling-Hammond and Youngs (2002), for example, reported that several dimensions of teacher qualifications have been shown to bear a significant relationship to student achievement, including teachers' knowledge of subject matter, knowledge about teaching and learning (as reflected in their teacher-preparation experiences, including teacher education coursework), teaching experience, academic skills, and certification.

The program directors I interviewed all called for better and more consistent preparation for ABE teachers. Their sentiments were mixed, however, when it came to making certification a prerequisite for teaching ABE. Many ABE teachers have years of experience in elementary and secondary school classrooms but no preparation for teaching adults. Others may have extensive backgrounds working with adults in other capacities (the Peace Corps, for example) but no formal teacher training. Thus, some ABE teachers are classroom novices, whereas others are experienced educators. Several program directors I interviewed expressed the opinion that ABE teacher preparation can take place within the context of professional development activities—that is, once people are already working in the field. Most directors believe, however, that ABE teachers should have at least a college degree prior to teaching. Still, a degree alone does not confer the ability to be an effective basic education teacher.

Certification.   Certification is the process through which states license their classroom teachers. Teacher certification processes assure the public of a teacher candidate's competence in providing instruction. Generally, to obtain K–12 certification, a candidate must have a bachelor's degree from an accredited teacher education institution, and clinical experiences (e.g., student teaching), and must pass a formal skills test, such as Praxis I and Praxis II, which are administered by the Educational Testing Service. Each state determines its certification requirements, and there is much variability across the states. Despite the lack of uniformity in credentialing teachers, most full-time K–12 public school teachers (93%) were fully certified in their main teaching assignment in 1998 (Lewis et al., 1999). According to data from the National Center for Education Statistics' 1993–1994 Schools and Staffing Survey (NCES, 1997a), only 5% of teachers held provisional or probationary teaching certificates, and 2% held either temporary or emergency certificates. Usually, emergency certificates are given in order to fill teacher vacancies in areas where there are critical shortages.

How important is teacher certification to teacher effectiveness? Analyses of state-level data have demonstrated that the strongest predictor of students' achievement is the proportion of well-qualified teachers—that is, those teachers who hold full certification and a major in the field being taught (Darling-Hammond, 2000). Furthermore, teacher certification has a greater effect on achievement in subject areas such as math and science than does having a content-area bachelor's or master's degree (Goldhaber & Brewer, 2000), and students taught by certified teachers have higher achievement than those taught by noncertified teachers (Hawk, Coble, & Swanson, 1985). Also, certified teachers report feeling better prepared for the challenges that they face in the classroom than do noncertified teachers (Darling-Hammond, Chung, & Frelow, 2002; Laczko-Kerr & Berliner,

2002). Finally, studies show that the students of teachers who acquire their credentials through nontraditional means and alternative certification procedures do not fare as well on standardized achievement tests (Laczko-Kerr & Berliner, 2002), and such teachers are more likely to leave teaching after only 2 years in the classroom (Andrew & Schwab, 1995; Raymond, Fletcher, & Luque, 2001). These data illustrate that K–12 teachers who hold certification are better prepared than are noncertified teachers, and students of certified teachers outperform students of noncertified teachers. Thus, the idea that ABE teachers should be certified—and perhaps certified specifically for ABE—is worthy of further consideration.

One survey of ABE professionals found general agreement with the idea that state credentialing for ABE teachers is important (Perin, 1999). Problems can arise whenever teachers are not certified, including the public's perception that uncertified teachers lack an appropriate degree and have insufficient theoretical and practical knowledge to teach well. For example, one ABE program director I interviewed described a situation in which her agency had applied for a grant to fund a back-to-school program for teenage mothers. During discussions with other supporting agencies and the local school district, a concern was raised that if the students' coursework were supervised and evaluated by ABE teachers, who are not state-certified instructors, the high school teachers might not give the students credit for their work.

The program directors in favor of certification for ABE teachers believed that it should be distinct from K–12 certification. Holding certification in elementary or secondary education, they argued, is no guarantee that teachers can work successfully with adults. Still, a few directors were not convinced that better quality instruction would necessarily follow from ABE certification. Whether or not certification in ABE is ever mandated universally, ABE teachers, like their K–12 counterparts, need ongoing professional development. Until ABE certification is required, professional development will continue to be an important vehicle for teacher preparation.

Professional Development. The goal of professional development is to improve student learning. Perin (1999) notes that professional development can be used to improve teacher competence. Competent teachers, in turn, produce competent learners (Joyce & Showers, 1995). Experts agree that, for professional development to be effective, it must be embedded within the everyday activities of teachers, rather than offered through occasional "one-shot" workshops and seminars (National Center for Education

Statistics, 1998), and practitioners should be "active participants in determining their own learning needs, and in designing and implementing appropriate learning activities" that contribute to their teaching abilities (Kutner & Tibbets, 1997, p. 1).

The outcomes of professional development should be increased knowledge and improved classroom skills for teachers. Teachers should emerge from professional development training with a good grasp of learning strategies that can be imparted to students, and greater knowledge about how to teach content and assess student achievement. State departments of education require K–12 teachers to engage in ongoing professional development activities that include attending state and regional professional conferences, local workshops, and summer institutes, and completing university courses.

Teacher Preparation: What Type?

Unique Skills and Knowledge.   Teaching adults requires at least some unique skills and knowledge beyond what is required for elementary and secondary teaching. By some accounts, the learning needs of adults are considered to be fundamentally different from those of children and youth (Knowles, Holton, & Swanson, 1998). In addition, adults in ABE programs may have a history of failure in school and can be distrustful of the educational system. ABE educators, therefore, need to be well prepared to work with the unique learning needs of ABE students. A significant portion of the ABE population may have undiagnosed learning disabilities, for example. Some estimates suggest that more than 50% of the ABE population may consist of adults with one or more learning disabilities (Ryan & Price, 1993). Qualified teachers should have adequate preparation to ensure that they know how to work effectively with such learners. ABE teachers should also possess a good understanding of the core theories of adult development and learning (Merriam & Caffarella, 1998). No research has been conducted, however, to demonstrate that teachers with specific preparation and/or certification in teaching adults, compared to teachers with K–12 certification or teachers without any certification, are more effective in regard to student persistence and achievement.

Despite the lack of research in ABE about specific teacher knowledge and skills associated with teacher quality and student achievement, efforts have been made to identify important adult educator skill domains. Several states, and at least one national effort, have produced lists of competencies that describe what qualified ABE teachers should know and be able to do (Bureau of Adult Basic & Literacy Education, 2001; Sherman, Tibbetts,

Woodruff, & Weidler, 1999). Royce (1998), for example, identified sets of teacher competencies that categorize four levels of qualification: trainee, entrance, experienced, and expert. She identified five sets of standards for competencies:

1. *Adult theory in practice*—creates and sustains a positive learning environment; promotes independent, lifelong learning.
2. *Instructional expertise*—exhibits command of content; designs and plans instruction; assesses and monitors learning.
3. *Community interaction*—utilizes community resources; encourages adult learner community involvement; understands the relationship between program and community.
4. *Professional development*—participates in professional development activities; models lifelong learning.
5. *Program operations*—understands the goals, policies, and procedures of agencies; exhibits accountability; functions as an effective team member.

The program directors I interviewed identified several skills as essential to effective teaching. These include the ability to individualize instruction to meet the unique and diverse learning needs of students and to diagnose student learning problems. Teachers should also possess adequate content knowledge in the areas they are teaching and have good literacy skills themselves. Although the Royce standards incorporate 13 units, 29 performance indicators, and a three-tier checklist of 139 instructor competencies, none directly addresses ABE teachers' knowledge of content.

Teaching reading is a challenging and complex activity under the best of circumstances. Knowledge of adult learner characteristics and classroom management skills alone are likely not sufficient to teach reading and related literacy skills to adult nonreaders. A recent review of the literature on K–12 and adult reading instruction and acquisition (Kruidenier, 2002), for example, points to the use of explicit comprehension strategy instruction, multiple readings of the same text to increase reader fluency, and the need for phonemic awareness instruction with adult nonreaders. ABE teachers need to know about these instructional strategies and how to teach reading to adults. However, among the ABE teachers who hold teacher certification in K–12, only those who have certification in elementary education are likely to have had specific coursework in reading instruction.

Some adult educators (Brookfield, 1990) disdain the search for models of effective instruction and suggest that teaching effectiveness is context-specific, value-laden, and not amenable to codification or standardization. Practicing adult educators, however, *want* to know how to increase their effectiveness and are eager to learn more about their content areas and the uses of technology, to obtain better instructional resources, and to improve their classroom management skills (D'Amico, 1995; Sabatini, Daniels, Ginsburg, Limeul, Russell, et al., 2000; Smith, Hofer, Gillespie, Solomon, & Rowe, 2003).

In addition to a basic set of competencies and specific training or licensure related to teaching adults, adult education experts identify specific dispositions or attributes of teacher personality and character that they argue may be more important to student achievement and persistence than certification (Cantor, 2001; Johnson, 1998; Knowles et al., 1998). Dedication to adult education, patience with struggling readers, sensitivity to gender and cultural differences, enthusiasm, and the ability to convey caring feelings for students have been identified as important qualities for teachers of adults (Cantor, 2001; Galbraith, 1990; Johnson, 1998; Kazemek, 1988; Leineke & Francisco, 1999; Shanahan, Meehan, & Mogge, 1994). Leineke and Francisco (1999) suggest that teachers should hold high expectations for their students but be flexible, be able to cope with changing circumstances, and adapt their instructional approaches to meet student needs. Several program administrators I interviewed echoed the importance of these characteristics. They value ABE teachers who are able to create a sense of community in the classroom, an atmosphere that is "safe, open, and student-focused, where successes are celebrated," in the words of one ABE director I interviewed. Administrators indicated that they wanted to hire people who are committed to adult education; who demonstrate a positive, can-do attitude; who are ebullient, creative, open to new experiences, and able to display empathy and a sense of caring about adult learners. Such individuals are thought to be the best instructors, and several administrators agreed that they often find these personal attributes to be more important than teaching credentials or previous work experience with adults. However, I could locate no research that has tied adult student persistence, achievement, or other outcomes to such dispositions.

Stability of the ABE Workforce

Berliner (1988) and others (Ericsson & Charness, 1994) claim that it requires up to a decade of intense, focused effort within a domain to develop expertise. Therefore, establishing an ideal teacher workforce in ABE necessitates creating conditions that encourage people to remain in the profession over the long term so they can acquire both the skills and experiences to become truly expert instructors.

Despite the myriad challenges that K–12 teachers encounter in their day-to-day practice, nearly two of every three public school teachers indicate that they plan to stay in the profession as long as they are able, or until they qualify for retirement (NCES, 1996). Only about 7% of public and private school K–12 teachers, in fact, left the field between 1993–1994 and 1994–1995, according to data from the Schools and Staffing Survey of 1993–1994 conducted by the National Center for Education Statistics (NCES, 1997a). Thus, the K–12 teacher workforce appears to be very stable. More than 91% of public school K–12 teachers are employed full-time as are nearly 80% of private school teachers, according to an NCES survey (NCES, 1996).

Obviously, there are characteristics of the work of teaching in K–12 settings that make these jobs very appealing and rewarding for teachers. Slightly more than one third of teachers (33.8%) in the 1993–1994 Schools and Staffing Survey indicated that they were "highly satisfied" with their teaching job, and another third (34.5%) were "moderately satisfied." (By contrast, one survey of adult education staff in one metropolitan literacy program found 85% of respondents rated their jobs as "satisfactory" or "very satisfactory; D'Amico, 1995.) The factors that contribute to K–12 teacher satisfaction include having control over the work environment, having administrative support, student behavior, and teacher compensation (NCES, 1997b). It is likely that the same factors influence teacher satisfaction in ABE settings and play an important role in determining the overall stability of the ABE workforce.

WHAT *DOES* THE ABE TEACHER WORKFORCE LOOK LIKE?

As I have established, the ideal ABE workforce should be well prepared and certified. Retaining that workforce once it is in place is also crucial. Is the current workforce meeting those criteria? In this section, I describe the current conditions of ABE teacher preparation, and what is known about the stability of the workforce.

Teacher Preparation

Formal Education. Presently, teacher training in the ABE field primarily consists of preparation for teaching in Grades K–12. Various surveys of ABE programs and staff find that the majority of ABE teachers hold teacher certification in elementary and secondary education (D'Amico, 1995; Mackin, Dwyer, Godin, Schenck, & Seager, 1996; Sabatini et al., 2000). States' requirements for adult education are not as uniform as are those in place for K–12 teaching, and there is little consensus as to the amount of education or training that should be required for becoming an ABE teacher. One program director that I interviewed hired former ABE and GED students as instructors (even though they did not have a high school diploma), but most states require ABE teachers to be certified in some field, which means that they have at least a 4-year college degree. ABE instructors in Alabama, for example, must hold a teaching certificate in any field and must have completed an approved master's level ABE program. Yet states such as Alaska, Colorado, and South Dakota, by contrast, have no certification or credential requirements for ABE teachers. Generally, even when there is no state requirement for teacher certification, such as in Hawaii, Montana, and North Dakota, there is usually either a requirement or preference for a bachelor's degree, although not necessarily in education (Kutner & Tibbets, 1997).

Although there are little data on the subject, it appears that relatively few ABE teachers are graduates of formal programs that have been designed to prepare teachers for the ABE classroom (Mackin et al., 1996). The exception is teachers of ESOL, who often hold baccalaureate and/or graduate degrees in bilingual education or ESOL (Crandall, 1993). Individuals who earn undergraduate degrees in ESOL or bilingual education can obtain K–12 teacher certification in a number of states (Pelavin Associates, 1991). A survey by Pelavin Associates of college and university ABE graduate programs found no evidence of undergraduate training in ABE (Evans & Sherman, 1999). Programs in generic adult education (which also includes human resource development) generally focus on leadership and administrative training at the graduate level. Eighty-six institutions of higher education in the United States offer graduate degrees in adult education, according to the Evans and Sherman report, but it is not clear how many of these programs specifically prepare teachers for ABE rather than for generic adult education.

The Mackin et al. (1996) survey of 634 adult basic educators found that 85% of surveyed personnel had earned a bachelor's or an advanced degree. Four percent had an associate's degree and 7% had not obtained any college degree (the remaining 4% were categorized as "other"). Only 12% of the personnel surveyed by the Mackin group had earned a degree in adult education (or a closely related field). D'Amico (1995) found that

TABLE 6.1
Educational Attainment of U.S. Adult Basic Education
and Public School Teachers

	< Bachelor's Degree	Bachelor's Degree	Master's Credits, Degrees, or Higher
Mackin et al. (1996) (n = 634)	7%	45%	40%
D'Amico (1995) (n = 360)	7%	28%	64%
Sabatini et al. (2000) (n = 423)	6%	53%	41%
NCES (Bandeira de Mello & Broughman, 1998)*	< 1%	52%	47%

Note. *Data pertain to K–12 teachers in both public and private schools.

64% of New York City's Adult Literacy Initiative (NYCALI) paid staff had earned a master's or doctoral degree and another 28% had completed college (bachelor's degree). Among the remaining staff members having less than a 4-year college degree, 5% had not earned a high school degree (it was not clear if these staff members were teachers or held other jobs). Sabatini and colleagues (2000) reported that 41% of their sample of ABE teachers had completed a master's degree or higher, 53% had a bachelor's degree, and 6% had earned only a high school diploma or GED.

The educational credentials of the adult education teachers in these three samples compare favorably to the national population of teachers in U.S. public schools (the educational attainment of ABE teachers across the three studies, in comparison to NCES data, are shown in Table 6.1). For example, 45% of the teachers in K–12 schools held a master's degree in 1998, according to data from the National Center for Education Statistics (Lewis et al., 1999).

Certification.   ABE is one of the few fields in education in which individuals may become classroom teachers with only a modest amount— perhaps only a few hours—of preparation. According to the National Institute for Literacy (2000), however, there has been a surge of interest in professionalizing the field in response to recent demands for accountability and higher standards. As a result, several states' departments of education are now moving toward requiring or recommending certification for ABE teachers. Whereas 20 states have no mandatory criteria for hiring adult educators, 11 states have credentialing systems in place for adult educators (Payne, Thornton, & Falk, 2001). Each state among this latter group requires a minimum of a bachelor's degree in any field, and at least two of these states require certification in K–12, as well as ABE certification. As previously noted, Alabama requires a master's degree in adult education. The remaining states require some adult education coursework (from 4 to 15 credits) in addition to the bachelor's degree.

Presently, there is no national uniform standard or minimum requirement for hiring teachers in ABE, although in many states, most ABE teachers who have certification hold it in either elementary or secondary education because in only a few states is ABE certification possible (Payne et al., 2001). Twenty-three states do not require ABE teachers to hold teacher licenses (National Institute for Literacy, 2000).

Of the personnel surveyed by Mackin and colleagues (1996), 31% were certified in adult education. Sixty-three percent of staff was certified in an area other than adult education. Sixty-one percent of surveyed personnel in the Sabatini et al. (2000) study were certified teachers, but they did not indicate whether they held certification in elementary, secondary, or adult education. Nearly all public school teachers are fully certified in their primary teaching field (93% in elementary education and 92% in a departmentalized field, such as math or science), and two thirds (66%) of high school teachers and 44% of middle school teachers have an undergraduate or graduate major in their teaching area (Lewis et al., 1999). It appears that a smaller percentage of ABE teachers than K–12 teachers can be characterized as certified in ABE.

Professional Development. Professional development should lead to increased knowledge and enhanced teaching skills that can be readily applied within the ABE classroom. A few states require ABE teachers to engage in ongoing professional development activities, including participation in state and regional conferences, workshops, and summer institutes, and to complete university coursework. Orientation programs for new ABE teachers are mandated in several states (Leineke & Francisco, 1999). Typically, states' departments of education or other state-level entities responsible for ABE provide these professional development workshops and programs.

The U.S. Office of Adult and Vocational Education sponsored a study that surveyed the variety of training approaches for ABE and ESOL instructors in the 50 states and the District of Columbia (Pelavin Associates, 1991). This survey found that the typical forums for professional development training are workshops, seminars, and brief training sessions, usually offered through summer institutes and conferences (Pelavin Associates, 1991; see also Belzer, Drennon, & Smith, 2001). The content covered at workshops and training seminars is usually determined at the state or local level. Some states require credit or noncredit coursework that may be obtained at local colleges or universities. In most cases, these programs and seminars are directed at those already in the field, rather than individuals who are preparing to become ABE teachers.

Participants in professional development are able to obtain a smattering of knowledge in a diverse selection of topics. Typical offerings include content instruction (such as basic reading, methods of teaching mathematics, writing instruction, ESOL instruction, and life skills), adult learning theory, and the characteristics of adult learners (such as motivation, learning disabilities, learning styles, special-needs learners, and cultural diversity). Other workshop and seminar topics include methods of classroom management (such as planning for instruction), student assessment, and application of technology (Pelavin Associates, 1991). ABE teachers have expressed interest in learning about these topics (D'Amico, 1995; Sabatini et al., 2000), and they rate workshops as preferable to university coursework or online learning (Payne et al., 2001; Sabatini et al., 2000).

In states where ongoing professional development is not required, ABE teachers voluntarily attend workshops and seminars when they are convenient and accessible to them. Mackin et al. (1996) found that 57% of ABE staff reported having participated in statewide and/or regional conferences, and 40% took part in single-session workshops. About one third of ABE teachers in a study by Smith et al. (2003) reported that they had provided professional development training to other ABE teachers (e.g., leading workshops, mentoring, and coaching). The high level of participation in conferences, workshops, and training attests to ABE teachers' commitment to increasing their skills and knowledge, assisting other teachers in their professional development, and thereby helping students acquire literacy.

However, one could question the extent to which a teacher can become an expert educator through only occasional participation in workshops. Research in K–12 has documented the inability of one-shot workshops to increase teachers' knowledge and skills without follow-up or ongoing assistance for teachers once they return to their classrooms (Joyce & Showers, 1995). Little research in K–12 exists about how teachers change as a result of professional development. Mackin et al. (1996) asked ABE teachers to list a professional development activity that had a significant impact on their work. More than one third (37%) felt that none of the activities in which they had participated had a significant impact. Among those who rated professional development activities as significantly affecting their work, 25% said that participation in state or regional conferences was the primary activity. Nearly half (47%) of Mackin et al.'s respondents indicated that participation had positive effects on curriculum and instructional methods, and 42% indicated that positive outcomes for adult students were achieved. Smith et al. (2003), in a study of ABE teacher change and professional development, found that after 18 hours of participation in professional development, most teachers gained at least some knowledge on the topic, but only 24% changed significantly over time as a result.

Stability of the ABE Workforce

Two other aspects of the makeup of the ABE teacher population describe who teachers are in this field: employment status (full-time and part-time employment) and employment stability (the amount of staff turnover and job migration within the ABE field).

A survey of adult education programs (Young, Fitzgerald, & Morgan, 1994) reported that 41% did not employ full-time staff. One half (50%) of the respondents in D'Amico's (1995) survey of NYCALI staff were full-time employees, although these full-time staff members were over-represented in the sample, according to D'Amico. This was likely due to the manner in which the survey was distributed to staff, resulting in a biased sample of administrative and central-office staff members (some of whom were also ABE teachers). Seventy-two percent of the sample were employed as teachers, 22% were program managers, 8% were counselors, and 15% were employed in "other" positions. Some held multiple positions, including teaching. Most of the part-time staff members held full-time positions in other settings. Thirty-six percent of ABE teachers in the Mackin et al. (1996) survey were employed in their teaching positions on a full-time basis. Sabatini et al. (2000) reported that 59% of the ABE teachers in their survey were employed on a full-time basis (because full-time staff were overrepresented in the Sabatini et al. study, this percentage likely overestimates the extent of full-time employment in ABE).

These data on employment status are confirmed by available federal statistics that show most ABE teachers are either employed on a part-time basis or are unpaid volunteers (U.S. Department of Education, 1999; Young et al., 1994). More than 165,000 persons worked in state-administered ABE programs in 1999, and a sizeable portion of these individuals included classroom personnel. Of this population, only 11% were full-time staff, including program administrators, many of whom do not teach. Slightly more than 10,000 full-time teachers (6% of total ABE personnel) were employed in local ABE programs.

Many teachers simultaneously work in several part-time ABE positions to achieve full-time employment (D'Amico, 1995). Some full-time elementary and secondary education teachers also moonlight as ABE teachers to supplement their incomes (Foster, 1988). Other ABE teachers are retired K–12 teachers, and some have left public school jobs because of dissatisfaction with the work and a perceived lack of fit between their skills and the demands of teaching in public schools. Still others—particularly women—have taken extended time away from full-time teaching to raise children. While their children are young, and even once their children are older, many wish to return to the classroom and find ABE to be a suitable alternative because of the flexible hours offered. However, others return to K–12 when their children are older so they can get the full-time work and employee benefits that many ABE programs are unable to offer (Smith et al., 2003).

As already indicated, a sizeable portion of the ABE teacher pool consists of part-time staff members. Although funding levels to support ABE programs and personnel have increased over time, some experts claim that these funding levels are too low to support the employment of full-time teachers (Liebowitz, Robins, & Rubin, 2003; Sticht, 2000). Therefore, short-term employment, job migration, and high staff turnover might be expected to be the norm. However, no national random sample survey of ABE teachers has looked at the issue of turnover. D'Amico (1995) found that length of service in ABE ranged from a mean of 11 years (among staff at the NYC Board of Education) to a mean of 4 years (among City University ABE staff). (It should be noted that the mean is not the best measure for these data because the range for length of service can be very broad; the median value in the distribution for "years of present employment" is the preferable indicator. Unfortunately, this statistic was not reported.) Mackin et al. (1996) found that the average number of years in the field of ABE was 9.5 among their survey respondents, and these persons had been employed for 7.8 years, on average, at their current adult education program. Sabatini et al. (2000) reported that 65% of full-time and 57% of part-time ABE personnel had been working in the field for 6 or more years.[1] No data were reported on length of service in the current teaching job. Young, Fleischman, Fitzgerald, and Morgan (1995) found that part-time ABE staff turn over more frequently than full-time staff: 80% of

---

[1] Special care should be taken when interpreting the results of this survey in terms of demographics because the researchers specifically sought to sample full-time teachers from programs identified by state staff.

full-time, but only half of part-time instructors had taught in ABE for more than 3 years, meaning that half of all part-time instructors had taught in adult basic education for less than 3 years.

WHAT CONDITIONS CONTRIBUTE TO THE CURRENT MAKEUP OF THE ABE TEACHER WORKFORCE?

Compared to the ideal—a largely full-time, well-trained, and stable teaching workforce—the ABE workforce, unlike the K–12 workforce, falls short. The majority of ABE teachers have not had formal preparation, work in part-time positions, and may be less experienced in teaching adults. In this section, I look at why this is the case at this time. I also look at the effects of a possible teacher shortage on the ABE workforce.

Lack of Formal ABE Teacher Preparation

As indicated previously, there are no undergraduate teacher education programs to prepare future ABE teachers. Graduates of generic adult education master's programs are likely to take full-time administrative positions, which pay more than K–12 positions and provide benefits. Many teachers who end up in ABE programs do so because the positions offer them flexibility and freedom; they are part-time jobs that are generally free from many of the bureaucratic and curricular constraints present in K–12 schools. Teacher education is largely post hoc in ABE, occurring through the various professional development programs that are offered to ABE teachers. It is through these programs that teachers first become aware of the field of adult education (Smith et al., 2003).

Lack of Well-Supported Jobs in ABE

Few incentives, such as competitive starting salaries, fringe benefits, and tenure, exist to motivate individuals to consider careers in ABE teaching. Until more powerful and attractive incentives are offered, the field will continue to rely on K–12 teachers and others who have not been schooled in adult education. Some program directors I interviewed attributed their difficulties in hiring teachers—on either a full- or part-time basis—to the lack of competitive salaries, rather than a shortage of qualified personnel.

Dependence on Part-Time Teachers

Many of the administrators I interviewed held the opinion that part-time teachers staff much of the ABE field. Having to rely on part-time teachers is viewed by several of the administrators as necessary because (a) funding is inadequate to support the employment of full-time teachers, (b) programs must offer classes at night for those students unable to attend during the day, and (c) student attendance is erratic, necessitating flexible class schedules. Having part-time staff allows programs to offer a variety of classes and services efficiently. Program directors noted that it would be impossible for them to offer these services without part-time teachers. For example, an adult learning center might have several small grants that fund workplace-training programs for a few hours per week on a limited basis in far-flung locations. It would be inefficient to use full-time staff to cover such piecemeal teaching assignments.

Yet this argument ignores the fact that most full-time college and university faculty members actually teach part-time (Chronicle of Higher Education, 1999)—anywhere from one to several classes per week, often at different times of the day. The remainder of their time is devoted to other responsibilities, such as research, advising students, and committee work. Although colleges are better funded than most ABE programs, the same might be possible for full-time ABE teachers. They could be flexibly deployed to teach daytime, evening, or weekend classes. Time not spent in the classroom could be devoted to other professional activities, such as curriculum development, instructional and program planning, and professional development.

One director I interviewed indicated that she hires only full-time teachers for her program because it is difficult to find suitable candidates who want to work for what she described as the low pay (and lack of benefits) that is typical of part-time teaching. She hires fewer teachers but pays them more and offers a benefits package. She had learned from previous experience that the diverse schedules and assignments of part-time teachers made it difficult to organize them into a cohesive team. Further complicating matters for program administrators, according to this director, part-time staff may teach full-time in other schools or programs, or may work in other kinds of jobs, and so are generally not available for staff meetings and often cannot or do not participate in professional development activities. Frequently, part-time teachers are unable to complete essential tasks outside the classroom, such as filling out paperwork for student performance assessments. This is a significant problem for pro-gram directors because documenting student progress has become critical in an era of mandated accountability.

Possible Teacher Shortage

Teacher shortages in the K–12 system may also play a role in shortages of ABE teachers. The U.S. Department of Education (2001) claims that the nation will face such a shortage of K–12 teachers in the coming years, particularly in mathematics, science, foreign languages, ESOL, reading, and special education. There is, however, little consensus as to whether a teacher shortage exists now or is likely to develop in the near future. Feistritzer (1998), for example, points to projections from the National Center for Education Statistics that illustrate annual declines in the num-ber of teachers that will be needed as the current school enrollment surge dissipates over the next decade. Also, more people are awarded bachelor's degrees in education each year than there are teacher vacancies, according to Feistritzer. Darling-Hammond (2000) also claims that the number of students in teacher-preparation programs each year is more than enough to satisfy the demand for teachers in the K–12 system. These graduates represent a pool of potential ABE teachers and, with the proper incentives, might be encouraged to become ABE teachers.

I asked the program directors I interviewed if their efforts to find new teachers were being hurt by local teacher shortages. None believed this to be true at the present time, although a few thought that the potential for staffing problems did exist.

WHAT COULD HELP MOVE ABE TOWARD A QUALIFIED TEACHER WORKFORCE?

Moving the field toward the realization of an ideal teacher workforce will require ABE to train and retain qualified teachers. Establishing certifi-cation requirements is one approach; hiring experienced K–12 teachers to work in ABE programs is another. Professional development can be improved so that new ABE teachers can quickly gear up for teaching adult learners and continue to improve their skills.

Retaining qualified teachers may require several actions, including unionization. Collective bargaining could result in higher salaries and improved benefits, thereby making the field more attractive to potential teachers.

The ABE field can also learn and apply lessons from the early childhood education profession, particularly in regard to creating a more visible field through public awareness campaigns.

Preparing an Ideal Workforce

A report from Massachusetts, *New Skills for a New Economy* (Massachusetts Institute for a New Commonwealth, 2000), recommends several ways in which ABE might help to prepare a workforce that can meet the demands of that state's dynamic economy. These recommendations include improving teacher quality, increasing the number of full-time teachers and recruiting new teachers, increasing teacher salaries and benefits to attract a skilled teaching staff and encourage long-term commitment to the profession, and recruiting retired K–12 public school teachers to fill part-time ABE positions. However, the report says nothing about the need for such teachers to be credentialed in ABE.

Professional development opportunities may be an appropriate avenue for experienced K–12 teachers to acquire an ABE teaching credential. On employment in an ABE program, teachers could participate in professional development programs and courses to accumulate a sufficient number of hours to obtain ABE certification. The required number of hours of professional development will vary from state to state, although consensus regarding the minimum number of hours should be achieved. States without licensure for ABE teachers should consider such a requirement.

Although continuing professional education is important in most areas of teaching, it is critical to ABE, given the diverse experience and degree of preparedness that ABE teachers bring to the classroom, and lack of training in reading instruction. One survey of program administrators and teachers shows professional development to be among the highest priorities for ABE teachers (Sabatini, Ginsburg, & Russell, 2002). As already noted, several efforts have been made to identify types of teacher competencies that could be developed through staff development programs and activities (Payne et al., 2001; Royce, 1998). Once the competencies are identified and staff development programs have been put in place, procedures and instruments must be established to assess the degree to which teachers have achieved these competencies.

As yet, little effort has been made to determine how long it would take for ABE teachers to acquire the identified competencies or to advance from a level of minimal proficiency to "experienced" and then "expert," or "master," teacher. However, one expert, a professional development trainer who is evaluating the teacher competencies identified by Royce (1998), estimates that ABE teachers in Pennsylvania spend from 10 to 20 hours to achieve minimal proficiency in any two competency areas (Bootsie Barbour, personal communication, July 30, 2001).

Identifying requisite competencies for ABE teachers is useful in order to establish a more systematic approach to professional development. Program administrators and teachers can work collaboratively to achieve competency goals. Teachers can develop personal action plans and portfolios that document how they have reached the competency goals. These portfolios can be vehicles for professional planning, teacher–supervisor discussions, and teachers' self-evaluations. Program directors can also use lists of competencies as criteria for making hiring decisions or for evaluating teachers. The competencies can be combined with teacher-training activities to ensure that teacher candidates are appropriately prepared before entering the classroom.

Retaining Quality Teachers

To improve the stability and availability of quality teachers, the ABE field could consider unionizing the workforce. Some writers (Perin, 1999) have suggested that unionizing would help ABE teachers gain recognition as professional educators and receive the requisite salary increases, benefits, and other forms of compensation. In fact, some efforts at bringing ABE teachers into teachers' and other labor unions have been taking place, although these efforts are as yet few (D'Amico, 1995). According to Kerchner, Koppich, and Weeres (1997), "Unions are potentially powerful collaborators because they negotiate the allocation of time in school and define a teacher's . . . dut[ies] . . . and . . . work role relationships" (p. 173). Most ABE teachers who are union members are employed in community colleges that have collective bargaining units representing the faculty and/or operating staff (although there are ABE teachers who teach union members in literacy programs run by the unions, and these teachers are sometimes also union members; National Education Association, 2001). The largest teachers' unions—the National Education Association (NEA) and the American Federation of Teachers (AFT)—appear not to have devoted significant attention to ABE teachers' concerns. According to Sticht (2002), NEA's Department of Adult Education separated from AFT in 1951 and joined with the American Association for Adult Education to form the Adult Education Association of the United States. Thus, for the latter half of the 20th century, NEA was removed from the adult education business altogether and from the professionalization of adult educators. ABE teachers' best hopes for unionizing may, therefore, reside with other labor organizations. Historically, the labor unions representing crafts, trades, and manufacturing employees have taken more than a passing interest in adult education, including ABE (Timm, 1996). Recently, the United Auto Workers (UAW) became the official bargaining unit for graduate assistants at New York University (Smallwood, 2001). It is not hard to imagine how the UAW or an organization such as the American Federation of County, State, and Municipal Employees (AFCSME) might come to represent the professional interests of ABE teachers, especially those employed in ABE programs at community colleges (D'Amico, 1995).

Unionization of ABE teachers is likely to lead to higher pay, benefits such as health care and life insurance, and more stable, longer term employment. These are the kinds of incentives that are likely to bring more qualified and committed individuals into the field. Unionization is not without its potential drawbacks, however. Among the concerns mentioned by program directors was that differences between administrators and teachers regarding professional development priorities might lead to grievance processes. Such actions could lead to fewer opportunities for teacher learning and professional development. A recent study examining contracts for K–12 teachers in 100 school districts, for example, found that only about a quarter of these agreements contained explicit language on professional development (Bredeson, 2001). Unionization is thus no guarantee that the best interests of ABE teachers (or of their students) will be served.

To meet the unique needs of the populations they serve, above all else, ABE programs must be flexible. A few of the program directors I interviewed voiced concerns that union contracts might restrict class scheduling or limit teacher contact hours or class size, thus hindering the delivery of services. Also, in colleges where the faculty is represented by unions, cooperation and understanding between regular college and ABE faculties is necessary in order to avoid conflicts over issues such as course load and staff development. Because ABE teaching is distinct from college-level teaching, college faculty need to be informed about, and sympathetic to, the field's unique demands.

Lessons Learned From Early Childhood Education

It is useful to consider what ABE can learn from teacher preparation initiatives in other fields. Teacher training in the field of early childhood education (ECE), for example, may have some implications for teacher preparation in ABE. ECE shares with ABE many of the problems associated with trying to prepare and retain a professional workforce. The conditions of ABE and ECE teacher training, and opportunities for professional practice, are remarkably similar.

ABE teachers can identify with the many frustrations that early childhood educators encounter in their professional development. As is true in ECE, the attempts to professionalize ABE teachers have not been coordinated across states. Both professions are perceived to have lower status compared with other fields of education. Historically, salaries have been very low for adult and early childhood educators, and fringe benefits are poor or nonexistent (Isenberg, 2000). Neither field offers clearly defined career paths, and employment opportunities are frequently limited to part-time positions because programs lack the necessary state and federal funding to employ full-time staff. Funding disparities leave teachers in ABE and ECE vulnerable to budget cuts that threaten their jobs.

In several respects, however, ECE is ahead of ABE and has advanced well beyond ABE as a recognizable profession. The ECE field has a national organization—the National Association for the Education of Young Children (NAEYC)—that represents the interests of early childhood professionals and advocates for the provision of high-quality early childhood programs.

A major advantage of ECE over the ABE field is that the population served by ECE is easy to identify (i.e., children under age 5). ABE, on the other hand, serves a highly diverse population (age 16 and older) with a much broader array of learning needs.

ECE also enjoys generally widespread public support for its goal of securing the healthy development of all young children through high-quality early childhood programs. In contrast, the public in general neither acknowledges nor understands the important role of ABE, and the field has no single organization that advocates on its behalf. As ECE professionals have done in the past, ABE teachers should build public relations campaigns to educate the nation about the crucial contributions that highly qualified and fairly compensated professional ABE educators can make to the U.S. education system (Sticht, 1998).

WHAT ARE THE IMPLICATIONS FOR RESEARCH, POLICY, AND PRACTICE THAT WILL ADDRESS THE ISSUES REGARDING THE ABE TEACHER WORKFORCE?

The final section of the chapter recommends directions in research, policy, and practice that will advance the field of ABE teaching by attracting and retaining qualified adult educators.

Research

It is imperative that researchers gather accurate data on four topics: characteristics of existing ABE teachers, the connection between preparation and teacher quality, the factors that support retention of teachers, and the connection between teacher quality and retention.

We have little knowledge of the current workforce. Without knowing ABE teachers' background characteristics and employment status and stability, we cannot know how far we have to move toward achieving the ideal workforce and how much money we need to invest to meet this goal. Having reliable and valid data on the characteristics of ABE teachers could help to negate stereotypes about this group of educators (such as the belief that "All you need is a degree of caring"—rather than an actual degree and specific preparation to teach adult learners). Valid data would also be useful in informing policies that influence teacher-hiring practices. The U.S. Department of Education's Office of Vocational and Adult Education should conduct a survey of a nationally representative sample of ABE staff or use the national NRS system, which collects data from each state and each program, to determine how many teachers are employed in full- and part-time teaching positions. We need data on ABE teachers' educational preparation, prior work experience with adults, certification status, and turnover rates.

Research is also needed to determine the characteristics that predict success in teaching ABE. For example, are individuals with extensive teaching experience in K–12 schools more effective ABE teachers than teachers who do not have K–12 teaching experience? Does having a graduate degree or specific academic preparation in adult education make a difference in teacher effectiveness? How beneficial is professional development in helping teachers use teaching techniques or strategies that research has proven to be effective? Are there measurable differences in the quality and effectiveness of full-time versus part-time ABE teachers (i.e., do students of full-time teachers have better outcomes and achievement than students of part-time teachers)? More research that examines the ways in which ABE teachers develop competencies for effective instruction needs to be conducted.

Research to determine what factors support retention should also be studied. For example, researchers should ask if there is a higher level of teacher attrition in ABE than in K–12, and if so, what are the chief factors that contribute to that attrition in ABE? They should also look at what conditions within programs support ABE teachers to teach well, increase their professional development, and serve to lower staff turnover in those programs where high attrition exists.

Policy

Sticht (1998) argued that ABE should be recognized as the third leg of a three-part system of education in the United States, an educational system that is on par with the P–12 and higher education systems. To be recognized as such, ABE needs qualified teachers. Research in K–12 consistently indicates that teacher ability is significantly related to student achievement, but teacher skill is not the only critical factor. Having highly qualified teachers alone is not sufficient to ensure the quality of the ABE system (Darling-Hammond, 1997; Murnane & Phillips, 1981; Rosenshine & Stevens, 1986). ABE teachers must also have opportunities for full-time, well supported, and long-term employment, including access to high-quality professional development programs to continue to develop their skills, as K–12 teachers do.

If research shows that hiring qualified teachers also leads to improved student performance, programs will likely struggle to be successful in meeting the literacy needs of adult learners unless qualified, knowledgeable teachers can be hired and retained. The effect of underprepared teachers on student achievement is unknown. Given the lack of evidence that ABE leads to significant increases in adults' literacy skills (Beder, 1999; Friedlander & Martinson, 1996; Sheehan-Holt & Smith, 2000), adult educators must recognize the problems inherent in the present system of teacher training. Of course, there are many influences on student learning, as has been shown in the K–12 student achievement literature (e.g., class size, socioeconomic status, school resources, culture, and leadership, and teachers' working conditions). Still, having high-quality adult educators in ABE classrooms is fundamental to establishing an effective system of adult education.

Establishing a stable high-quality workforce of ABE teachers will require changes in attitudes on the part of national ABE policymakers, state-level bureaucrats, local program administrators, and teachers. Funding priorities must be reordered so that teacher salaries are sufficient to sustain a professional workforce and professional development activities can be fully supported. The field needs its own systems for preparing teachers for adult education, rather than relying on K–12 preparation. Adult educators have long argued that the practices and philosophy of adult education are fundamentally different from those of primary and secondary education (Knowles et al., 1998; Lindeman, 1926/1989). Yet ironically, ABE predominantly employs part-time and volunteer teachers who lack specific preparation for instructing adult learners in literacy development.

If research results demonstrate that ABE-certified teachers are more effective than noncertified teachers, as has been shown in K–12, then K–12 teachers who want to teach in ABE should be required to have specific ABE certification based on relevant coursework. The unique characteristics and needs of adult learners must be recognized and steps taken to ensure that only those with knowledge and training in adult education methods will be sanctioned to teach adult learners who are enrolled in formal, state-supported literacy education programs.

Presently, multiple pathways lead into the ABE teaching field. Although this approach may have some advantages for obtaining a diversified workforce, this strategy has also had the singular disadvantage of keeping teacher salaries low. If anyone (including those lacking education beyond high school or any formal teacher preparation) can become an ABE teacher, then why should a premium salary be paid to those individuals who hold advanced degrees and have ABE teacher training and certification?

The ABE field may be better served by restricting some of the avenues to becoming a teacher. Limiting the number of individuals who are qualified to teach may lead to more competitive salary and compensation packages. In this regard, the field needs to work closely with adult education faculty at colleges and universities to revamp and redirect graduate programs in adult education to include ABE teacher training. Efforts should also be made to establish undergraduate programs in adult teacher education. Undergraduates who might otherwise be attracted to fields such as special education, family studies, or social work could be recruited into these programs. It is likely that many college students are unaware that the field of adult education exists and so never consider it as a career choice.

Teacher training and professional development activities should be broadened so teachers can move more fluidly between the K–12 and ABE systems. If research shows that full-time teachers have better student outcomes than part-time teachers, opportunities for full-time employment must be increased. In that case, lobbying efforts must be directed toward increasing funding levels for ABE programs so these programs can employ a core of qualified, full-time teachers. Or, policymakers should put in place requirements that increase the per capita student costs.

If research shows that adequate supports (good salaries and benefits, paid professional development time) lead to attracting and retaining quality teachers, then such supports should be widespread. Job security issues must be addressed through long-term funding commitments to programs from the federal government and the states. Teachers' unions representing ABE teachers have an important role to play in negotiating more secure employment commitments, increased salaries, and improved benefits.

Practice

Recruiting and retaining qualified teachers to ABE requires several actions. First, research should provide policymakers with information they need on what contributes to a quality, stable workforce. Second, ABE teaching must be established as a professional field that is on a par with early childhood and K–12 teaching. Teachers must be empowered to make decisions about and to effect changes in their programs, which can happen only if they are viewed as capable professionals. Third, ABE teachers must be better compensated with comparable salaries and benefits (e.g., medical care, retirement plans) and increased job security (brought about by stable funding allocations). This may ultimately require that ABE teachers organize, join professional unions such as NEA, and engage in collective bargaining. Fourth, access to teaching resources and professional development activities must be improved. The development of high-level teaching skills depends on increased opportunities for collaboration with trainers and fellow teachers. ABE advocates must press for changes to federal and state policies regarding the professional development opportunities for ABE teachers. Fifth, professional associations such as the Commission on Adult Basic Education (COABE) should strive to increase participation of rank-and-file ABE teachers and work with other adult education organizations to raise the stature of the field.

For too long, ABE has relied on an "anyone we can get" approach to hiring teachers. This is a poor model for recruiting, developing, and retaining qualified practitioners. Steps should be taken to increase the visibility of ABE teaching as a legitimate career in education through public awareness campaigns. A field that concerns itself with increasing the educational, social, and economic opportunities of adults—to the betterment of a democratic society—has every right to claim legitimacy on a par with early childhood, K–12, and higher education.

REFERENCES

Andrew, M., & Schwab, R. L. (1995). Has reform in teacher education influenced teacher performance? An outcome assessment of graduates of eleven teacher education programs. *Action in Teacher Education, 17,* 43–53.

Bandeira de Mello, V., & Broughman, S. P. (1998). *1993–1994 school and staffing survey: Selected results.* Washington, DC: U.S. Department of Education.

Beder, H. (1999). *The outcomes and impacts of adult literacy education in the United States.* NCSALL Reports No. 6. Cambridge, MA: National Center for the Study of Adult Learning and Literacy.

Belzer, A., Drennon, C., & Smith, C. (2001). Building professional development systems in adult basic education: Lessons from the field. In J. Comings, B. Garner, & C. Smith (Eds.), *The annual review of adult learning and literacy* (Vol. 2, pp. 151–188). San Francisco: Jossey-Bass.

Berliner, D. C. (1988). *The development of expertise in pedagogy.* New Orleans, LA: American Association of Colleges for Teacher Education.

Bredeson, P. V. (2001). Negotiated learning: Union contracts and teacher professional development. *Education Policy Analysis Archives, 9*(26). Available at http://epaa.asu .edu/epaa/v9n26.html.

Brookfield, S. D. (1990). *The skillful teacher.* San Francisco: Jossey-Bass.

Bureau of Adult Basic & Literacy Education. (2001). *Pennsylvania adult teacher competencies: User's guide.* Harrisburg, PA: Pennsylvania Department of Education.

Cantor, J. A. (2001). *Delivering instruction to adult learners* (Rev. ed.). Toronto, Canada: Wall & Emerson.

Chronicle of Higher Education. (1999, September 3). Faculty attitudes and characteristics: Results of a 1998–99 survey. *Chronicle of Higher Education, 46*(2), A20–A21.

Crandall, J. (1993). Professionalism and professionalization of adult ESL literacy. *TESOL Quarterly, 27*(3), 497–515.

D'Amico, D. (1995, October). *Staffing patterns in New York City Adult Literacy Initiative programs: Data and directions.* New York: Literacy Assistance Center.

Darling-Hammond, L. (1997). The quality of teaching matters most. *Journal of Staff Development, 18*(1), 38–41.

Darling-Hammond, L. (1999). *Teacher quality and student achievement: A review of state policy evidence.* Seattle, WA: University of Washington.

Darling-Hammond, L. (2000). Teacher quality and student achievement. *Education Policy Analysis Archives, 8*(1). Available at http://epaa.asu.edu/epaa/v8n1/.

Darling-Hammond, L., Chung, R., & Frelow, F. (2002). Variation in teacher preparation:

How well do different pathways prepare teachers to teach? *Journal of Teacher Education, 53*(4), 286–302.

Darling-Hammond, L., & Youngs, P. (2002). Defining "highly qualified teachers": What does "scientifically-based research" actually tell us? *Educational Researcher, 31*(9), 13–25.

Ericsson, K. A., & Charness, N. (1994). Expert performance: Its structure and acquisition. *American Psychologist, 49,* 725–747.

Evans, A., & Sherman, R. (1999). *Guide to ABE in graduate programs.* Washington, DC: Pelavin Research Institute.

Feistritzer, C. E. (1998, January 28). The truth behind the "teacher shortage." *The Wall Street Journal* (online).

Foster, S. E. (1988). *Professionalization of the adult literacy workforce.* Washington, DC: Office of Educational Research and Improvement, U.S. Department of Education. (ERIC Document Reproduction Service No. ED302 680)

Friedlander, D., & Martinson, K. (1996). Effects of mandatory basic education for adult AFDC recipients. *Educational Evaluation and Policy Analysis, 18,* 327–337.

Galbraith, M. W. (1990). *Adult learning methods: A guide for effective instruction.* Malabar, FL: Krieger.

Goldhaber, D. D., & Brewer, J. (2000). Does teacher certification matter? High school teacher certification status and student achievement. *Educational Evaluation & Policy Analysis, 22*(2), 129–145.

Hawk, P., Coble, C. R., & Swanson, M. (1985). Certification: It does matter. *Journal of Teacher Education, 36*(3), 13–15.

Isenberg, J. P. (2000). The state of the art in early childhood professional preparation. In National Institute on Early Childhood Development and Education (Ed.), *New teachers for a new century: The future of early childhood professional preparation* (pp. 15–58). Washington, DC: U.S. Department of Education.

Johnson, D. P. (1998). Adult educators need to have enthusiasm. *Adult Learning, 9*(4), 11–14.

Joyce, B., & Showers, B. (1995). *Student achievement through staff development* (Rev. ed.). White Plains, NY: Longman.

Kazemek, F. (1988). Necessary changes: Professional involvement in adult literacy programs. *Harvard Educational Review, 58,* 464–487.

Kerchner, C. T., Koppich, J. E., & Weeres, J. G. (1997). *United mind workers.* San Francisco, CA: Jossey-Bass.

Knowles, M., Holton, E. F., & Swanson, R. A. (1998). *The adult learner: The definitive classic in adult education and human resource development.* Woburn, MA: Butterworth-Heineman.

Kruidenier, J. (2002). Literacy assessment in adult basic education. In J. Comings, B. Garner, & C. Smith (Eds.), *Annual review of adult learning and literacy* (Vol. 3, pp. 84–151). San Francisco: Jossey-Bass.

Kutner, M., & Tibbets, J. (1997). *Looking to the future: Components of a comprehensive professional development system for adult educators.* Washington, DC: Pelavin Research Institute.

Laczko-Kerr, I., & Berliner, D. C. (2002). The effectiveness of Teach for America and other under-certified teachers on student academic achievement: A case of harmful public policy. *Educational Policy Analysis Archives, 10*(37). Available at http://epaa.asu.edu/epaa/v10n37/.

Liebowitz, M., Robins, A., & Rubin, J. (2003, March). *Rising to the challenge: Building adult education systems in New England.* Quincy, MA: Nellie May Education Foundation.

Leineke, W., & Francisco, C. (1999). *Credentialing adult educators in Illinois: A white paper for the field.* Found online January 25, 2001 at http://www.coe.ilstu.edu/ipdpc/credentialing.htm. (Document no longer available online.)

Lewis, L., Parsad, B., Carey, N., Bartfai, N., Farris, E., Smerdon, B. et al. (1999). *Teacher quality: A report on the preparation and qualifications of public school teachers* (NCES 1999–080). Washington, DC: U.S. Department of Education.

Lindeman, E. C. (1989). *The meaning of adult education in the United States.* Norman: University of Oklahoma. (Original work published 1926)

Mackin, K., Dwyer, M. C., Godin, K., Schenck, A., & Seager, A. (1996). *National evaluation of the Section 353 set-aside for teacher training and innovation in adult education.* Portsmouth, NH: RMC Research Corporation.

Massachusetts Institute for a New Commonwealth. (2000). *New skills for a new economy: Adult education's key role in sustaining economic growth and expanding opportunity.* Cambridge, MA: MassInc.

Merriam, S., & Caffarella, R. (1998). *Learning in adulthood* (2nd ed.). San Francisco: Jossey-Bass.

Murnane, R., & Phillips, B. R. (1981). Learning by doing, vintage, and selection: Three pieces of the puzzle relating teaching experience and teaching performance. *Economics of Education Review, 2,* 453–465.

National Center for Education Statistics. (1996, July). *Schools and staffing in the United States: A statistical profile, 1993–1994.* Report No. 96–124. Washington, DC: U.S. Department of Education.

National Center for Education Statistics. (1997a, July). *America's teachers: Profile of a profession, 1993–1994.* Report No. 97–460. Washington, DC: U.S. Department of Education.

National Center for Education Statistics. (1997b, July). *Job satisfaction among America's teachers: Effects of workplace conditions, background characteristics, and teacher compensation.* Washington, DC: U.S. Department of Education.

National Center for Education Statistics. (1998, July). *Toward better teaching: Professional development in 1993–1994.* Report No. 98–230. Washington, DC: U.S. Department of Education.

National Education Association. (2001). *Newsmakers: In the labor movement. Will part-timers win parity?* NEAToday Online. Available at http://www.nea.org/neatoday/9811/inlabr.html.

National Institute for Literacy (2000). *The professionalization of adult education: Can state certification of adult educators contribute to a more professional workforce?* NIFL State Policy Update. Washington, DC: Author.

Payne, E. M., Thornton, T., & Falk, K. (2001, May). *Texas adult education credential model.* Available at http://cie.ci.swt.edu/credential/coverpage.htm.

Pelavin Associates. (1991, February). *Study of ABE/ESL instructor training approaches: State profiles report.* ED No. 338 605. Washington, DC: Office of Vocational and Adult Education.

Perin, D. (1999). Professionalizing adult literacy: Would a credential help? *Journal of Adolescent and Adult Literacy, 42,* 610–627.

Raymond, M., Fletcher, S. H., & Luque, J. (2001). *Teach for America: An evaluation of teacher differences and student outcomes in Houston, Texas.* Stanford, CA: The Hoover Institution, Center for Research on Education Outcomes.

Rosenshine, B., & Stevens, R. (1986). Teaching functions. In M. C. Wittrock (Ed.), *Handbook of research on teaching* (3d ed., pp. 376–391). New York: Macmillan.

Royce, S. (1998). *The adult teacher competencies study.* Lancaster, PA: Royce and Royce.

Ryan, A. G., & Price, L. (1993). Learning disabilities in adult basic education: A survey of current practices. *Journal of Postsecondary Education and Disability, 10*(3), 31–40.

Sabatini, J., Daniels, M., Ginsburg, L., Limeul, K., Russell, M., & Stites, R. (2000). *Teacher perspectives on the adult education profession: National survey findings about an emerging profession.* NCAL Technical Report TR00–02. Philadelphia, PA: National Center on Adult Literacy.

Sabatini, J., Ginsburg, L., & Russell, M. (2002). Professionalization and certification for teachers in adult basic education. In J. Comings, B. Garner, & C. Smith (Eds.), *Annual review of adult learning and literacy* (Vol. 3, pp. 203–247). San Francisco, CA: Jossey-Bass.

Shanahan, T., Meehan, M., & Mogge, S. (1994). *The professionalization of the teacher in adult literacy education.* Technical Report TR94–11. Philadelphia, PA: National Center on Adult Literacy.

Sheehan-Holt, J. K., & Smith, M C. (2000). Does basic skills education affect adults' literacy proficiencies and reading practices? *Reading Research Quarterly, 35*(2), 226–243.

Sherman, R., Tibbets, J., Woodruff, D., & Weidler, D. (1999, February). *Instructor competencies and performance indicators for the improvement of adult education programs.* Washington, DC: U.S. Department of Education.

Smallwood, S. (2001, July 6). Success and new hurdles for T.A. unions. *Chronicle of Higher Education, 47*(42), A10–A12.

Smith, C., Hofer, J., Gillespie, M., Solomon, M., & Rowe, K. (2003, November). *How teachers change: A study of professional development in adult education.* Cambridge, MA: National Center for the Study of Adult Learning and Literacy.

Sticht, T. G. (1998, April). *Moving adult literacy education from the margins to the mainstream of educational policy and practice.* Paper presented for the International Conference on How Adults Learn, Washington, DC.

Sticht, T. G. (2000, May). *Examining the funding picture in ABE.* Found online December 19, 2003, at http://www2.wgbh.org/MBCWEIS/LTC/ALRI/stichttwo.html.

Sticht, T. G. (2002). The rise of the adult education and literacy system in the United States: 1600–2000. In J. Comings, B. Garner, & C. Smith (Eds.), *Annual review of adult learning and literacy* (Vol. 3, pp. 10–43). San Francisco: Jossey-Bass.

Timm, S. A. (1996). Workers' education: The connection between adult and business education. *Thresholds in Education, 22*(3), 13–16.

United States Department of Education. (1999). *State-administered adult education program 1999 adult education personnel.* Washington, DC: Office of Vocational and Adult Education.

United States Department of Education. (2001, October 2). *Secretary Paige announces $31 million in grants to recruit and train new teachers.* Press release. Washington, DC: U.S. Department of Education.

Wilson, S., Floden, R., & Ferrini-Mundy, J. (2001). *Teacher preparation research: Current knowledge, gaps, and recommendations.* Seattle, WA: University of Washington.

Young, M. B., Fitzgerald, N., & Morgan, M. A. (1994, December). *National evaluation of adult education programs: Executive summary.* Arlington, VA: Development Associates.

Young, M. B., Fleischman, H., Fitzgerald, N., & Morgan, M. A. (1995). *National evaluation of adult education programs: Executive summary.* (Contract No. LC 90065001). Arlington, VA: Development Associates.

7

Overview of the Adult Literacy System in Ireland and Current Issues in Its Implementation

Inez Bailey

INTRODUCTION

It is only since 2000 that adult literacy has had a place in the education system in Ireland in a meaningful sense.[1] Prior to this Ireland had no national literacy policy and only a very small fund to cover minimal adult literacy services. Today, literacy is the top priority in national policy on further education[2] and is firmly embedded in policy agendas outside of the education sector. This change has been largely the consequence of the Irish results of the first-ever national adult literacy survey, the International Adult Literacy Survey (IALS), which was carried out in 1995. It showed

---

[1] The term *adult literacy* is most commonly used in Ireland, particularly in policy. There is concern, however, that adult literacy is often interpreted too narrowly and excludes numeracy. Some practitioners use the term *adult basic education* to overcome this difficulty and not to denote something different from adult literacy.

[2] Further education is defined as "systematic learning undertaken by adults who return to learning having concluded initial education or training" (Department of Education and Science, 2000, p. 12).

that one in four of the Irish adult population scored at the lowest level of literacy on a scale of one to five (Morgan, Hickey, & Kellaghan, 1997). The IALS also showed how poor literacy skills among the adult population negatively affected family, community, and work life. This led to government recognition of the importance of improving adult literacy levels for wider social and economic development.

Since the publication of the IALS, the funding has increased 18-fold and participation in literacy services has increased almost 6-fold. The National Development Plan (NDP) 2000–2006 outlines a vision of the future that provides for greater economic and social development. Adult literacy is part of the NDP as a clear contributing factor to upskilling the workforce and facilitating greater participation of those on the margins of society (Government of Ireland, 1999, pp. 191–192). Also, in 2000, the Department of Education and Science (DES) published the first-ever policy on adult education, containing a national adult literacy strategy as the top priority in the document. This policy document, *Learning for Life,* recognizes that adult education can make a major contribution in meeting the skill requirements of a rapidly changing workforce, as well as improving social cohesion and equity in the emergence of a broadly inclusive and proactive civil society. The inclusion of a philosophy of literacy as broader than just workforce development distinguishes literacy in Ireland from the market-driven rhetoric that is dominant in U.K. and U.S. policy in this area (Hamilton, Macrae, & Tett, 2001, p. 32). A further distinguishing element of adult literacy in Ireland is that the core national body overseeing the development of the sector is a membership-based nongovernmental organization with relatively good public funding and influence.

This chapter provides an overview of adult literacy in Ireland, beginning with where adult literacy is situated in the Irish education system and outlining the key stakeholders involved. The chapter traces the development of adult literacy policy and practice over the last 35 years and then describes the philosophy of literacy and the core service provided in Ireland today. It also highlights the innovative work being carried out to address the diverse needs of adult learners and the issues and opportunities in adult literacy as it moves forward.

HISTORICAL BACKGROUND

The Republic of Ireland is a small, trade-dependent country that is slightly larger than West Virginia and about three times the size of Massachusetts, with a population of almost four million (2002 census). The vast majority of the population is Irish-born and Roman Catholic, with non-Irish-born residents coming mostly from other European Union countries. After a period of heightened economic growth between 1995 and 2001 (9% growth rate), the growth rate has slowed to about 4%. Unemployment currently stands at around 4% and poverty is estimated at around 10%.

1960 to 1972: Before Entering the European Communities (EC)

Vocational Education Committees (VECs) were established in 1930 to provide vocational education and training to young people and adults, with most funding and subsequently provision available for people aged 12 to 18.

Prior to the 1970s, there was no official recognition of the adult literacy problem in Ireland. There was no commitment to equality of educational opportunity nor to a critical evaluation of the effectiveness of the national school system. Sean Moylon, Minister for Education (1951–1954) stated, "It is my opinion that this system of ours, of which there is no comparable system on earth, is very appropriate to this country" (O'Buachala, 1988). By 1960, Charles McCarthy, then General Secretary of the Vocational Teachers' Association of Ireland, said that the population in Ireland ". . . is almost universally literate; or more accurately . . . only the unteachable are illiterate. I have nothing more to say on illiteracy . . ." (O'Buachala, 1988).

Free second-level education (similar to high school in the United States) was introduced in Ireland in 1967, far later than in most of its European counterparts (Clancy, 1999). The government increased spending at this level and made a concerted effort to develop the higher education system, leaving few resources for further education. There was no state-funded adult literacy provision; however, in 1969 a group of people interested and involved in adult education established the National Association of Adult Education (AONTAS). Local communities organized a community development movement, including an educational aspect.

With the benefits of economic expansion that began in the 1960s, Ireland entered the European Communities, as it was then known, in 1972. This heralded a period of great social and economic development, during which Ireland strove to emulate the wealth and prosperity it saw in other countries. The soundest route out of poverty for a nation with few natural resources was through its educated people. Therefore, the government and the general population placed a high premium on education. People who did not have a good education themselves worked hard to ensure that the next generation would get the opportunity to have one.

1973 to 1992: Efforts to Build an Adult Literacy Service

In 1969, the government set up a commission, chaired by Con Murphy, a Rights Commissioner in the Labour Court and one of those involved in establishing AONTAS, to advise on the development of adult education in Ireland. The findings of the commission, known as the Murphy Report and titled *Adult Education in Ireland* (1973), detailed 22 points necessary to develop the adult education system in Ireland, including the need for a special report on how to address the needs of adults with low literacy. This was the first national acknowledgment of an adult literacy problem in Ireland, although little resulted from the report.

At a community level, however, people were beginning to volunteer as tutors for individuals who wanted help developing their literacy skills. Because of the stigma attached to having a literacy difficulty, much of this activity was done on a covert basis in people's homes, protecting the identity of learners. One-to-one tuition was the dominant form of instruction at the time, keeping the adult literacy movement low-key and the problem invisible.

In the 1970s, Britain launched the *Right to Read* campaign to raise awareness about adult literacy, encourage participation in learning opportunities, and secure greater resources for literacy programs. The British media supported the campaign, which raised awareness of adult literacy in Irish society because many households had access to British television stations. The British campaign also had an impact on the Irish state broadcasting station (RTE), which produced a radio program on adult literacy entitled *Helping Adults to Read,* subsequently used as a resource for tutors.

In 1974, the Archdiocese of Dublin set up the first adult literacy service, the Dublin Literacy Scheme, in their Dublin Institute of Adult Education, spearheaded by the Director, Fr. Liam Carey, who had returned from adult education studies at Colombia University in 1967 and had been instrumental in establishing AONTAS. Cork, the second-largest city, established a similar service at the same time, using funds from a wider program aimed at addressing poverty in disadvantaged communities, establishing one of the first links between literacy and antipoverty work.

By the mid-1970s, as the numbers of people using the Dublin Literacy Scheme increased, AONTAS set up a subcommittee on adult literacy, which recommended the establishment of a separate body to focus solely on adult literacy. As a result, in 1980, the National Adult Literacy Agency (NALA) was formed. NALA was set up as a membership organization for all those interested or involved in adult literacy. After 5 years of lobbying the government, the Department of Education gave NALA a small grant to open an office and employ three staff.

NALA acted as a coordinating body, harnessing the efforts of all those involved in adult literacy, raising awareness, and lobbying the government for funding and recognition of the issue. NALA organized annual campaigns, targeted at the Government, to achieve the three Rs: resources, recognition, and representation. To this end, NALA mailed questionnaires in 1982 and 1983 to voluntary literacy providers, training centers catering to people with a disability or who were unemployed, and psychiatric hospitals, to ascertain the extent and organization of adult literacy services in Ireland. The data they collected was not complete but showed there were approximately 1,000 learners involved in one-to-one tuition (NALA, 1987).

In 1983, the government appointed another commission on adult education, this time chaired by Dr. Ivor Kenny, Director General of the Irish Management Institute. The Kenny Report, *Lifelong Learning* (1984), was the first state report to have lifelong learning as its central theme. It highlighted the importance of developing a structured adult education system, catering to the needs of all adults, including those with basic education needs. This report noted that such developments were an economic imperative, not just a narrow educational issue. Unfortunately:

> the report had little impact on an education system already straining to cope with a greatly expanded provision for a rapidly increasing youth population and the financial crisis of the mid-1980s. This led the Organization for Economic Cooperation and Development (OECD) to conclude that, despite considerable reference to the ideal of lifelong learning, as in nearly all other countries, there is no evidence of any concerted efforts to render it a reality. (DES, 2000, p. 54)

In 1985 the government granted NALA its first funding and provided the VECs with the first dedicated resources for adult literacy and community education. This enabled VECs to cover some of the costs of an Adult Literacy Organizer (ALO), an individual who organized tuition, trained volunteers to work with individual learners, and provided tuition to small groups of learners.

In 1986, the Department of Education circulated a discussion document, *Adult Education in Disadvantaged Areas,* which contained the estimate that 110,000 adults had very serious literacy difficulties and a further 286,000 had insufficient skills for everyday life. However, the Department then concluded that their official had employed a flawed methodology in determining the statistics and so the document was never formally published. In the same year, NALA conducted another, wider survey of adult literacy provision, sending questionnaires to the adult literacy services, which were now receiving funding from their local VEC. They also sent the survey to state employment training workshops, Traveler's workshops (a small indigenous minority group), centers for people with disabilities, prison educational units, community groups, and psychiatric hospitals. The findings of the survey revealed that 3,022 learners were involved in literacy tuition, over half of whom were in the adult literacy service. The remainder was receiving tuition in the other education and training centers mentioned earlier as part of their broader vocational education and training program. The survey also showed that although most learners and tutors were working within the adult literacy service, the other education and training centers were using most of the available resources. NALA hoped that the findings of the survey would influence the Department of Education to increase funding for literacy provision, which was described as "grossly inadequate and of a temporary nature" (NALA, 1987, p. 37). However, a change of government in 1987 and an economic crisis led to major cutbacks in government spending, including cuts in spending on adult literacy.

During the economic crisis of the late 1980s, unemployment levels spiraled upward. Ireland was beginning to lose much of its low skilled and manual industry to economies with cheaper labor. In addition, Ireland had a growing number of young people and, despite high levels of emigration, far more educated people than jobs, leaving those with the lowest levels of educational attainment—employed or not—most vulnerable.

In an attempt to lift the country out of recession, in the late 1980s, the government initiated a partnership to galvanize the nation into collective action. In the National Social Partnership (NSP) agreements, the Irish government brought together three groups—employers, trade unions, and farmers—and got them to agree to a common agenda for employment conditions, such as wage increases. The government also recognized the need to address the adult literacy issue; this resulted in increased resources being channeled into adult literacy.

In 1990, Dr. Patrick Hillary, President of Ireland, agreed to act as patron of the work of NALA and the following year, his successor, President

Mary Robinson, took on the role. At the same time, the Department of Education established a Consultative Group on Adult Education that provided a forum for meetings between NALA, the VEC adult literacy service, and themselves. The adult literacy service was by now established throughout Ireland, and those involved participated in NALA work to document their practices. NALA published guidelines on good practice in adult literacy that outlined the philosophy underpinning the work of the sector, and in 1991 it established a major 2-year training of trainers in adult literacy services programs. Despite a very small budget, determined, committed individuals, most of whom worked on a voluntary basis, were making progress toward gaining increased funds and recognition of the work of the adult literacy service.

1993 to 1997: Building a Foundation for Adult Literacy

Although adult educators in Ireland had always subscribed to the idea of lifelong learning as an integral part of the philosophy of adult education, and the European Union (EU), through a series of publications and policy documents (European Parliament and Council, 1995; OECD, 1996), promoted it as necessary for industrialized countries to survive in a global context, the government in Ireland had always viewed education and training as a linear progression from school to college or training center. Adult educators felt that a government policy embracing lifelong learning would bring about the infrastructural change to set up a permanent adult education system that would include adult literacy.

The government was focused on training for workers. In 1993, the Irish government submitted a national development plan to the European Commission, in which one of the two central objectives of the Community Support Framework for Ireland, 1994–1999, was to reintegrate long-term unemployed people (and those at risk of becoming so) into the economic mainstream. The government built their strategy around the priority of developing "the skills and aptitudes of those in work and those seeking employment by both addressing the needs of the productive sectors and by integrating those who are marginalized and disadvantaged" (Government of Ireland, 1999, p. 272). Under its Operational Program, which ran from 1994 to 1999, the government provided a significant percentage of the population with education and training courses.

By the mid-1990s, the Irish economy experienced an unprecedented boom, with growth rates outstripping most, if not all, of its trading partners.

The education and training system, specifically the Operational Program, played an important role in providing trained people in sufficient numbers to contribute to employment growth at this time (Government of Ireland, 1999). The government marketed the educated Irish workforce around the world, attracting foreign direct investment, particularly in the software and pharmaceutical industries.

The incoming tide, however, did not lift all boats, and government still had concerns about the number of people at risk in society. Persistent long-term unemployment and poverty led the government to conduct a study to determine how to combat poverty; although educational disadvantage was among the contributing factors highlighted, the study concentrated on primary and secondary school education and not on the adult population already poorly served by the mainstream education system (Department of Social Welfare, 1997). As a result of this study, the government introduced the National Anti-Poverty Strategy (NAPS), a nationally agreed-upon set of policy targets, proposals, and programs to eliminate the main factors contributing to the prevalence of poverty and social exclusion in Irish society. It has as its mandate the inclusion of all those marginalized socially, culturally, and economically. One of the key targets was addressing educational disadvantage by ensuring that programs were in place for people wishing to improve their level of literacy.

Another study, a 1992 survey by the OECD, revealed that the proportion of adults in Ireland who had left school at or before the junior cycle of second level (state examination at the age of 15) stood at 58% (just over 930,000 people), which was among the highest in the EU at the time (OECD, 1996). The OECD survey also highlighted the role of adult literacy in promoting competitiveness and employment, addressing poverty, promoting democracy and social cohesion, building a knowledge society, and strengthening people, families, communities, and ultimately nations.

However, in 1995, the government issued a White Paper on Education, *Charting our Education Future* (Department of Education, 1995) that, although referencing the importance of lifelong learning, was mainly concerned with primary, secondary, and higher education.

From 1993 until 1997, provision of adult literacy services grew incrementally each year. However, the rate of annual increase in the Adult Literacy and Community Education budget declined each year, dropping most significantly in 1996. By 1997, although there were approximately 5,000 adults participating in the adult literacy service, the adult literacy service relied on a "totally inadequate" budget, according to the Minister of State at the Department of Education and Science (Houses of the Oireachtas, 1998, p. 43).

The International Adult Literacy Survey

The International Adult Literacy Survey (Morgan et al., 1997), conducted in 1995 and published in 1997, provided Ireland with its first profile of the literacy skills of adults aged 16 to 64. The survey found that about 25% of the population, or at least 500,000 adults, scored at the lowest level (Level 1), performing at best tasks that required the reader to locate a simple piece of information in a text, with no distracting information, when the structure of the text assisted the task. A further 30% of the population was at Level 2. Ireland thus had a total of 55% of those aged between 16 and 64 scoring below the minimum desirable threshold for a Western industrialized nation. The survey showed, however, that people in the older age quintiles had poorer performance than those in the younger age groups. The survey concluded that one reason for this was that many older Irish people had not participated in second-level education, because it was fee paying until 1967 (Department of Enterprise, Trade and Employment, 1997). The findings were met with shock and disbelief (Houses of the Oireachtas, 1998).

The publication of IALS, which provided a comparative analysis of the numbers of adults in many Western industrialized populations who have difficulties with everyday reading tasks, greatly affected the adult literacy sector in Ireland. Up to that time, there had been no published adult literacy survey and very little attention paid to the area by successive Irish government administrations. NALA prepared a campaign to publicize the IALS results and suggest solutions; the campaign attracted considerable media attention. In addition, NALA set up meetings with, and prepared papers for, identified policy representatives and service providers, who heretofore had little or no involvement in the adult literacy issue, including the Department of An Taoiseach, Department of Enterprise, Trade, and Employment, and FÁS (the State Employment and Training Agency).

In 1997, as a result of the OECD survey, constant lobbying by NALA, and the initial ranking of Ireland as second-last in the first IALS publication, the government budget for literacy increased by 16%, starting a trend that was to continue for the next 5 years. Provision for adult literacy increased from a base of $1.2 million (€1 million) in 1997 to $21.6 million (€18 million) in 2003. Literacy had become a top priority. At the launch of the NALA International Literacy Day conference in 1999, our government leader, An Taoiseach, Mr. Bertie Ahern had the following to say:

I am convinced that literacy is one of the key ways to build an Ireland where people have the chance to build their own futures and have full access to a full and decent life. The Government I lead is determined to work with you to put in place a forward looking strategy in order to ensure that, as a society, we promote higher standards of literacy for all. I can assure you that the National Development Plan currently being finalized will reflect this priority. . . . [A]n underfunded and underresourced service too easily gets the label of being a service about a special problem. A problem that affects one in four of us is not a special problem, but a problem for all of us and we need to start saying so even more loudly and clearly and unapologetically. (NALA Newsletter, November 1999)

Also in 1997, the Government introduced another group to the partner-ship process, the Community and Voluntary pillar, through the "Partner-ship 2000" agreement. The agreement, consisting of tax measures to assist those with low incomes, and specific funding for equality initiatives on gender, people with disabilities, and members of the Traveling commu-nity (a small, indigenous minority group that is nomadic), was in essence a social inclusion package.[3] The Partnership 2000 agreement coincided with the publication of the Government White Paper on Human Resource Development (Department of Enterprise, Trade and Employment, 1997), which highlighted the comparatively low levels of education of Irish adults within an OECD context and signaled the negative impact on the economy and the labor market. Acknowledging that the link between educational disadvantage, unemployment, and social exclusion was well documented at the time, this agreement served to orient education policy "in such a way as to give priority in the allocation of resources to those in greatest need" (Government of Ireland, 1996).

1998 to Present: Adult Literacy Service Expansion and Improvement

First National Adult Literacy Strategy

In the past 6 years, numerous policy initiatives and dedicated fund-ing from the government through a variety of schemes has permitted the

---

[3] The Combat Poverty Agency (CPA), a statutory body, defines social inclusion as "ensuring the fullest participation of the marginalized and those living in poverty in deci-sion-making processes as a means to raise their standard of living and improve their qual-ity of life." The CPA defines social exclusion as "the process by which certain groups are pushed to the edge of society and prevented from participating fully by virtue of their poverty, inadequate education or lifeskills" (CPA, 2002, p. 42).

adult literacy service to expand and improve, reaching a greater number of adults. This has been accomplished through three primary components: national policy on adult education, *Learning for Life;* the first national strategy on adult literacy; and the inclusion of an adult literacy target in the National Anti-Poverty Strategy.

In 1997, the new government appointed the first ever Minister for State at the Department of Education and Science, with responsibility for Adult Education. After discussions with key stakeholders involved in adult education, the new administration published a Green Paper on Adult Education (DES, 1998), including a broad definition of adult literacy that encapsulated the philosophy of Irish adult literacy practice. It outlined the requirements necessary for the development of the adult literacy service to meet the needs of a greater number of adults wishing to improve their basic education.

Learning for Life. After 2 years of consultation concerning the Green Paper, and advances to the adult literacy budget, the Department of Education and Science (2000) published the first ever White Paper on Adult Education, *Learning for Life,* with adult literacy policy as its top priority. The approach to adult literacy developed since the 1970s thus became embedded in national policy, an important victory for adult literacy.

Learning for Life sets out a holistic approach to the development of a national program of adult education, recognizing its contribution to the six priority areas:

1. Consciousness raising
2. Citizenship
3. Cohesion
4. Competitiveness
5. Cultural development
6. Community building

Three core principles underpin this framework for adult education: lifelong learning as a systemic approach, equality, and interculturalism. This broad vision of adult education equally applies to adult literacy and highlights that both areas are not just about the development of skills and the resultant effect on the economy, but the role of adult learning in the development of social, cultural, and civil society as well.

The qualities that characterize good adult literacy practice are outlined in *Learning for Life:*

- A holistic curriculum.
- A view of the student as a self-directed, self-motivated learner.
- A recognition of the learner as the center of the learning process; that is, learning as construction rather than as instruction.
- A core-learning objective of preparing the learner for a life of learning rather than for a terminal, end-of-learning examination.

The National Adult Literacy Program. The *Learning for Life* White Paper also established the National Adult Literacy Program, a strategy to improve adult literacy levels among the adult population in Ireland. This is the first strategy of this kind in Ireland and represents the blueprint for adult literacy development up to 2006. The goals of this plan over 6 years are:

- Increase the number of clients reached so that by the end of 2006, an estimated 113,000 will have benefited from these services.
- Prioritize those with the lowest literacy levels.
- Implement a quality framework to monitor the effectiveness of the service.
- Develop new modes of reaching out and recruiting people.
- Ensure adult literacy education is available for the unemployed.
- Develop new strategies to address the underrepresentation of men in adult literacy classes.
- Explore the potential of Information Communication Technology and broadcasting.
- Continue to develop specific initiatives for disadvantaged groups.
- Expand provision of workplace literacy.
- Increase collaboration with the public library service, as well as other organizations working with relevant sections of the population.

The current National Development Plan 2000–2006, with a commitment to provide comprehensive and diverse education and training opportunities, catering to the needs of specific groups from early childhood through adulthood, particularly those experiencing social disadvantage, funds the National Adult Literacy Program at $106 million (€93.7 million). Since 2000, the program has ensured that:

- The clients catered to annually have increased from 5,000 to 28,000 from 1997 to 2003, surpassing published targets.

• Provision includes free nighttime and daytime classes, typically of 2 to 4 hours duration per week.

• The adult literacy service is developing a continuum from one-to-one voluntary tuition to group work to progression to certified learning options, in recognition of the need to provide a suite of learning options.

• The adult literacy service is expanding and strengthening referral networks and typically includes libraries, farming organizations, community groups, trade unions, social welfare centers, and so forth.

• Additional practitioner training programs provided by NALA are underway on a modular in-service basis, as part of a higher education accreditation framework for adult literacy practitioners.

• NALA is mainstreaming the Quality Framework, a strategy to guide and monitor quality standards, for the adult literacy service after a 3-year development process involving learners, practitioners, and senior management.

• In conjunction with adult literacy practitioners and learners, NALA has developed a national assessment framework, building on the Equipped for the Future program from the United States.

• NALA has successfully piloted and evaluated literacy and dedicated numeracy programs broadcast on radio and television, which are now part of the mainstream provision, most notably the *READ WRITE NOW* television series.

• Adult literacy services and their local authority are rolling out national workplace basic education programs for local authority workers in the public sector, after pilot programs were 50% oversubscribed.

• The DES has established an Inter-Departmental Group on Literacy for the Unemployed to develop an integrated response to addressing the literacy needs of the unemployed. *Return to Education* programs have been expanded throughout Ireland, providing long-term unemployed people with an opportunity to combine supported employment with a 9-hour basic education course.

• The adult literacy service is successfully running a small number of family literacy groups and piloting open learning centers, along with literacy groups for migrant women, the Traveling community, and supported programs for the unemployed.

• The adult literacy service is developing ESOL to meet the needs of an ever-increasing number of asylum seekers and refugees. NALA has published a set of guidelines for ESOL work drawn up by a national working group made up of adult literacy and ESOL practitioners, as well as representatives of agencies supporting the integration of non-nationals.

National Anti-Poverty Strategy (NAPS).   In line with the government policy just outlined, the current NAPS, *Building An Inclusive Society* program (2002), includes a greater focus on educational disadvantage and more specifically, literacy, and sets out three targets:

1. To halve the proportion of pupils in primary school with serious literacy difficulties by 2006.

2. To reduce the proportion of the population aged 16 to 64 with restricted literacy to below 10% to 20% by 2007 (restricted literacy being defined as falling into Level 1 on the IALS scale or equivalent).

3. To reduce the number of young people who leave the school system early, so that the percentage of those who complete upper secondary level or equivalent will reach 85% by 2003 and 90% by 2006 (p. 12).

This is the first time a target has been set for adult literacy, and there has been some debate about how this target came about and how it will be measured. The target is to be achieved by 2007 and as yet there are no plans for a further survey of adult literacy levels of the adult population.

The national policy context outlined here shows the government of Ireland's commitment to addressing the adult literacy issue in Ireland, and for the first time ever it has security for the future. However, it is not possible to ascertain where Ireland would rate in a future IALS, and the Irish government has not signed up to be part of the Adult Literacy and Lifeskills Survey (ALLS), the successor to the OECD's IALS, which not only covers literacy skills but measures a broader range of skills in the adult population. However, the inclusion of a quality framework devised by adult literacy learners, practitioners, and senior management has given previously unknown legitimacy to the sector and ensured that the ethos of adult literacy work in Ireland will underpin all developments in the area in the future.

THE PRESENT SYSTEM: PHILOSOPHY, THE ROLE OF NALA, AND STRUCTURE OF ADULT LITERACY SERVICES

Two aspects of the adult literacy services that are unique to Ireland are the philosophy underpinning adult literacy and NALA, which is a nonprofit membership organization concerned with national coordination, policy, and training in the adult literacy sector. The structure of the current system is also detailed in this section.

Philosophy

The NALA (2002a) definition of literacy states:

> Literacy involves the integration of listening, speaking, reading, writing, and numeracy. It also encompasses aspects of personal development—social, economic, emotional—and is concerned with improving self-esteem and building confidence. It goes far beyond mere technical skills for communication. The underlying aim of good practice is to enable people to understand and reflect critically on their life circumstances with a view to exploring new possibilities and initiating constructive change. (p. 8)

This definition encapsulates the main approaches to adult literacy work in Ireland, namely, that it is learner centered and promotes social action. It is the definition used by adult literacy providers.

The need to ensure respect for the dignity and autonomy of adult learners in all aspects of adult literacy work is central to national adult literacy policy and practice. In order to support the development of this ethos in adult literacy programs, NALA provides a wide variety of training and development opportunities, funded by the DES and designed in consultation with the key stakeholders. Moving away from the school model, the adult literacy service embraces new approaches to tutoring and new learning materials. Trainers discourage the deficit model—identifying a learner's weaknesses in order to develop an individualized learning plan—as it often reinforces the feeling of failure experienced by learners when they attended school. Instead, practitioners are trained to identify both strengths and weaknesses and to develop programs that build on the individual's strengths while addressing their literacy problem.

Maintaining the Philosophy

Can the adult literacy service remain truly learner-centered in a rapidly changing environment? Will adult literacy be seen merely as the skills of communication and not also as a means by which people critically reflect on their lives? As one practitioner stated:

> The ethos of the Irish Adult Literacy service is grounded in one to one tuition where the student is the central point. The individualised approach is integral to the provision. With the rapid expansion of the service over the last few years organisers are determined to hold dear to this ethos.
>
> —*Frances Ward*

Embracing change while holding onto this philosophy is a great challenge and one that needs to be built into adult literacy work through in-service training and development opportunities, but also should be enshrined in policy. With increasing numbers engaging in tuition, it will not be possible to offer one-to-one tuition to all new entrants.

To maintain the philosophy, NALA consults with all those involved in adult literacy, particularly the learners themselves, not just senior management. *Learning for Life* reflects that position, which is testimony to a bottom-up consultative process involving learners, practitioners, and other key players. Because NALA is a membership organization, broad views are present, not solely those of providers or funders. Training is another vital part of keeping the ethos central to adult literacy practice, and this is equally valid for paid professionals as it is for the much-valued volunteers. In addition, the accredited training framework for practitioners and the quality and assessment frameworks that have been developed in Ireland are all infused with the ethos of adult literacy work and to that end, they are key elements of sustaining the philosophy into the future.

It can be said that the adult literacy philosophy in Ireland is the antithesis of the dominant education ideology of an economically driven society, where the focus is strongly on the acquisition of knowledge and skills for the sustenance of the labor market. In that context, such an ethos will have to be guarded on an ongoing basis.

The Role of NALA

NALA, as already mentioned, is a unique, nonprofit membership organization concerned with national coordination, policy, and training in the adult literacy sector. A key objective of NALA, enshrined in its constitution, is to encourage the involvement of adult learners in all aspects of planning, organization, and research, which is a departure from the overly protective policies of the past.

The transition of the adult literacy service from a purely small-scale voluntary activity to a professionalized national service was the primary focus of NALA's work for the last 20 years. NALA acted as a national engine in the development of qualifications for practitioners, lobbied for additional resources for adequate staffing and resourcing of the service, and developed new ways of providing literacy tuition. This has been achieved in cooperation with adult literacy practitioners within the VEC sector—the VECs are the largest and most active NALA membership group. The Irish Vocational Education Association (IVEA)—the VEC sector's own national engine who have a greater focus on the development and integration of the service as part of the wider VEC provision—now have greater involvement in the service. This will be the most effective means by which the adult literacy service will embrace the future and continue its development.

NALA has been responsible for disseminating this philosophy of adult literacy, most notably through the *Guidelines for Good Adult Literacy Work* in 1985 (with an updated version in 1991), which became *the* manual for adult literacy services. This publication came about as a result of facilitated discussion between practitioners and learners about how they work together. The document sets out four basic principles that underpin good adult literacy provision:

1. Adult literacy work encompasses aspects of personal development—social, economic, emotional. It covers much more than reading and writing skills.

2. Adult literacy workers must always recognize and respect the adult status of the learners. All of their work must be developed with this in mind and should never rely on procedures and materials developed for children.

3. Adult literacy students need to become active, not passive, learners. They should always be enabled to contribute their skills, knowledge, and experience, both to the learning process and to the organization of provision at all levels. Students not only have the right to learn but also the right to choose how to learn.

4. Learning is a lifelong process. Adult literacy provision needs to establish links with other existing educational activities and to initiate new developments in continuing education. (NALA, 1991)

Each of these principles are further detailed within the guidelines, which also cover areas such as how to respond to the needs of learners in relation to their learning and encourage their involvement in how literacy instruction is provided. The manual also describes how literacy services should be organized (and the resources required), which include the need to:

- Provide full-time tuition.
- Enhance numeracy provision.
- Address special needs.
- Provide accreditation for learners and tutors.
- Embrace counseling skills.
- Conduct research.

A Profile of Learners—Access and Participation
in Irish Adult Literacy Programs

From 1996 to 1998, NALA conducted research into access and participation in adult literacy programs in Ireland, with the aid of EU funding (Bailey & Coleman, 1998). The rationale for this research lay in the very low participation rates in adult literacy programs in Ireland and abroad. One hundred fifty-nine learners participated in interviews in which they outlined their experience of having a literacy difficulty and deciding to do something about it. The study found that young people were leaving school early due to poverty, overcrowded classrooms, alienation from the curriculum, inadequate support for those with special learning needs, and ill health. The major cause of low literacy is linked to broader socioeconomic indicators and not due to large numbers of the population experiencing learning disabilities (the term *learning difficulties* is used in Ireland). However, there has been no survey to estimate the number of adults with a learning disability in Ireland and data that exist give an estimate of between 4% and 7% (http://www.dyslexia.ie/; http://www.aspire-irl.com).

Based on the interviews done during the study, *Access and Participation in Adult Literacy Schemes in Ireland,* the main barriers to participation were categorized as follows:

- Dispositional (e.g., negative attitude toward education, learning seen as irrelevant)
- Informational (e.g., material was too difficult to read or understand, lack of appropriate information)
- Institutional (e.g., difficulties using applications forms, dislike or distrust of traditional classroom setting)
- Situational (e.g., not enough time, lack of child care)

Before attending the adult literacy programs, many of the interviewees reported negative views of themselves as learners, acute embarrassment and shame about their low educational attainment, and crippling memories of their school days. As a result, they avoided situations where their literacy difficulties might be discovered. It is not surprising, therefore, that most adult education courses in Ireland are of a formal nature and utilized by those who have found success in the formal school system.

You'd feel you wouldn't be as educated as other people and you'd be shying away from getting into a conversation. I was always looking at courses but being that I knew I had difficulty with spelling I never went into any course that involved writing.

—Man in his 20s

And you were constantly told you were stupid . . . when they asked us was there anybody who would clean the toilets, we'd put up our hands, just to get out of the class. About four of us, who were pals. It was pointless trying to teach us, the teachers said. And it wasn't pointless.

—Woman in her 40s

In almost all cases, the dominant barrier was dispositional. A quote from one of the interviewees illustrates this.

Well to tell you the truth, I don't even try to tell my friends. I wouldn't even tell my next-door neighbour that I'm coming here. There was a chap from our road here and when I seen him first I wanted to hide, like I felt ashamed. I had a chat with him and he said he wouldn't breathe a word. . . . You just feel that people might look down on you.

—Man in his 30s

Many of the interviewees highlighted how their experience of poverty had contributed to their literacy difficulty. As children, they knew that "better off" children were given the attention in school. The attitude of the interviewees' parents was also highlighted, as many regretted that their parents did not play a more significant role in their education.

These people returned to the local adult literacy service in order to help their children, improve their job prospects or change jobs, and simply to meet their own developmental needs. For almost 60% of those interviewed, joining the adult literacy program was their first experience of any form of education and training since leaving compulsory schooling. All the learners who participated in the survey provided ample evidence that nonformal adult basic education is having a profoundly positive outcome on people who are regarded as "hard to reach." All detailed a variety of benefits that ensued, including the pleasure of reading the newspaper, increased participation in social and community activities, improved mental health, and empowerment.

There were few adults seeking employment within the 16 literacy programs that participated in the survey. Almost half of the research participants were in paid employment (mainly men), and a significant number of those not in paid employment were working full time in the home (mainly women). Many spoke about their frustration with their jobs or lack of them and felt that their education levels had severely limited their lifestyle options.

In relation to those who were not in adult literacy programs, the survey identified certain groups who were underrepresented. These included the unemployed, women under the age of 30, men over the age of 50, and older people in general. NALA began a number of initiatives to provide opportunities to those adults and to increase participation rates generally, including the *Return to Education* program for people on Community Employment, radio and television tuition, and referral networks; these became the core of the National Adult Literacy Program (DES, 2000), already outlined.

Many of the factors that in the past have led people in Ireland to seek adult literacy services now have been addressed. There is free second-level education, class sizes are smaller, and there are a variety of support measures that address educational disadvantage caused by poverty. In addition, there is greater awareness in schools of learning disabilities, and specialist teachers and resources are on hand. Despite all of this, a recent survey carried out by the Education Research Centre estimated that one in ten children are finishing primary school with insufficient literacy skills (Kellaghan, Cosgrove, Forde, & Morgan, 2000).

Structure of Adult Literacy Services

The education system in Ireland consists of five main components:

1. Early childhood (nursery).
2. Primary (elementary): starts at the age of 4 or 5 and finishes by the age of 12.
3. Secondary (high): 5 or 6 years of education; requires two state examinations.
4. Higher (college).
5. Further (adult), which includes adult literacy services.

The Department of Education and Science (DES) is responsible for all of these areas and funds most primary and secondary schools directly. Early childhood and further education are the newest additions to the education family. Further education is administered through the following infrastructure:

• The DES funds the bulk of the further education sector through Vocational Education Committees (VECs), of which there are 33 throughout Ireland. VECs are made up of locally elected councilors, as well as parents and representatives of students and staff. Each VEC is an autonomous and independent body, so there are differences in how each provides service. Further education provision within the VECs includes programs targeted at early school leavers (those receiving welfare benefits and those not) and people wishing to improve their adult literacy or get a post Leaving Certificate qualification. All VECs, as well as their individual literacy services, are members of NALA.

• The Irish Vocational Education Association (IVEA), a national representative employer body, formulates policy and advances the cause of the VECs by advocating with the DES. In 2002, the IVEA established a National Literacy Forum, which is comprised of representatives from various groups, within the VEC sector, concerned with provision of education services. This is the first time the core provider body of the VEC adult literacy service in Ireland has come together to address adult literacy issues.

• An Adult Literacy Organizer (ALO) manages the adult literacy service within the VEC.

• NALA, the umbrella organization concerned with adult literacy, includes individual learners, tutors, and those involved in adult literacy that work outside the VEC sector. From its membership, individuals are elected for a 2-year term to the NALA Executive Committee to guide the policy direction of the Agency and monitor the work as outlined in the organization's strategic plan. On an annual basis, NALA applies to the DES for core funding to carry out work, identified through consultation with members, and research into best practices in adult literacy internationally.

Adult Literacy Services in Ireland

The core adult literacy service is provided by the VEC in 135 locations. Although each VEC is unique in its approach to the provision of adult literacy, especially in structural matters, in most cases service is available during the day and in the evening, Monday to Friday. Adult Literacy Organizers (ALOs) manage the service, working alongside paid group tutors and volunteer one-on-one tutors. Most adult learners are now in tuition groups, although some are given the option of starting with a tutor on a one-on-one basis. Most services offer classes on a 2-hour-a-week basis; some services are able to offer more where requested. However, in a small number of locations, only 1-hour sessions can be offered, due to a shortage of facilities.

Some programs have private rooms for one-to-one tuition. Other programs, usually in urban areas, offer one-to-one tuition workshops, where several one-to-one pairs work in the same room. This can be a more sociable and less isolating way of offering one-to-one tuition for both the learner and the tutor. In many cases, a support tutor—an experienced group tutor who provides back-up support to the tutor as required—is also available in the room. Adult literacy services also have a resource room, of varying quality, which can be used by learners and tutors.

Tutor Profile. The NALA survey of adult literacy provisions published in 1987 showed that of the 1,255 tutors in the service at the time, the vast majority were volunteers and 82% were female. Today there are just over 4,000 volunteer tutors and 1,500 paid tutors. A recent NALA-commissioned survey, undertaken in order to inform a training-needs analysis, found that the majority of paid tutors work part-time, averaging between 5 and 10 hours per week (CHL Consulting, 2002). Most tutors are women, making up 95% of all paid tutors. Two-fifths of tutors are between the ages of 45 and 60, with another third between 31 and 45 years of age. Almost three quarters of tutors have been working for fewer than 5 years.

The educational background of tutors is generally of a high standard. Over three quarters of tutors, paid and voluntary, have a higher education qualification and another 13% have postgraduate certification. In addition to existing qualifications, 31% of tutors are currently studying for some type of additional qualification. As might be expected, this group is made up of a greater number of paid tutors.

Although the adult literacy service has gained funding through VECs, the service has retained volunteer tutors as the only feasible means by which to provide one-to-one tuition. In addition, there is a strong feeling within the NALA membership that volunteer involvement in the adult literacy service adds value, enriches the type of service provided, and maintains its deep roots in civil society. As funding for adult literacy has increased over the last 6 years, the role of the volunteer tutor has not been eroded, as was feared by some practitioners.

Adult Literacy Organizer Profile. When CHL Consulting conducted the NALA-commissioned training-needs analysis survey, they also surveyed Adult Literacy Organizers (ALOs). The role of the ALO has changed as a result of the rapid growth and development of the adult literacy service. Originally, the ALO worked on a part-time basis recruiting and teaching learners, as well as training volunteer tutors to work on a one-to-one basis with learners. Over the years, the role has evolved to include the management of a larger number of paid tutors, as well as volunteers.

This has brought up a range of management issues, including managing staff and reporting to line managers, integrating the adult literacy service into the wider further education service provided by the VEC, as well as other provisions beyond the VEC. The number of learners entering the service has also increased, requiring ALOs to secure additional facilities and provide more diverse programs. With heightened public awareness of the adult literacy issue, ALOs are also directly involved in local development groups representing their service. These groups include local area development committees and drugs task forces, as well as education networks.

As a result of these changes, ALOs, through their professional association (the Adult Literacy Organizers Association—ALOA), devised a new role outline, which was presented and accepted by their employer's representative body, the IVEA, and the DES. ALOA's aims are to: enhance the status of adult literacy provision within the adult education system; promote a high quality adult literacy service; and secure recognition of the social, cultural, and economic context of adult literacy (ALOA, 2001).

The national average number of tutors per ALO is just over 36, with the number of literacy clients per ALO averaging 129. Over half of the ALOs are between the ages of 45 and 60, with another third between 31 and 45 years of age. The overwhelming majority of ALOs are female. Two thirds of ALOs have been working for up to 5 years, with another fifth working for 6 to 10 years. Most ALOs have been recruited from the ranks of tutors.

The majority of ALOs hold a third-level qualification, with almost half holding postgraduate degrees. A relatively small number of ALOs stated they had qualifications specific to literacy and adult basic education. However, almost half of ALOs surveyed are currently studying for some type of qualification, the majority through the NALA/WIT project, which is discussed later in this chapter.

Career Structure. For the most part, there are no full-time permanent tutors or resource workers assisting ALOs employed within the VEC adult literacy service, which is a major gap in the infrastructure of the service. Many tutors working part time eventually find more secure employment in other parts of the education-and-training sector. Losing its most experienced and competent practitioners is not a new phenomenon, but is less acceptable at a time when the service has ample financing.

The adult literacy sector does not appear to be attracting people to work in the area due to the lack of career structure. Although this was the case when most of the present incumbents became involved, the Irish economy and society were also very different at the time. When the current generation of practitioners retires, it will be interesting to see who is there to take their place.

Recently, paid professional tutors organized an association, the Basic Education Tutors Association (BETA), which is principally concerned with advancing tutors' terms and conditions of employment within the VEC sector.

Key Components of the Current System

Teacher and Tutor Preparation and Certification.   *Learning for Life* (DES, 2000) acknowledges the unique and invaluable contribution made by volunteers (over 70% of all tutors) to the development of the adult literacy service and commits to providing opportunities to upgrade their knowledge and skills and help them gain certification through flexible procedures. With additional funding and staff in the 1990s from the DES, NALA devised a professional development program that enabled local literacy organizers to train their own tutors locally and to then use NALA in-service training to train tutors in additional areas. The most common of these 1-day sessions, delivered by experienced tutors, covered creating materials and group work.

Adult literacy tutors need a thorough understanding of the basic principles that underlie the philosophy and methods of adult education, as set out in the *Guidelines for Good Adult Literacy Work* (NALA, 1991). Therefore, the initial tutor training course includes three types of learning—attitude, skills, and knowledge—and allows sufficient time to explore the development of these areas in adult literacy work. During the training course, tutors also examine what it means to be an active learner, exploring the process by which learners can identify what they want to learn, how they as learners can best learn, and how to assess the learning that has taken place. The tutor training employs methods the tutors themselves will use in their teaching, such as role-play, practical work, and group discussion. During the training, the trainers evaluate the course through participant feedback during and immediately after the session, and trainers are encouraged to conduct a follow-up meeting with tutors after they have had time to implement what they have learned. The materials used for tutor training cover getting started with reading and writing using the language-experience approach, using cloze passages, and the Look Say Cover Write Check method of developing spelling skills (NALA, 1995). Initial tutor training is generally delivered over 20 hours, by experienced tutors or ALOs once or twice a year. Adult literacy learners are often involved in the design and delivery of initial tutor training.

During the 1990s, practitioners realized that if the service were to become more professionalized, they would need recognized qualifications in order to attain permanent, better-paid jobs. With this in mind, practitioners mandated NALA, through a resolution at the NALA Annual General Meeting in 1992, to develop such qualifications with the relevant authorities, ensuring that there would be recognition of prior experiential learning. Waterford Institute of Technology (WIT) agreed to work in partnership with NALA to provide accreditation for adult literacy workers. NALA and WIT spent considerable time working through—with practitioners and academics—the content of this university-level program, ensuring that it built on and was respectful of, the previous training developed over the years through NALA (McSkeane, 1998, p. iii). NALA and WIT developed a number of certificate and diploma programs, in response to an identified need for university-level training courses that would assist literacy organizers and tutors in upgrading their skills and also in gaining accreditation for the knowledge and skills they had accumulated during their years of work in the field of adult literacy.

The NALA/WIT project was established initially on a pilot basis, with funding from the DES. NALA/WIT now provides full certificate and diploma programs, as well as single-certificate modules, and is developing degree and postgraduate qualifications. The certificate program requires students to complete 12 modules (out of a possible 20) and the diploma program requires completion of 6 out of 8 modules. Each module contains 50 contact hours, 35 with a tutor and the remaining 15 made up by group work, peer learning, and support. The program is offered to VEC-based practitioners who usually are released by their employer to attend. There is no nationally agreed-upon VEC protocol that supports practitioners to attend training, so some do pay their own registration fee and attend on their own time; however, they must have approval from their manager to take the course.

The NALA/WIT program qualifications are designed for practitioners currently serving as tutors, but NALA and WIT are considering making them entry qualifications. NALA/WIT are also considering how to include field practice in the program, as they designed the existing body of qualifications for people with a minimum period of job experience. Also, the DES would likely require that trainees agree to serve a designated time with the adult literacy service in exchange for participation in the program. The current career structure does not extend to tutors, who at best find themselves on part-time contracts that run according to the academic year.

The recognition of the NALA/WIT qualifications by the IVEA is a key objective. Although the DES funds the project, it is the VECs who are the main employer for adult literacy workers and therefore it is important that they recognize and value these specific qualifications. To date the IVEA has mandated that ALOs possess the relevant NALA/WIT qualification, or an unspecified adult education equivalent, within 5 years of taking a full-time position.

The Quality Framework for Adult Literacy. In the late 1990s, McDonagh (1999) found that standards of practice were inconsistent across programs and that those involved in adult literacy services felt that the development of quality standards would improve their practice. NALA, working with learners, practitioners, senior management, and the DES, subsidized by the European fund Socrates, developed the Quality Framework, a strategy to guide and monitor quality standards in adult literacy.

The Quality Framework has five guiding principles or values:

- The adult literacy program will support the learner's right to attend on a voluntary basis and to set his/her own goals.
- The organization will operate under an ethical code of confidentiality, respect, and trust.
- All levels of the organization will respect cultural differences.
- The adult literacy program will pay particular attention to creating and maintaining an atmosphere of social interaction, informality, and enjoyment.
- The organization will enable learners to participate in all aspects of the program, including evaluation.

The framework provides a way of looking at five main quality areas involved in running a local adult literacy service. Within each of these five quality areas—Resources, Management, Teaching and Learning, Outreach and Promotion, and Progression—are statements of quality. Combined, these statements of quality are the standards a program should work toward. Each statement describes a key element of a quality adult literacy program. For example, in relation to the quality statement on assessment, a quality local service will:

- Assess the learner's needs and level of literacy during an initial interview and/or in the course of the first few tuition sessions, as appropriate.
- Ensure that tutors engage in ongoing assessment with learners.
- Refer learners with specific needs for an appropriate professional assessment.

The Quality Framework can be used as a tool for self-evaluation of adult literacy sites, promoting planning and continuous improvement, and improving accountability. Over half of programs in Ireland (28 out of 33) are now using the Quality Framework, following an initial piloting of this new system. NALA has developed a mainstreaming plan that gives details of supports it provides to adult literacy services wishing to use the Quality Framework. These include funding for a team facilitator, an anchorperson to support the process, and the expenses of participating learners and volunteers, as well as advice and guidance.

The programs that do not use the framework most often cite the burden of other work commitments as the reason for not doing so. Therefore, the adult literacy service is promoting its use and detailing the benefits reported by VECs who are using the framework. The current national reporting requirements for local literacy services are quantitative biannual reports to the DES, which fails to capture true indicators of quality at the local level that translate to the national level. The DES's endorsement of the process-oriented Quality Framework in *Learning for Life* and the adoption of the Quality Framework by programs highlight this point. The challenge ahead, therefore, is how to develop a link between the Quality Framework and the national reporting system in order to strengthen the connection between quality and accountability.

Structure Challenges

Raising capacity is a difficult task facing the adult literacy service. ALOs are developing and implementing strategic plans for their programs that cover (in two phases) the period of funding and targets set out in the National Development Plan 2000–2006. These plans are being incorporated into wider strategic plans for each VEC, which will enable practitioners to answer the burning question in Ireland at the moment, "When is a literacy program full?" In order to attract new learners, practitioners need to provide a wider range of services to adults with literacy difficulties, including more flexible instruction times. This will also entail an expansion of family and workplace initiatives, as well as an increased usage of Information Communication Technology (ICT) and open and distance-education modes of learning.

Each local VEC needs to develop the local infrastructure. There is a shortage of existing premises for adult learners, and the national capital budget made available to the VECs does not cover expenses. VECs are seeking local solutions, with the emphasis on greater utilization of all local public premises; however, these facilities are often temporary and do not meet ideal standards.

VECs also need to provide classes on weekends and during the summer and other holiday periods. (Traditionally, literacy services closed completely for 3 months over the summer.) Different staffing arrangements will be required to facilitate greater access.

The adult literacy service also needs to review how it provides services. Most VECs provide classes in cities and towns. There has been little exploration of how services could be expanded to provide support to people engaged in self-study and what would be required to make this happen.

Adult literacy providers have, however, increased their capacity to use ICT. A NALA ICT survey showed that access to ICT equipment has risen by 50% since 2001, and access to the Internet has risen to 80% (NALA, 2003). Approximately 51% of tutors integrated ICT into their teaching, primarily by using Microsoft Word and other literacy packages. However, ICT is mainly delivered separately, as an ICT course. Providers will need training, not just in ICT skills, but in integrating ICT in the learning situation.

OTHER ADULT LITERACY PROGRAMS

In addition to the traditional method of provision of adult literacy services—through the VECs—there are a number of other literacy programs in Ireland.

TV and Radio Distance Education— The Low-Tech Approach to Reaching the Hard to Reach

Since 1997, the number of adults participating in local VEC literacy centers has increased from 5,000 to almost 30,000. However, with a potential target population of 500,000 adults with literacy difficulties, there is a need to look at providing alternative options for adults wishing to improve their skills. At a time when high-tech solutions to adult literacy (e.g., CD-ROMS) were being explored in other countries, NALA turned its attention to what low tech could offer.

In 1998, NALA and a local commercial radio station teamed up to provide *Literacy over the Airwaves,* in cooperation with two local VECs. To raise awareness of the adult literacy issue in general, and to aid recruitment, it was felt that even if the radio series did not succeed in enabling people to learn, it would be of benefit on these other fronts. The DES and the Independent Radio and Television Commission provided funds for the program.

The radio broadcast was available in three rural provincial towns only, from 7–8 P.M. and then repeated from 8–9 P.M., Monday to Friday. *Literacy over the Airwaves* registered a total of 145 participants; 19 (or 13%) were independent learners. Participants reported some progress in their reading and writing skills. The specific gains made by learners varied, according to their level of skill before starting the program, their interests, and requirements. The most frequently mentioned gains included: filling out forms, writing letters, using the dictionary, and increasing vocabulary. Learners also reported general benefits from the programs; for example, feeling that they were not the only one with a problem in reading and writing and feeling that they were doing something about the problem.

With the success and the learning from this small-scale initiative, NALA, with the support of the DES, approached RTE, the national state broadcaster, and proposed a TV literacy series. The DES committed funding to the project and RTE donated two time slots for the proposed series. One was a late-evening slot to allow adults to watch the program—children would be in bed and most people would be free of home and work commitments—the other was a daytime repeat slot that would accommodate a different audience. The media company AV Edge won the contract to develop the series, in close collaboration with NALA.

READ WRITE NOW was broadcast in the autumn of 2000. It was accompanied by a learner pack, which was distributed free to the general public on request and supported by experienced tutors available via a free telephone line.

After the program concluded, NALA commissioned an evaluation and concluded that the series had successfully attracted an audience of new independent and existing center-based learners. Viewing numbers for these television programs were very high, averaging 136,000 viewers for the evening timeslot and 19,000 viewers for the repeat, morning broadcast.

Viewing figures for the *READ WRITE NOW* series were equivalent to other mainstream programs broadcast at these times. This was an achievement for an educational broadcast aimed at adults with low literacy levels.

Of the 30,000 learner packs distributed in conjunction with the program, significantly, 11,000 were sent to independent learners. Participants interviewed by the NALA evaluation stated that the series and the learning pack helped them learn in a very practical and proactive way.

As a result of the success of the first TV broadcast, NALA commissioned *READ WRITE NOW 2* in 2001 and efforts were made to build on the lessons from the previous series. The series was designed to support an integrated approach to literacy work. For example, the learning points were situated in the context of everyday life, with each program covering different themes.

The evaluation report (McSkeane, 2002) concluded that the vast majority of learners surveyed favored contextualized learning rather than a skills-based approach and had learned things in addition to reading and writing skills. As a result, information about the learning process was integrated into the third series. *READ WRITE NOW 3* included a specific focus on the theme of "learning to learn," which influenced the format and structure of the programs. Each program contained new things to learn, new ways of learning, and learners telling their own stories. The fourth series was developed and broadcast in autumn 2003.

ESOL

Unlike the United States, the numbers of non-English-speaking people coming to live in Ireland has been very small. However, over the last 5 years, there has been a significant increase in people whose first language is not English, including refugee and asylum seekers, residing in Ireland. Asylum seekers do not have the right to work, and the state restricts their access to public educational services, except for the adult literacy service, which will provide asylum seekers with "free access to adult literacy, English language and mother culture supports" (DES, 2000, p. 173). To accomplish this, the adult literacy service has been developing an English for Speakers of Other Languages (ESOL) provision.

Much more research in the area of ESOL is needed, focusing on the effectiveness of provision and ensuring that ESOL tuition is meeting the needs of all potential learners. Anecdotal evidence shows that asylum seekers without the right to work who are taking ESOL classes want more than the 2 or 4 hours tuition per week currently offered. There is also an ongoing debate about how best to structure services in this area and it is unclear what the extent of the role, if any, of the adult literacy will be in the future, in particular if there is a dedicated ESOL service established. The DES needs to develop an interdepartmental approach to address the needs of asylum seekers, refugees, and nonnationals, as well as develop a national ESOL strategy.

Family Literacy

A key issue for research, training, and policy is to define an approach to family literacy that builds on the philosophy of adult literacy work, which recognizes and respects the experience and views of learners. This is particularly important as some family literacy programs are designed to increase the child's literacy skills, using the parent as an instrument in that process, whereas others are concerned with the literacy needs of both children and parents.

NALA has set up a project with the aim of developing a family literacy policy and guidelines for adult literacy services. NALA is undertaking this through research and consultation with parents, educators, and those working in family services. The coordinator working on this project outlined the work involved:

> Family learning in Ireland is at an early stage of development. At present the key issue is to define an approach based on respect for a variety of family life and the learning that happens in all homes. Just as adult literacy work in Ireland is based on a learner-directed ethos, so family learning programmes aim to involve families in planning programmes and approaches that best support their learning.
>
> —Jenny Derbyshire

Over the last decade, a small number of adult literacy services developed family literacy programs to meet particular needs. For example, in the early 1990s, one VEC developed a family literacy program for parents of children up to 12 years, with the focus on preschool. Important features of this project included day care provision for younger children and an emphasis on an adult education approach to working with parents and caregivers.

Another model that has become a popular feature of family literacy work in various settings involves encouraging and supporting parents and caregivers to read to babies and young children. The National Reading Initiative promoted this in 2000 and it has been adapted to suit local needs and conditions. Recent programs, such as "Dads and Lads" courses, have also focused on encouraging fathers to become more involved in their children's learning, as most family literacy participants are women.

At present, about half of the 135 adult literacy services provide family literacy programs, drawn from the models outlined. However, development has slowed recently due largely to limited funding for such outreach work. In particular, lack of funding for day care makes it difficult to run family-literacy courses with parents of preschool children, especially as preschool care is, in general, underdeveloped in Ireland. However, it may now be possible to move forward through the promotion of partnerships between adult literacy services and schools, preschools, libraries, and training centers for young people, as well as community development and family centers. Schools in particular expend considerable energy trying to involve parents in their children's education, while many of the same parents are involved in local adult literacy and community projects. Linking educational and other community services is also part of a wider phenomenon of joining government and public services, aimed at providing a better service to those who need it. From an adult literacy perspective, this is a great opportunity to be part of a wider educational agenda, sharing experience and expertise with other educators.

Workplace Basic Education (WBE): Return to Learning Workplace Project in the Local Authorities

Ireland is divided into 34 local government administrations (called Local Authorities) that have responsibility for housing provision, sanitation, planning, roads, and amenities in their area. The Local Authority sector employs approximately 30,000 people across a range of disciplines, and provides education and training opportunities to their workforce.

The *Return to Learning Project,* supported by NALA (through the provision of a template for the program, as well as training and contact with a national coordinator), is a partnership initiative between the Local Authority National Partnership Advisory Group (LANPAG) and the DES. The focus of the *Return to Learning* program is on ensuring that employees have an opportunity to access training in literacy, communications, computers, numeracy, personal development, and job skills. The objective of the workplace literacy program is to create a "safe" and supportive learning environment for staff.

In 2000–2001, the project was piloted in five counties, with a budget of $150,365 (€133,000), funded 50% by LANPAG and 50% by DES. The local VEC literacy service provided the program in each of these areas, and the VEC appointed Project Coordinators who ran the program in conjunction with the VEC ALOs.

The program consisted of 4 hours per week over a 20-week period, on work time. NALA designed and VEC adult literacy service delivered the program in a flexible and adaptable way to meet the needs of the participants. The course cost an estimated $10,062 (€8,900) for each group of seven to eight people. This included 80 hours of promotion/awareness and recruitment by the Project Coordinator.

In the pilot project, a total of 120 people (twice the anticipated number), mainly men, completed the course in the five pilot areas. The evaluation (Conboy, 2002) shows that employees benefited from the course in the following ways:

- Increased self-confidence, as well as improved communication and interaction with others.
- Literacy skill development (e.g., filling out forms, writing letters, and reading the newspaper).
- Greater familiarity with computers and some development in computer skills.
- A positive influence on their home and family lives.
- Reawakening of interest in learning.

The VEC adult literacy service and NALA have begun making efforts to extend WBE into the private sector, with a very small number of projects operating in local areas in large industry. It remains difficult to implement these types of programs in Ireland due to a weak culture of workplace learning, especially in regard to basic education, as well as the lack of entitlement to paid educational leave. In addition, there is no dedicated fund for WBE initiatives available to employers or the adult literacy service. However, with EU funds covering in-company training, NALA and one of the VECs are currently developing a model of WBE for small-to-medium enterprises.

Unemployment: Return to Education—An Intensive Basic Education Model for Unemployed People With Adult Literacy Needs

The 1997 OECD survey concluded that an Irish person at Level 1 would experience a higher incidence of unemployment than people who scored at Level 1 in any other country surveyed (OECD, 1997). The ratio of unemployed to employed people scoring at the lowest literacy level in the Irish survey was 2:1.

Research done in Belgium (Sterq, 1993) highlighted the fact that many social-inclusion measures targeted at the long-term unemployed actually excluded the participation of those with insufficient basic skills. Irish initiatives targeted at such a group also appear to mirror this experience. It is clear that the integration of basic skills development within existing training programs targeted at disadvantaged groups is highly beneficial to the participant, as it ensures a planned approach to the development of literacy in the context of the overall program, as well as wider access to such programs for people with literacy needs.

The *Return to Education* program was initiated by NALA to provide for the needs of unemployed adults with literacy difficulties. NALA brought together FÁS, the national employment and training authority, and the VECs, to see how mixing their expertise and resources could result in better provision for this client group. Community Employment (CE), funded and administered by FÁS, is the main state-funded work-experience program for unemployed people. People unemployed for more than 6 months are eligible to apply for supported work in their local area and are paid a salary for 19.5 hours of work. In addition, participants are given a small budget to pay for limited specific training they might require. For participants with literacy difficulties, the training available was insufficient to meet their needs, and a barrier to their progress into mainstream employment resulted.

Return to Education aims to give participants in CE programs an opportunity to attend a basic reading and writing skills course as part of their CE work-experience program. Participants are released from their CE work for 9 hours per week to attend this course. CE participants receive the same entitlements as if they were working for the full 19.5 hours.

The course was designed to ease participants, no matter what education level, back into education. Participants receive accreditation in some cases, depending on level achieved. Due to the nature of the course, a flexible approach is adapted to suit the requirements of each student. One-on-one or small-group instruction is available to suit the needs of the students. The program concentrates on English, communication skills, computers, and numeracy. It also teaches personal-development and job skills.

An external evaluator (McArdle, 1999), rating the pilot programs from March to June 1999, highlighted a variety of gains from this program for long-term unemployed adults with literacy difficulties: educational advances, including certification in many cases; increases in self-confidence; changes in outlook in terms of further education/training or work; and, in some cases, actual movement of learners into mainstream training or jobs (subsequent to the evaluation).

The program continues to expand and at the start of 2003, there were 46 CE programs in 26 VEC areas, catering to approximately 700 participants with literacy difficulties.

Integration of Adult Literacy Into Vocational Education and Training Targeted at the Socially Excluded

In addition to the local VEC adult literacy programs, adult literacy tuition takes place in a number of other settings, including the Prison Education Service, Centers for the Unemployed, Youthreach (early school leavers), SIPTU (trade union), Community Training Centers, Travelers' Workshops, and centers providing services for people with disabilities. In most cases tuition is an "add on" to the main vocational-training program and is therefore not fully integrated.

An integrated approach to the teaching of adult literacy within vocational education and training programs is an effective way of providing more intensive basic education to a greater number of people. Vocational education and training programs aim to help participants acquire specific work-related skills and were designed for people with a minimum of upper-second-level education (Sterq, 1993). However, some individuals may not possess the level of adult literacy required to successfully complete the training program. Many training programs have sought to address this by providing separate literacy instruction. The isolation of literacy skills in this manner "is in conflict with current thinking regarding good practice" (City of Limerick VEC, 1998, p. 19).

However, NALA has been promoting the integration of adult literacy within the core-training framework. The integration of adult literacy into training programs combats social exclusion by ensuring that no person is, or feels, excluded from these programs because of a literacy difficulty. Integration also ensures that programs help every participant to develop the literacy skills necessary for successful completion of the course and for progression in further education, training, or employment. In order for this to be effective, NALA identified that trainers needed to make these skills an explicit part of their program, which requires a planned and purposeful approach.

NALA, in conjunction with the National University of Ireland Maynooth, has developed a training program for vocational-skills educators and trainers, to enable them to integrate adult literacy into their programs. NALA also published *Guidelines on Integrating Literacy* (NALA, 2002b), which outlined the key features of an integrated, whole-center approach to literacy within vocational education and training programs. The document presents 10 guidelines, indicating (a) the systems and procedures needed to ensure that adult literacy development is built into every phase of an education and training program, from induction through to progression, and (b) methods individual trainers and teachers can use to build adult literacy into their program delivery. Education and training centers are using the *Guidelines,* particularly in vocational training programs for young people, as an aid to developing integrated, whole-center policy and practice on literacy.

To complement the *Guidelines,* NALA recently published *Skillwords* (NALA, 2003), a resource pack of literacy materials related to vocational training areas. These are edited versions of materials developed by vocational trainers from FÁS Community Training Centers, VEC Youthreach Centers, and Senior Travelers' Training Centers, in cooperation with their learners. They are offered as resources that can be photocopied, but can also be used as models and examples of integrated adult literacy materials. The pack also provides further guidelines for vocational trainers on how to design and use vocationally relevant adult literacy materials.

CURRENT ISSUES AND CHALLENGES

One could say that the adult literacy movement in Ireland has come out of obscurity and into an intense spotlight in the past 35 years. Under such scrutiny, practitioners and providers, despite getting a lot of what they have lobbied for, may feel somewhat overwhelmed by current challenges, as well as those that lie ahead. Fundamental to ensuring that their fears are heard and addressed is the availability of a range of forums for debate and support, as well as a means by which they can feed into the policy realm. Following are some key areas of debate.

Adult Literacy Policy in the European Union

Individual members states of the EU have responsibility for their own education and training systems; however, the EU has taken a strong role in the promotion of lifelong learning for many years. Lifelong learning is now seen as an "overarching strategy of European co-operation in education and training policies and for the individual" (Commission of the European Communities, 2002, p. 4).

The EU's focus on adult literacy is of great benefit to an area that has traditionally had a low profile. The EU has prioritized adult literacy in the context of their work in stimulating and supporting the implementation of lifelong learning across the European area and this has raised several issues, both positive and negative:

• Developing basic skills and upgrading existing skills are eligible for support under the European Social Fund (ESF) and this is currently providing the bulk of resources for adult literacy work in Ireland (although these funds come with some restrictions).

• Adult literacy is now firmly embedded in the EU agenda for lifelong learning and is fully supported by Ireland, which provides additional security to adult literacy development into the future.

• The EU focus on new basic skills (such as foreign languages and computer skills) may overshadow the traditional areas of literacy and numeracy, as well as lose sight of the needs of adult learners. In the wider context of what the EU wants to achieve, there needs to be a focus on both the traditional and new basic skills as the foundations for EU citizens in the knowledge society.

• The approach to adult literacy work in Ireland, which is beyond a skills approach, may be threatened by an overriding narrower focus on upskilling the labor force. A critical factor in achieving common goals within the EU is that all involved can agree on priorities for future action.

Staffing

Adult Literacy Organizers established their own association, primarily so they could join a trade union to negotiate for better pay and conditions at a time of mass expansion. The Teachers Union of Ireland (TUI) represents the ALOs and has recently offered membership to paid, part-time tutors as well. The TUI negotiates from the position that members with mainstream teaching qualifications are entitled to a permanent job and the appropriate pay scale. However, members that do not hold such qualifications but do have adult education qualifications are not guaranteed permanent jobs because they are not entitled to new jobs if their current jobs cease to exist. In a climate of relatively low unemployment and high inflation, it remains difficult to recruit and retain staff—paid and voluntary—pending the development of attractive career structures and better employment conditions, and joining trade unions has not greatly enhanced the career structure for adult education practitioners.

Certification

Certification systems for adult learners used in the 1990s set the bar too high; many adult learners were not able to achieve them through their coursework and thus could not get on the qualifications ladder. In 2003, the National Qualifications Authority of Ireland (NQAI) launched the National Qualifications Framework, which will bring about significant changes in the systems and structures of education and training. It is the single entity through which all learning achievements may be measured and related to each other in a logical way (NQAI, 2003). The framework defines the relationship between all education and training awards. The result is a clearer and more understandable qualifications system, enabling and encouraging learners to achieve awards for learning on a lifelong basis. The framework contains a grid of level indicators, which cover knowledge (breadth and kind), skill (range and selectivity), and competence (context, role, learning to learn, and insight) and denote learning outcomes within these areas. The framework has 10 levels covering a very low level of learning up to a PhD. This has created an opportunity for people to get recognition for smaller learning achievements and is particularly useful for adult literacy learners.

NALA is launching an assessment framework for adult literacy called *Mapping the Learning Journey* (NALA, 2005). It has been designed and developed from consultation with key stakeholders, best practice in assessment in Irish adult literacy services, and international research, particularly the *Equipped for the Future Assessment Framework* in the United States. *Mapping the Learning Journey* has four main cornerstones that complement the knowledge, skill, and competence structure of the Qualifications Framework.

Funding

The slowdown in Ireland's growth over the last 18 months has seen a decrease in public spending across all government departments. As a result, the adult literacy budget for 2004 fell short of projected requirements. This creates challenges to the adult literacy service to meet the demands, not just from learners seeking to join programs but also from employers and other vocational training providers.

The vast majority of the current funding for the adult literacy service in Ireland has come from the European Social Fund. However, with more countries joining the EU on May 1, 2004, there is increasingly less aid available to current EU countries. The Irish government will need to ensure that current levels of expenditure on adult literacy will be at least maintained, through state expenditure, in the future.

Research and Evaluation

As a result of the poor funding of adult literacy work in Ireland in the past, there is a dearth of research and evaluation publications in the area. Most of the published material has come through the DES and NALA, with a small but increasing contribution from some VECs. There has been no national evaluation of the adult literacy service, primarily due to the size and nature of the service. At the local provider level, there has always been great interest in evaluation, evidenced by demand for training in the area and related publications (Conlan, 1994). However, with increased expenditure in the area, and the need for greater accountability that comes with it, the DES will need to place a greater emphasis on research and evaluation in the future.

The NALA/WIT project is generating research through coursework and assignments at both certificate and diploma level. This will be added to as the program extends to develop degree and postgraduate qualifications. Furthermore, the project aims to engage in more research and build up an adult literacy academic discipline, separate and distinct from adult or community education.

Partnership and Integration

Increased funding for adult literacy has attracted new players who are keen to be involved in this growth area. Adult literacy practitioners are experiencing competition in terms of their services and clients, and are grappling with ownership issues. The prioritization of adult literacy has also meant that it is no longer the preserve of only those who work in literacy, but now also involves the full range of statutory and voluntary-sector staff that also deal with "our clients." On the positive side, this has led to a greater emphasis on working in partnership at the local level, whereas previously, practitioners often worked in isolation. More people have gotten involved in and joined the adult literacy service through a greater emphasis on networking by ALOs with groups such as local social welfare and health authorities. However, it has also led to a rapidly increasing workload for ALOs beyond their original role, which now needs to be reviewed and amended as appropriate. It has also led to an increased workload for NALA, particularly in supporting the new people and organizations getting involved in this area.

NALA has convened a working group representing relevant stakeholders from the literacy service and government departments to develop an implementation plan for the literacy service with a focus on the development of a more structured and permanent adult literacy service. The group has drawn up a model for the adult literacy service, including a variety of other service providers within the VEC and outside, detailing how the adult literacy service should be integrated into the wider VEC and beyond. In addition, the group has developed staffing norms for adult literacy service, and although the VEC adult literacy service is a long way from putting these staffing structures in place due to lack of resources, having a blueprint available to those responsible for managing and funding the service should improve this situation and may be critical for future development.

CONCLUSION

Major developments have occurred in literacy in Ireland since the publication of the IALS, but that was 7 years ago and all concerned need to be focused on the next stage of development of the adult literacy sector. In the current economy in Ireland, the future is more uncertain and funding for education is under threat, as it is in all other public services. Although the adult literacy services have not yet felt the adverse affects, many adult literacy practitioners fear that after only a recent spell in the political limelight, the position of adult literacy is set for the same fate as the economic boom, and the bubble may be about to burst. In looking at the future of the adult literacy sector, there will need to be greater collaboration between stakeholders. The ongoing government support of the adult literacy sector, particularly the DES, is critical to the future of adult literacy.

Accountability is an increasingly important part of funding debates. Literacy providers are faced with the inevitability of a transparent system that provides taxpayers with evidence of success and value for money. How to achieve this while ensuring that the quality of the service is not undermined is a growing concern among many involved in adult literacy work. To these people, the learner-centered ethos of adult literacy work in

Ireland is its most vital characteristic and, indeed, the key to its success to date. It must be retained as the adult literacy sector embraces the changes being brought about by the knowledge society.

We can no longer assist people with literacy difficulties with just one core service, nor can we look at this issue in a narrow and linear fashion, as this does not reflect the diversity of people in today's society. People with adult literacy needs often may have other, more important concerns, and therefore adult literacy will most successfully be addressed within those contexts, not by a referral to a dedicated adult literacy service. This, in short, is the theory behind an integrated approach. Any strategy for raising adult literacy levels will need to provide a range of options and opportunities. This will require research and innovation, both of which have been chronically underfunded. It will also require greater levels of partnership across the public, private, and voluntary sectors. It is hard to find an organization that would not be able to assist in this area; however, no single organization or sector has the definitive answer. The social partnership process in Ireland continues to be instrumental in continuing this kind of work. Working together may be the greatest challenge for us all, but the most effective in terms of individuals with literacy needs.

APPENDIX

Useful Contacts

Adult Education Organisers' Association (AEOA)	http://www.adulteducationorganisers.org
Adult Literacy Organisers' Association (AEOA)	http://www.literacyireland.org
AONTAS (National Association of Adult Education)	http://www.aontas.com
Department of Education and Science (DES)	http://www.education.ie
FÁS (national training and employment authority)	http://www.fas.ie
Further Education and Training Awards Council (FETAC)	http://www.fetac.ie
Irish Vocational Education Association (IVEA)	http://www.ivea.ie
National Adult Literacy Agency (NALA)	http://www.nala.ie

National Qualifications Authority   http://www.nqai.ie
    of Ireland
NALA/WIT project   http://www.wit.ie/literacyproject

Journals

The Adult Learner. Published by AONTAS. Available from AONTAS, 2nd Floor, 83–87 Main Street, Ranelagh, Dublin 6, Ireland.
NALA Newsletter and Journal. Published by NALA. Available free from NALA, 76 Lower Gardiner Street, Dublin 1, Ireland.

REFERENCES

Adult Literacy Organisers Association. (2001). *ALOA constitution.* Dublin: Author.
Bailey, I., & Coleman, U. (1998). *Access and participation in adult literacy schemes in Ireland.* Dublin: National Adult Literacy Agency.
CHL Consulting. (2002). *Training needs analysis of adult literacy practitioners.* Dublin: National Adult Literacy Agency.
City of Limerick VEC. (1998). *Developing core skills — The Trialogue Experience.* Limerick: Author.
Clancy, P. (1999). *Declining a third level offer.* Dublin: Higher Education Authority.
Combat Poverty Agency. (2002). *Combating poverty in a changing Ireland. Agency strategic plan, 2002–2004.* Dublin: Author.
Commission of the European Communities. (2002). *European report on quality indicators of lifelong learning.* Brussels: European Commission.
Conboy, P. (2002). *The Return to Learning Initiative: Evaluation report and implementation guidelines.* Dublin: National Adult Literacy Agency.
Conlan, S. (1994). Evaluating literacy work. *The Adult Learner: Adult and Community Education in Ireland, 2*(5), pp. 42–45.
Department of Education. (1995). *Charting our education future: White paper on education.* Dublin: Stationery Office.
Department of Education and Science. (1998). *Green paper on adult education: Adult education in an era of lifelong learning.* Dublin: Stationery Office.
Department of Education and Science. (2000). *Learning for life: White paper on adult education.* Dublin: Stationery Office.
Department of Enterprise, Trade and Employment (1997). *White paper on human resource development.* Dublin: Stationery Office.
Department of Social Welfare. (1997). *Sharing in progress: National Anti-Poverty Strategy.* Dublin: Stationery Office.
European Parliament and Council. (1995). Decision no. *95/2493/EC* of 23 October 1995 establishing 1996 as the European Year of Lifelong Learning. *Official Journal L256,* October 26, 1995.

Government of Ireland. (1996). *Partnership 2000 for inclusion, employment and competitiveness.* Dublin: Stationery Office.

Government of Ireland. (1999). *Ireland: National Development Plan, 2000–2006.* Dublin: Stationery Office.

Hamilton, M., Macrae, C., & Tett, L. (2001). *Powerful literacies: The policy context.* In J. Crowther, M. Hamilton, & L. Tett (Eds.), *Powerful literacies* (pp. 23–42). Leicester: National Institute of Adult Continuing Education.

Houses of the Oireachtas. (1998). *First report of the joint committee on education and science on literacy levels in Ireland.* Dublin: Author.

Kellaghan, T., Cosgrove, J., Forde, P., & Morgan, M. (2000). *The national assessment of English reading with comparative data from 1993 assessment.* Dublin: Education Research Centre.

McArdle, M. (1999). *Evaluation of the NALA return to education course in Mullingar and Ballyfermot.* Dublin: National Adult Literacy Agency.

McDonagh, O. (1999). *NALA-Socrates project consultation on quality.* Dublin: National Adult Literacy Agency.

McSkeane, L. (1998). *National certificate in training and development (Adult basic education—management) 1997–98 evaluation report.* Dublin: National Adult Literacy Agency/Waterford Institute of Technology.

McSkeane, L. (2002). *READ WRITE NOW TV SERIES 2: Evaluation report.* Dublin: National Adult Literacy Agency.

Morgan, M., Hickey, B., & Kellaghan, T. (1997). *Education 2000, International Adult Literacy Survey: Results for Ireland.* Dublin: Education Research Centre/Department of Education.

National Adult Literacy Agency. (1987). *Adult literacy provision—NALA survey report 1987.* Dublin: Author.

National Adult Literacy Agency. (1991). *Guidelines for good adult literacy work.* Dublin: Author.

National Adult Literacy Agency. (1995). *New ideas for training in adult literacy.* Dublin: Author.

National Adult Literacy Agency. (1999). *NALA Newsletter, November 1999.* Dublin: Author.

National Adult Literacy Agency. (2002a). *The national adult literacy agency strategic plan 2002–2006.* Dublin: Author.

National Adult Literacy Agency. (2002b). *Integrating literacy—NALA guidelines for further education and training centres.* Dublin: Author.

National Adult Literacy Agency. (2003). *Skillwords—integrating literacy: A NALA resource pack for vocational education and training programmes.* Dublin: Author.

National Adult Literacy Agency. (2005). *Mapping the learning journey: User guide.* Dublin: Author.

National Anti-Poverty Strategy. (2002). *Building an inclusive society.* Dublin: Office for Social Inclusion.

National Qualifications Authority of Ireland. (2003). *The national framework of qualifications: An overview.* Dublin: Author.

O'Buachala, S. (1988). *Education policy in twentieth century Ireland.* Dublin: Wolfhound Press.

Organization for Economic Cooperation and Development. (1996). *Lifelong learning for all.* Paris: Author.

Organization for Economic Cooperation and Development. (1997). *Literacy skills for the knowledge society: Further results from the International Adult Literacy Survey.* Paris: Author.

Sterq, C. (1993). Literacy, socialisation and employment. London: Jessica Kingsley Publishers.

8

Beyond Single Interests: Broad-Based Organizing as a Vehicle for Promoting Adult Literacy

Michael A. Cowan

INTRODUCTION

For the past 30 years, community organizers and citizen leaders in the United States have built powerful, enduring, and diverse collectives that deliver funding and other resources consistently on issues that matter to their members, including affordable housing, community policing, public education reform, and workforce preparation. I characterize the form of community organizing to be highlighted here as "broad-based" because, at its heart, community organizing is a deliberate effort to cross lines of race, class, religion, and geography to build organizations with sufficient power to stand for the whole and address common-good issues in local communities. It does so not by bringing individuals together, but by connecting mediating institutions such as congregations, neighborhood associations, and other local voluntary associations. These organizations have not only led successful action campaigns in San Antonio, Baltimore, New

York, Los Angeles, Chicago and elsewhere on issues such as those listed here but also, and as importantly, have fostered more inclusive civil and political cultures within those communities. A dramatic example of the latter occurred less than 3 months after the tragedy of September 11, 2001, when on November 18, 2001, 2,000 Muslims and 2,000 non-Muslims came together in a public event called "Chicagoans and Islam," created by the broad-based organization called United Power for Action and Justice. Here is an excerpt from one eyewitness account:

> The meeting was co-chaired by Muslim and majority-group leaders. The event began and ended with Muslim and non-Muslim leader pairs speaking to each other on stage about their cultures, families, and why they came to this event. Its centerpiece was 2000 one-to-one relational meetings between 4000 Muslim and non-Muslim participants lasting 25 minutes each. Self and other, Muslim and non-Muslim, city and suburb dialogued. The action began with one black leader reading an excerpt of the Declaration of Independence, and ended with 4000 people reading the same passage in unison. (Chambers, 2003, p. 123)

At a moment when America was still in shock and reports of anti-Muslim threats and acts appeared daily in news broadcasts, one broad-based citizen organization built a bridge instead of a wall. The event was only possible because Muslim organizations had participated in United Power from its beginning and because preexisting relationships based on mutual interests and respect were there to be mobilized at a critical moment.

Although adult literacy organizations have an issue every bit as compelling as those addressed by broad-based organizations, they typically lack the clout to secure the resources necessary to make a large, sustainable impact. In explaining public funding streams to members of the board of a local metropolitan literacy alliance in a recent meeting, one board member referred to adult education as the "bottom feeder" among publicly funded education programs. Such language surely arises from a sense of relative powerlessness.

The intention of this chapter is to:

• Identify, by way of a limited but significant example, the role of adult literacy as one critical component of a major quality-of-life issue.

• Outline what is widely regarded by both practitioners and scholars as the most efficacious framework that has evolved in the United States to date for bringing social issues to prominence and garnering the resources to address them in an effective and sustained manner.

- Locate broad-based community organizing within emerging theory and research on "social capital."
- Consider adult literacy from the perspective of a classic sociological description of how social problems gain public attention and attract resources.
- Illustrate basic principles of the organizing framework explained here with examples drawn from a metropolitan-wide, broad-based organizing effort on behalf of adult literacy now underway in one of America's historic cities, and offer suggestions for first steps for community leaders interested in implementing such an approach in other places.

LITERACY AND QUALITY OF LIFE

Before outlining the significant role that a particular form of community organizing can play as an instrument for advancing adult literacy, let me make the personal and social stakes plain by way of an example. Jobs are a critical factor in the equation of a good life, and their significance cuts two ways in every community. From the worker's side, a "good" job (defined here as one that pays approximately twice the minimum wage, provides basic fringe benefits, and opens up pathways for career growth and promotion) is the usual entry point to full and productive participation in society. Health care, home ownership, reliable and convenient transportation, retirement security, effective involvement in children's education, and civic engagement are difficult, if not impossible, to achieve for those who do not have access to good, secure jobs. The significance of work that promotes dignity and provides fair compensation should not be too quickly dismissed from the debate on adult literacy as a capitulation to a dominating "human capital" ideology; on the contrary, access to such work is, first of all, a question of justice.

From the employer's side, the absence of an adequate number of qualified people to fill available jobs forces choices from a limited and limiting set of options: importing workers from outside the community, paying a stiff premium for contract laborers, burdening current workers with excessive mandatory overtime, or being unable to grow a business. In a chronically undersupplied labor market, neither workers, nor local businesses, nor the larger community for which they constitute the economic base can prosper. When good jobs are not available to most adults of working age in a community, the quality of life of the community as a whole, and of every person and institution within it, are inevitably put at risk (Wilson, 1996).

The following example from metropolitan New Orleans illustrates this double-edged dilemma, presenting one local variation on a theme recurring throughout the U.S. economy today. The training director of Louisiana's largest private employer, a builder of ocean-going transport ships, reports that a lack of qualified local applicants forces the shipyard to import about one sixth of its 6,000-person workforce from outside the local community under contract-labor arrangements. Under these contracts, the shipyard pays a premium of about $8 for every clock hour logged by 1,000 contract workers, or $320,000 per 40-hour week. Available entry-level jobs for pipefitters, electricians, welders, and grinders start at nearly $10 per hour with benefits. Reliable workers who upgrade their skills can move steadily beyond entry-level wages through participation in the company's comprehensive advancement program in all crafts to salaries more than two times higher than the starting level. The shipyard also has a union to protect workers' interests. According to company officials, workers who reach the 3-year mark usually become career employees. About 40% of the shipyard's current workforce is from the city of New Orleans, and company officials estimate that at least 500 of the jobs now being filled by contract workers could be taken by local residents who are in good health, drug free, report on time, take supervision, and are *able to read and do math at the sixth- to eighth-grade level.* Whereas there are local programs available through social service agencies to deal with the other challenges just listed, the literacy barrier has proven to be the most difficult to address—the Achilles heel of efforts by this company to find the workers it needs, and for workers to gain access to these good jobs.

Coupled with labor-market projections that indicate a significant long-term shortage of qualified workers in other identifiable industry clusters in the region,[1] such as health care and food processing, this dramatic example suggests that the shortage of qualified labor will continue unless and until the New Orleans metropolitan area commits to and creates a comprehensive, integrated system to provide motivated un- and underemployed adults with access to the education, training, and other supports necessary to qualify for the good jobs already available in this area and those that will be created in the future—*if* such a system is created and the local economy prospers. Current discussions among employers, educators, workforce-investment boards, community groups, workforce-preparation providers, and government officials about what it will take to create that

---

[1] MetroVision Economic Development Partnership/New Orleans Chamber of Commerce, 2000; Louisiana Department of Labor, 2001.

system all point to the need to address low levels of adult literacy as the critical missing piece in local workforce programs.

How significant is that missing piece in New Orleans? The 1991 national projections of adult literacy levels estimate that in the city of New Orleans about 39% of people aged 16 years and older—136,000 adults—function at Level 1 literacy, and an additional 31%—116,000 people—at Level 2 (NIFL, 1998). If functioning at Level 1 literacy means that people cannot get entry-level jobs with significant career potential and Level 2 means that they have little hope of advancing if they do (Quigley, personal communication), then these harsh figures suggest that a staggering 70% of the adult population of New Orleans is at high risk of economic marginalization, of being relegated to low wages and job insecurity—with all the ramifications for themselves, their families, and their neighborhoods. It is equally clear that these educational levels will function as a governing parameter on economic growth in the community, because employers will simply not be able to recruit the workers they need to grow their businesses. Matters of race and justice are significant here because the vast majority of the 70% of people at Level 1 or 2 are of African-American descent and living in poverty. This is just one more indication of continuing racial disparities in America on a whole host of quality-of-life indicators relative to education, health care, home ownership, income, wealth, and criminal justice (Brown et al., 2003).

Clearly there is an entire web of "organizable" issues here, and they are not specific to New Orleans. A report from Columbia University's American Assembly on the future of the U.S. workforce notes, "More than one third of the nation's current workforce lack the basic skills needed to succeed in today's labor market" (Giloth, 2003). How does a whole community, rather than an isolated segment, mobilize to address such an issue?

BROAD-BASED ORGANIZING AS A VEHICLE FOR ENHANCING ADULT LITERACY

During the last half of the 20th century, "community organizing" became part of the everyday vocabulary in the United States. The term ordinarily conjures up one of two images in the popular imagination: people coming together in a neighborhood or some other local geographical unit to address a common concern (e.g., a "Neighborhood Watch" program), or marches and demonstrations orchestrated, on varying scales, for the purpose of bringing public pressure to bear on decision makers about a particular issue. The practice of community organizing has, in fact, moved beyond these familiar forms over the past 30 years, as broad-based organizations tracing their roots to the work of Saul Alinsky have transformed the theory and practice of organizing. Drawing on the lessons of the burgeoning labor movement in the United States under the tutelage of the legendary John L. Lewis, Alinsky crafted the first democratic citizen organizations in Chicago's infamous Back of the Yards neighborhood in the late 1930s. He accomplished this by initiating what would come to be his organizing hallmark—an unlikely public partnership between local churches and labor unions based not in shared ideology but in mutual interests and respect. With the success of Alinsky's endeavor, the idea of community-based organizations began to spread. Experienced organizer Mike Miller explains the ultimate impact of Saul Alinsky on community organizing in the United States in this way:

> The three principal people who came out of Alinsky's earlier work—Tom Gaudette, Ed Chambers, and Fred Ross—then themselves mentored generations of new organizers. So there's not any community organizing that you can look at in the country today that probably can't be traced back to one of these three people. (Hercules & Orenstein, 1999)

Broad-based organizations in the Alinsky tradition now bring people together through mediating institutions like congregations, union locals, and neighborhood associations to create a common agenda and pursue a whole range of interests on an ongoing basis (Chambers, 2003). Mediating institutions stand between individual households and the large institutions of the state and the market. They give members a place where concerns can be registered and common positions forged around priority concerns. Alinsky (1972) identified two forms of power: organized people and organized money. Mediating institutions are organized people with some money, like a congregation. Broad-based organizations are collectives with institutional members.

Three key terms—interest, power, and broad-based—need further definition as background to this form of organizing. *Interest* is synonymous with motive. Our interests are what move us. Arendt (1958) points out that this English word comes from two Latin words, *inter* (meaning "between" or "among") and *esse* (meaning "to be"). Human interests, the things that move people to act, play out between and among us. The motivating interests of organizations are a mixture of survival and mission concerns. Contrary to the tenets of individualism, interests are thoroughly social or relational in character. How I pursue my interests inevitably affects others, and vice versa. Persons or groups who think that they can pursue their particular self-interest on an isolated, individual basis will not be capable of acting effectively on the interests of others or even in their own best interests. In the arena of differing interests, the great problem with self-interest is not selfishness, but rather, narrowness of understanding—the failure to recognize how various group interests are always interrelated. Recognizing shared interests and crafting a collective agenda inclusive of them drives all effective broad-based organizing.

Within the tradition of broad-based organizing, *power* is defined as the capacity to act effectively on an agenda, to accomplish chosen purposes. It has two faces: the capacity to *have* an influence and the capacity to *be influenced*. In its full-bodied form, power is relational, not unilateral (Chambers, 2003). The capacity to be influenced—to learn, to grow, to compromise, to change one's position based on new information—is as truly a sign of power as the capacity to influence others. Power is not a bad word; it simply names the ability to accomplish ends that matter to us. Its exercise is good or bad depending on the intentions and methods of those who employ it. To be without power is to be ineffectual, unable to pursue our values and the commitments they engender effectively. In fact, properly understood and practiced, power is such a good thing that all of us, particularly socially committed organizations, should have more. The failure of idealistic individuals and organizations to come to terms with power realistically leaves their best efforts at the mercy of those who do understand how power works, are not bashful about using it, and concede nothing voluntarily.

Broad-based here has two interrelated meanings. First, such organizations are *diverse* because they are intentionally built across racial, religious, and class lines. Second, they are *multi-issue* because their diversity means that the various partner institutions will inevitably bring differing interests to the table. Within the generic realm called "organizing," the broad-based approach has an unparalleled track record of initiating sustainable social change in communities around the United States, one that has been acknowledged, analyzed, and critiqued by sociologists (Wilson, 1999), political scientists (Warren, 2001), theologians (Lee & Cowan, 2003), journalists (Greider, 1992), and activists (Sen, 2003). Broad-based community organizations in every region of the United States have developed a reliable and replicable methodology for building relational power to act for social change on a wide range of public issues in their communities. More than 60 such organizations participate in the Alinsky-founded

Industrial Areas Foundation (IAF) Network. The following examples illustrate what these organizations are doing.

In Baltimore, Baltimoreans United in Leadership Development (BUILD) created the "Commonwealth Agreement," which guaranteed opportunities for advanced education or access to jobs with fringe benefits and a career path for all graduates of the Baltimore public schools who met attendance and grade standards. In Chicago, United Power for Action and Justice initiated the "Ezra Project," which provides affordable home ownership opportunities for thousands of low- and moderate-income Chicagoans who would otherwise be excluded from owning their own homes. In Jackson, Mississippi, The Amos Network took the lead in registering hundreds of low-income children for state-funded health care. In San Antonio, Communities Organized for Public Service (COPS) responded to the departure of a major employer of low-income Hispanics and African Americans by organizing and securing public and private funding for Project Quest, which is now widely regarded as one of the premier programs in the nation increasing access of low- and moderate-income people to jobs that pay family-sustaining wages and provide fringe benefits and career paths. In New Orleans, the Jeremiah Group initiated the public pressure that led to the creation of a special school in a local school district for students suspended or expelled from other institutions, and the creation of a youth drug court. Examples could be cited from other IAF affiliates, as well as two other national networks and hundreds of local organizing efforts across the length and breadth of the United States, all with roots in the Alinsky heritage (Warren & Wood, 2001).

A broad-based approach offers proponents of adult literacy an organizing strategy for making quality adult education available to all members of a community, regardless of race or class. This potential can be realized, however, only if adult literacy leaders begin to think and act not as a single-interest group with a righteous issue, but as members of larger collectives with a multi-interest agenda for social change. As the final section shows, that orientation requires that local literacy leaders identify other institutions as potential partners with complementary interests, understand the particular interests of those partners, and forge a larger shared agenda that includes, but is not limited to or controlled by, the interests of any of them, including adult literacy advocates. Done properly, this does not mean giving up one's identity and primary commitment, but rather, finding powerful allies with whom we can craft a larger agenda that includes the interests of all participants. The process of bringing differing institutional interests together in order to create social change is illuminated when the strategy of broad-based organizing is considered as an example of creating a particular form of social capital.

Broad-Based Organizing and Social Capital

It is useful to consider broad-based organizations as generators of what social scientists term *social capital,* and define as "connections among individuals—social networks and the norms of reciprocity and trustworthiness that arise from them" (Putnam, 2000). Playing off Marx's (1887) classic formula for the generation of capital, M-C-M′, where money is transformed into a commodity that is in turn transformed into a profit, IAF national director Ed Chambers (2003) offers the following description of broad-based organizations as creators of social capital:

> . . . the social (or political) capital of a citizens' organization is its power to win on its interests. Its power is rooted in the meanings, values, social knowledge and relationships that hold such groups together in a community of common interests. Social capital is the shared "wealth" of the body politic. By analogy [to Marx], its formula might be expressed as: TEP— CA—TEP′. In this formula TEP = Talent, Energy and Power; CA = collective action; TEP′ = more talent, energy and power. Kept in motion, collective talent, energy and power generate change for the common good. (pp. 68–69)

Our social (or political) capital is the web of connections we have established with others that we can mobilize to seek support, solve problems, and accomplish goals. Social capital involves both trust and shared values. Putnam (2000) distinguishes two forms of social capital: bonding and bridging. *Bonding* social capital is the form of connection that grows, for example, among members of a support or friendship group or small community of faith. Part of the power of membership in such groups is the way they create bonds of personal association and mutual support among their members. When a member of the group calls, a fellow member is often willing to help. As Putnam notes, bonding social capital has an inward-looking, exclusive focus. It is good for "undergirding specific reciprocity and mobilizing solidarity" (p. 22), but limited to those with whom one has developed face-to-face relationships around a shared personal interest or concern. Because such connections (e.g., in a 12 Step or a bible-study group) are based on personal preference and choice, they often become gatherings of people of common background in terms of income, religion, race, culture, or geography, groups that Bellah, Madsen, Sullivan, Swidler, and Tipton (1985) call "lifestyle enclaves," gatherings of the like-minded. Thus the relationships that make up bonding social capital tend toward the personal and exclusive.

Bridging social capital, by contrast, is the form of connection that develops among people who share a common social concern (e.g., members of a civic committee or a soccer-parents group). Bridging connections are less personally intense and, because what connects people here are not private experiences or interests but rather a common external concern, bridging social capital has an outward-looking, inclusive focus. As Putnam notes, this form of relationship is good for "linkage to external assets and . . . information diffusion" (p. 22). Bridging social capital can bring people who do not usually associate with each other together around matters of common interest, allow them to share information and resources, and eventually develop the capacity to act together.

In applying the concept of social capital to IAF broad-based organizations, Warren (2001) offers the following observation:

> Building strong local communities is a necessary, but not sufficient, strategy for democratic renewal. Fostering such within community "bonding" social capital provides the foundation for members of those communities to enter democratic life. But local communities can be isolated, even antidemocratic. In order to develop broader identities and a commitment to the common good, we need a strategy that brings people together across communities. . . . [W]e need bridging social capital as well, that is, cooperative connections across the lines, particularly those of race and class, that separate communities. (p. 25)

The power and effectiveness of broad-based organizations over time is rooted in their success in making and sustaining connections grounded in shared interests across lines of race, religion, class, and geography. Commenting on the IAF's remarkable national track record in generating interracial social capital, Wilson (1999) notes that, "In its successes the IAF provides a model for the development of a multiracial political coalition . . ." (p. 89). Here, we catch a glimpse of pluralistic democracy in action. Indeed, according to one respected social commentator, the IAF is the most promising current exemplar of democratic politics at work in a nation where electoral politics is now almost completely dominated by organized money (Greider, 1992). What lessons might the public successes of these organizations on a wide range of social issues provide for literacy's advocates? How do we move adult literacy from a vaguely acknowledged problem to a specific, "organizable" issue?

ADULT LITERACY AND THE
SOCIAL DEFINITION OF REALITY

Bronfenbrenner (1977) once cited what he regarded as "the only proposition in social science that approaches the status of an immutable law— W. I. Thomas's inexorable dictum: 'If men define situations as real they are real in their consequences'" (p. 516). Following that same line of thought, which would be characterized in today's academic vocabulary as "hermeneutical," Blumer's (1971) classic essay, "Social Problems as Collective Behavior," describes what Blumer calls "five discernible stages in the full career of social problems," that is, the process by which social problems come into being:[2]

1. Recognition of the existence of a problem.
2. Legitimation of a problem as worthy of public discussion.
3. Mobilization of action to address the problem.
4. Formation of an official plan of action by a society by creating social policy.
5. Implementation of the official plan of action.

Blumer's insight is at once simple and penetrating: Only to the degree that a society moves through these stages with respect to a particular social issue will the issue exist for that society. For those working in adult education, low levels of literacy are already perceived as real and are, therefore, real in their consequences. For many others in our communities, however, literacy issues are perceived dimly or not at all and, therefore, make no serious and sustained claim on community attention, energy, and resources. This perception gap appears to be one of the great frustrations of those committed to the work of adult literacy.

Quigley (1997) documented how recognition of, and response to, the realties of adult literacy has come into and out of the collective consciousness and conscience of America, pointedly describing the several and varied eras of adult literacy in the United States. His work also makes plain the quite different ways that America has interpreted, legitimated, mobilized, planned, and acted in the area of literacy. One can see plainly

---

[2] The author wishes to express his thanks to Professor Lydia Voigt of Loyola University New Orleans for calling this essay to his attention.

how various societal definitions of illiteracy have elicited varied national responses. For example, when a society comes, through Blumer's stages of collective problem definition, to define illiteracy as an individual moral failing, as America did in the 19th century, individual moral reeducation is prescribed as the solution. On the other hand, when a society comes, through those same stages of collective interpretation, to define illiteracy as a national economic development problem, as America has tended to do beginning in the last part of the 20th century, it construes and addresses literacy primarily as part of a workforce-development strategy, and sets funding priorities accordingly. Quigley's analysis makes it plain that the meaning of adult literacy and, therefore, the appropriate social responses to it, are historically contested matters. The outcomes of that ongoing contest are relevant precisely because the perception emerging as real will indeed be real in its formal and material effects on the issue of adult literacy.

The fundamental challenge for literacy advocates is not instructional but political; the challenge is to secure the social and financial capital necessary to address adult literacy in a holistic and sustained manner. This task may be understood as moving a large enough segment of their communities through Blumer's stages of collective definition of the social problem (i.e., illiteracy) to produce a substantial outcome. Literacy remains a marginal problem for a society or a local community as a whole as long as it continues to be the province of the relative few who have come to define it as significant enough to demand action. Unfortunately, those who already define literacy as a real problem constitute a relatively weak voice on the periphery of society's agreed-upon concerns, priorities, and power arrangements.

Unlike the United States, Ireland has recognized and addressed the problem of literacy. While acknowledging the enormous differences in population, geography, and cultural diversity between the two countries, we might still fruitfully compare the relative disorganization of the United States regarding the recognition of literacy as a significant social problem with the situation in Ireland. There, the process of collective definition of the problem of literacy, beginning in a crisis of recognition provoked by the release of the International Adult Literacy Study in 1997 (Blumer's first stage), culminated in the implementation of a comprehensive adult literacy plan with major grassroots input under the direction of the publicly funded but nongovernmental National Adult Literacy Agency (Blumer's fourth stage), leading to an 1,800% increase in government expenditure per annum from 1997 to 2003 (Blumer's fifth stage). As a result of this national process of collective definition of the problem of adult literacy, Ireland witnessed a five-fold increase in the number of adults participating in ABE programs from 1997 to 2003 (Bailey, chapter 8, this volume; National Adult Literacy Agency, 2001).

Each and all of the steps in the career of a social problem defined by Blumer—recognition and legitimation of a problem, mobilization of action, and formation and implementation of a plan—must be taken by someone, but who is capable of carrying them out? What sort of actor is required? Although powerful individual voices, like that of Kozol (1985) or Sapphire (1997), have their place in calling attention to the grim realities of life without literacy, it seems evident that a collective or collectives of some kind are required to generate sustained and focused action on this issue.

One possible collective actor would be an association of local literacy providers and adult learners. Those are in place in numerous communities around the country, yet the problem remains or grows, so it seems that a more powerful collective is required. The same may be said about local government, civic associations, and educational and philanthropic institutions. If local organizations on this scale could have solved the problem of adult literacy, surely they would have done so somewhere by now. At the other end of the scale, what about national organizations of literacy providers, adult learners, and other concerned stakeholders? These collectives are in place too, yet the problem remains. If low levels of literacy in the United States constitute a major problem for individuals and their families, employers, and whole communities, but the problem is not publicly recognized and systematically addressed (per Blumer's analysis), then a variation of the immortal words of Cool Hand Luke would seem to apply: What we have here is a failure to organize.

PRINCIPLES FROM BROAD-BASED ORGANIZING FOR ADULT LITERACY

Four key principles drawn from the practice of broad-based organizing by its professional practitioners suggest how community leaders can intentionally mobilize a broad-based strategy to address the issue of adult literacy (Chambers, 2003). This section illustrates each of the four principles with an example drawn from a broad-based metropolitan literacy

initiative, and offers a suggested initial action for communities considering such a strategy.[3]

Organizing Principle #1:
Power Precedes Program

Recall the definition of power previously offered: the capacity to act effectively on a particular agenda. Seasoned, broad-based community organizers insist that before anything sustainable can be done to address an issue
through programs or policies, the necessary base of financial and bridging
social capital must be built. Proceeding to action without that foundation
is a constant temptation for those fueled primarily by passionate concern
about a particular issue, and the predictable outcome of giving in to that
temptation is an organization that struggles to survive from the day it opens
its doors, or from the point where its initial funding is depleted. This seems
to be the chronic state of most adult literacy programs and indeed of many
other nonprofits attempting to address significant social issues today.

Through sustained collaborative work over an 18-month period, the
Literacy Alliance of Greater New Orleans was established in Fall 2002.
The Alliance's mission is to support, challenge, develop, and coordinate
literacy services in the greater New Orleans area in order to expand and
systematically improve available literacy education opportunities for
adults. It is a broad-based collective with a policymaking board composed
of a diverse group of community stakeholders, including literacy providers and learners, as well as leaders from business, local government, faith-
based organizations, higher education, and elsewhere. To insure a comprehensive base of power and a broad frame of reference for the Alliance,
its bylaws stipulate that none of the constituent groups may make up more
than 25% of the board. As a coalition founded intentionally on a broad

---

[3] The broad-based effort to address adult literacy in the greater New Orleans area was
convened by Loyola University's Lindy Boggs National Center for Community Literacy in
April, 2001, with planning grants from Baptist Community Ministries, a local private foundation, and consulting assistance from Margaret Doughty, former executive director of the
Houston READ Commission and a founder of the National Alliance of Urban Literacy
Coalitions. An invited gathering of literacy providers, adult learners, and other community
stakeholders divided into three working groups to build a solid foundation of data and
information on literacy needs, create an inventory and begin to evaluate the kinds and quality of literacy services currently available in the metropolitan area, and investigate national
and international best practices. An additional and critical goal was to build mutual respect,
trust, and collaboration among a diverse stakeholders group in order to address the situation once it had been understood.

base of institutional power, the Alliance is deliberately building the foundation of bridging social capital that will be required to implement sustainable change with a strategic focus and on a large scale—something that is simply not possible for disconnected, loosely connected, or competing individual literacy providers.

For community leaders considering using a broad-based organizing approach to adult literacy, an initial action is to identify potential partners—institutions and organizations, including but not limited to literacy providers and adult learners—with a significant stake in the literacy of adults. Such partners can be found in institutions and organizations whose success depends on having literate adults as participants. Businesses, schools, and churches are obvious starting points.

Organizing Principle #2: The Issue Underlying Any Particular Problem Is Recognition

An organization that approaches policymakers, funders, or community leaders for action on a particular matter is, at the same time, seeking their recognition of its legitimacy and authority to act on that matter (Chambers, 2003; Taylor, 1995). When a change in policy, funding of a proposal, or a commitment of support is garnered, so is a measure of recognition of the organization that initiated it. Powerful and experienced broad-based organizations constantly balance how much bridging social capital they have currently amassed against how much would be expended in action on a current priority issue of their member organizations. They learn to calculate both the timeliness and likely success of a campaign, and how the potential outcome will affect the social capital of the organization; that is, its capacity to act on other issues. Sometimes the decision is made not to act.

From the early stages of the existence of the Literacy Alliance of Greater New Orleans, the phenomenon of recognition was discernable in four salient examples. First, in his initial "state of the schools" address to the community in August 2003, the newly hired, reform-oriented superintendent of the New Orleans Public Schools pledged to carry out a complete restructuring of public adult education in concert with the Literacy Alliance. Second, the New Orleans Jobs Initiative, the area's premier work readiness agency for un- and underemployed local residents living in poverty, committed to partner with the Literacy Alliance in the creation of comprehensive, sector-specific programs integrating preemployment education, case management, hard-skills training for particular jobs, and workplace-based literacy assessment and education. Third, Greater New Orleans, Inc., the newly reorganized regional Chamber of Commerce, invited the Literacy Alliance to its planning table as a principal partner in addressing literacy questions as a critical component of what they regard as the controlling issue for the economic future of the metropolitan area— the development of the local workforce. Finally, the newly elected reform mayor of New Orleans highlighted the city's partnership with the Literacy Alliance in his comprehensive plan to create new worker readiness and job opportunities in the new economy for would-be and incumbent work- ers in New Orleans. All these connections constitute significant bridging social capital generated by the Literacy Alliance since its inception, and that capital, now in motion, is creating more.

An initial action for community leaders considering a broad-based orga- nizing approach to adult literacy consistent with the principle of the impor- tance of recognition is to identify key decision makers from organizations and institutions in the governmental, private, and nonprofit spheres, whose recognition and support would be crucial to the success of a broad-based organizing effort. Then, community leaders need to do the homework necessary to discover what priority interests of theirs must be explicitly acknowledged in order to command initial attention and ultimately receive recognition and support. Discovering and building on mutual interests is the key.

Organizing Principle #3: All Effective Broad-Based Organizing Starts by Discovering and Building Agendas for Action on Shared Interests

As already noted, organizations attempting to pursue a particular interest on an isolated, narrow basis will not be capable of acting effectively on either their own or others' interests. The typical problem here is failing to recognize how various stakeholders' interests are interrelated and could combine to generate a larger shared agenda. The legendary individualism of Americans is regularly mirrored in organizations that become trapped in passionate pursuit of single interests with little or no effort made to scan the environment for potential partners and a more inclusive agenda. In its simplest form, the question that can help would-be collaborators begin to build recognition of new bases for shared action is: What could we do—or do better—together that we cannot achieve separately?

The history of another local collaborative effort, one of the most successful in the city's history, profoundly shaped the shared-interest organizing strategy being deliberately pursued by the Literacy Alliance of Greater New Orleans, providing a clear answer to that question. Prior to an effort (sponsored by two prominent local corporations) to bring together programs providing services to the homeless, about $500,000 in federal funds was awarded each year to a number of disconnected, competing providers in the New Orleans area. The creation of Unity for the Homeless in 1992 allowed a multi-interest board of providers and other stakeholders from the business and nonprofit sectors to create a seamless "Continuum of Care" for the homeless in Orleans Parish, approach funding sources with one coordinated set of priorities, and hold funded providers accountable for their results. Unity's effective coordination, management, and oversight of grants created cooperation and trust among providers and credibility with funders and, as a result, $7–8 million dollars per year has come from a variety of public and private sources to support programs for the homeless in Orleans Parish in the past 7 years. The nationally recognized success of Unity for the Homeless provided the founders of the Literacy Alliance with a compelling example of the possible effects of addressing the challenge of adult literacy through the coordinating vehicle of a diverse, metropolitan-wide organization led by a stakeholders group representing a wide spectrum of interests but speaking in one voice to the community as a whole, as well as to public and private funders at all levels.

An initial action for community leaders considering a broad-based organizing approach to adult literacy is to make a serious effort, through preliminary research, to understand the organizational interests and priorities of the potential partners identified in connection with the first principle discussed ("power precedes program"), and then convene focused individual and group conversations with them in order to identify shared interests. Most institutions want to carry out their stated missions and also find the financial and other resources necessary for the organization to continue. Sometimes the latter concern comes into conflict with the former, and an institution sacrifices mission focus for funding. Perhaps the key sign that a would-be broad-based effort has grasped the logic of shared interests, which drives all effective organizing on this scale, is that its primary leaders will not insist on their particular organizations' interests, no matter how important, as *the* larger agenda around which other institutions and organizations must coalesce. In fact, in the practice of contemporary broad-based organizing, the term *primary leader* specifically denotes one with a demonstrated capacity to put the agenda of the larger collective first. Whether that larger collective is focused on adult literacy with workforce development as one constituent concern, or on workforce development with adult literacy as a constituent concern, or on comprehensive education reform with adult literacy and workforce development as constituent concerns matters only in a pragmatic sense: Which way of framing the collective generates the most bridging social capital, that is, brings the most power to the table to create and execute an inclusive, multi-interest agenda?

Organizing Principle #4: Don't Sacrifice the Possible for the Perfect

A hallmark of effective broad-based community organizing is a particular kind of political judgment; namely, the ability to recognize, and the maturity to accept, the best possible compromise available in a particular set of circumstances. Ideologues and single-interest advocates are too often prepared to pass up a partial victory as a "matter of principle." Although there may be times when an all-or-nothing position is required, in the real world of limited resources and competing interests, such a position usually reflects a failure to understand adequately how one organization's interests intersect with those of others, and to seek agreements of mutual benefit. The more challenges organizations face in terms of resources, the more necessary such agreements are and the more difficult they are to forge. Human service organizations in all fields are well acquainted with this particular vicious circle. In the world as it is, a good compromise gives nobody everything they wanted, and everybody something important. As significantly, it solidifies relationships among the partners for the inevitable next round of the struggle. When organizations fail to learn the demanding, definitive political art of compromise, they not only reduce the probability of winning a particular outcome, but also poison the water for potential future collaborations. Even when they "win," they lose.

When one reviews the statistics on adult literacy levels in urban America, and discovers dismaying numbers of adults functioning at the lowest level of literacy while only a small fraction are involved in current literacy programs, the temptation understandably arises either to take the position that we must stop what we are doing and begin again, or assert that we simply must fund what we are already doing at a higher level. In the world as it really is, however, neither of these positions is tenable. In following a broad-based approach to organizing multiple constituent groups with differing interests (providers, adult learners, employers, etc.) around the complex issue of adult literacy, the Literacy Alliance has been required to initiate, coordinate, and facilitate a tough dialogue aimed at compromise between those who are inclined toward using the "starting fresh" strategy (typically employers) and those who lean toward the "more funding" strategy (typically providers). From its first meeting, the Literacy Alliance's board has been forced to search for ways of innovating in the area of adult literacy, creating best-practice capacities that do not currently exist in the metropolitan region, while simultaneously focusing on increasing support and accountability of already existing programs on some discerning and principled basis.

An initial action for community leaders considering a broad-based organizing approach to adult literacy, consistent with the principle of the "possible," is to approach the multi-interest negotiating table with very deliberate consciousness of two kinds of interests: advancing the particular mission and survival concerns of organizations, and developing sustainable relationships based in mutual interest and respect with one's partners. Wise practitioners at the table of inevitably differing interests understand what single-issue advocates typically fail to recognize: Sometimes the other's interest or the larger collective's interests must lead.

Additional Principles

Two final principles drawn from broad-based organizing are nicely suited both to bringing this section to a close and to serving as a caveat to literacy advocates who would move in this direction. The first principle is that *all organizing is constant reorganizing.* Until their concerns are finally and fully addressed, multi-interest collectives must be prepared to scan the local horizon continually for new member organizations, new leaders, new allies, new enemies, and new focal points for action campaigns. Once organized, broad-based collectives must be continually reorganized. Finally, surprising as it may be to the passionate advocates of particular issues, who are quick to divide the world into good guys and bad guys, in the endless search for new partners on constantly shifting constellations of issues, *there are no permanent allies and no permanent enemies.*

OBJECTION AND CONCLUSION

One possible and plausible objection to the examples and suggested initial actions just presented is that, because the Literacy Alliance of Greater New Orleans has a particular focus—raising the level of adult literacy in its metropolitan area—it is not really broad-based in its approach. It is true that the Literacy Alliance is not a multi-issue organization in the same sense as the local IAF affiliate, the Jeremiah Group, which has dealt effectively with issues in the realms of public education, affordable housing, and family-sustaining jobs. Nonetheless, the Alliance must and does address multiple interests every time the designated representatives of its constituencies gather to deliberate. The members of its decision-making board—adult learners and literacy providers, leaders of faith-based institutions, employers, political officials, funders, and representatives of public and private education—obviously do not come to the Alliance table with the same organizational priorities. For example, employers and providers start from quite different perspectives based on different life experiences and social locations. The ultimate success of the Alliance requires that the common agenda that those negotiators forge over time be not only sufficiently inclusive of their differing interests, but also strategically focused and limited, in order to generate a feasible plan of action within the constraints of urgent need and available resources.

There is another and more subtle sense in which the social capital being created by the Literacy Alliance of Greater New Orleans is broad-based or bridging in character, and being mobilized in response to multiple issues. Some board members of the Literacy Alliance whose primary concern is adult literacy have agreed to become part of the comprehensive local workforce-development effort spearheaded by the business community, in which literacy has emerged as a major concern. Others have joined with local church leaders to explore the possibility that the long tradition of Bible study in African-American churches might become a potent vehicle for enhancing not only the faith but also the literacy of its regular participants. Still others have engaged with local health practitioners to discover effective ways and means of connecting literacy enhancement with health care. In each of these examples, and others that could be adduced, differing interests come together into larger wholes. Bridging social capital is being created. As the locus of connection, the Literacy Alliance is the immediate impetus for these partnerships. Each of them represents in miniature what the Literacy Alliance stands for writ large, and all of them reinforce its recognition and power, adding to its social capital.

A broad-based, multi-interest coalition among institutions crossing racial, religious, and class lines outlined here is possibly the strongest candidate now available to become the collective actor necessary to legitimate adult literacy as a critical issue in popular awareness, and to initiate, coordinate, and sustain the actions necessary to create effective plans to address that issue effectively in local communities. There are several avenues for such a coalition to come about. First, already existing coalitions, like the member organizations of Literacy USA (formerly the National Alliance of Urban Literacy Coalitions), may decide strategically to increase their bridging social capital by broadening their collective leadership and partnerships around a larger interest like economic development or comprehensive education reform. A second avenue for coalition building is for communities without existing literacy coalitions to establish collectives that gather from the outset under a larger interest umbrella like comprehensive education reform or regional economic development, including, but not limited to, adult literacy advocates.

Broad-based coalitions may provide a way to form creative, efficacious, and sustainable connections among literacy leaders and advocates for other community concerns. Whether or not this approach is feasible may be considered conceptually, as I have attempted to do here, and will certainly continue to be evaluated empirically in New Orleans and elsewhere. The verdict on this approach will prove in the end, however, to be a matter not of conceptual reflection or scientific inquiry, but rather of political praxis. Going down the broad-based road will require of those devoted to adult literacy the political wisdom and maturity to pursue that particular commitment to justice as one important concern among others. This will require that they enlarge the scope of their concern and be prepared for the act that defines the art of politics—compromise. The ultimate measure of coalitions attempting a broad-based approach to a significant social issue like adult literacy will come in the form that the Black church calls the "fruit test"; that is, their effectiveness will be judged by the biblical injunction that "a tree is known by its fruit." Here the fruit to be tested is how well coalitions that include literacy as one major issue answer in practice, amid the changing contingencies and conflicting interests that make up the messy real world of all communities, the question of shared interests articulated earlier: What could we accomplish through participation in a multistakeholder organization gathered around a more inclusive agenda that we have not been able to achieve by organizing around a single interest? If community leaders, including literacy advocates, can imagine no compelling answer to that question, a broad-based approach will generate no interest because it indeed demands a great and focused effort; if they can, such an approach will be required, because nothing less will do.

REFERENCES

Alinsky, S. (1972). Rules for radicals. New York: Vintage.

Arendt, H. (1958). *The human condition.* Chicago: University of Chicago Press.

Bellah, R., Madsen, R., Sullivan, W. M., Swidler, A., & Tipton, S. M. (1985). *Habits of the heart.* Berkeley: University of California Press.

Blumer, H. (1971). Social problems as collective behavior. *Collective Behavior, 18*(3), 298–305.

Bronfenbrenner, U. (1977). Toward an experimental ecology of human development. *American Psychologist,* 516.

Brown, M., Carnoy, M., Currie, E., Duster, T., Oppenheimer, D., Shultz, M., & Wellman, D. (2003). *White-washing race: The myth of a color-blind society.* Berkeley: University of California Press.

Chambers, E. (2003). *Roots for radicals.* New York: Continuum.

Giloth, R. (Ed.). (2003). *Workforce intermediaries for the 21st century.* Philadelphia: Temple University Press.

Greider, W. (1992). *Who will tell the people.* New York: Simon & Schuster.

Hercules, B., & Orenstein, B. (1999). *The democratic promise: Saul Alinsky & his legacy.* Chicago: Media Process Educational Films.

Kozol, J. (1985). *Illiterate America.* New York: Penguin.

Lee, B., & Cowan, M. (2003). *Gathered and sent: The mission of small church communities today.* Mahwah, NJ: Paulist Press.

Louisiana Department of Labor. (2001, April). *Top demand occupations for regional labor market area greater New Orleans.* Unpublished study.

Marx, K. (1887). *Capital: A critical analysis of capitalist production* (Vol. 1). (S. Moore & E. Aveling, Trans.). New York: International Publishers.

MetroVision Economic Development Partnership/New Orleans Chamber of Commerce. (2000, August). *The New Orleans region and the new economy: Preparing the workforce.* Unpublished study.

National Adult Literacy Agency (NALA). (2001). *A strategy for the way forward.* Dublin, Ireland: Author.

National Institute for Literacy (NIFL). (1998). *The state of literacy in America.* Washington, DC: Author.

Putnam, R. (2000). *Bowling alone: The collapse and revival of American community.* New York: Simon & Schuster.

Quigley, A. (1997). *Rethinking literacy education.* San Francisco: Jossey-Bass.

Sapphire. (1997). *Push: A novel.* New York: Vintage.

Sen, R. (2003). *Stir it up: Lessons in community organizing and advocacy.* San Francisco: Jossey-Bass.

Taylor, C. (1995). *The politics of recognition: Philosophical arguments.* Cambridge, MA: Harvard University Press.

Warren, M. (2001). *Dry bones rattling: Community building to revitalize American democracy.* Princeton: Princeton University Press.

Warren, M., & Wood, R. (2001). *Faith-based community organizations: The state of the field.* Toledo: COMM-ORG: The on-line conference on community organizing and development [http://comm-org.utoledo.edu/papers.htm]

Wilson, W. J. (1996). *When work disappears: The world of the new urban poor.* New York: Knopf.

Wilson, W. J. (1999). *The bridge over the racial divide: Rising inequality and coalition politics.* Berkeley: University of California.

Resources on Community Organizing

Michael A. Cowan

The following list of annotated resources includes books, articles, videos, and Web sites. It is organized as follows to facilitate access according to readers' primary interests:

I. Practical Resources for Community Organizing
II. Organizing and Literacy
III. Theory and History of Community Organizing
IV. Cultural, Social, and Historical Contexts for Community Organizing

PRACTICAL RESOURCES
FOR COMMUNITY ORGANIZING

Alinsky, S. (1971). *Rules for radicals.* New York: Vintage.

This, the better known of Alinsky's two books, is subtitled "A Pragmatic Primer for Realistic Radicals." (Alinsky's first book was *Reveille for Radicals* [New York: Vintage, 1946].) Alinsky's legendary pragmatism, as embodied in maxims like "No permanent allies, nor permanent enemies" indeed shines through in *Rules for Radicals.* The text addresses critical issues like self-interest, power, and the tension between means and ends. The seventh chapter, entitled "Tactics," is still regarded by professional community organizers as the classic statement of how ordinary citizens can get attention and response from the powers that be. Anyone interested in grasping the world-view of the founder of community organizing in the United States will want to read this controversial, provocative text.

Chambers, E. (2003). *Roots for radicals: Organizing for power, action, and justice.* New York: Continuum Press.

Edward Chambers was a protégé of Saul Alinsky and has directed the Industrial Areas Foundation (IAF), a national network of broad-based community organizations, for nearly 40 years (since Alinsky's death). In this book, which completes the Alinsky trilogy (see *Rules for Radicals*), Chambers shares the practical wisdom distilled from the work of IAF's broad-based organizations over the past 30 years. Of particular value are chapters on the central role of "relational meetings" in effective organizing, and on understanding the constit-uent elements of the tension between facts and values that motivates people to organize for social change. This is the voice of contem-porary community organizing's most experienced and authoritative leader.

COMM-ORG, *The on-line conference on community organizing and development,* University of Toledo at comm-org.utoledo.edu.

The membership of this ongoing online conference, which began as an online course on the history of community organizing, is roughly balanced between academics and practitioners, and includes some government officials and funders. COMM-ORG is sponsored by the Department of Sociology, Anthropology, and Social Work at the University of Toledo. As noted on its Web site, the COMM-ORG mission is to "help connect people who care about the craft of com-munity organizing; find and provide information that organizers, scholars, and scholar-organizers can use to learn, teach, and do com-munity organizing; involve all COMM-ORG members in meeting goals."
    COMM-ORG defines community organizing as:

- People without power getting power, both as individuals and as a community.
- Building relationships (sometimes this is its primary goal).
- Beginning in a local area, often as small as a neighborhood.
- Building on shared experience—rooted in a place or a cultural identity.
- Often leading to development activities and/or larger social movements when it succeeds.

The Web site invites and publishes the reflections of scholars and practitioners in the area of community organizing (see, e.g., Warren & Wood citation in the "Theory and History of Community Organizing" section of this bibliography).

Gecan, M. (1992). *Going public.* Boston: Beacon.

Here is a window into public engagement for the common good through the experience of a seasoned, accomplished professional organizer. The book is structured around four habits (or virtues) that the author regards as central to participation in life beyond the private sphere: relating, action, organization, and reflection. The teaching in this volume is done through powerful stories drawn from a lifetime of organizing experience.

Gustafson, R., & Sato, T. (Eds.). (2000). *Power, justice, faith: Conversations with the IAF.* Los Angeles: Center for Religion and Civic Culture, University of Southern California.

In 24 wonderful vignettes, ordinary people who became experienced community leaders in broad-based organizations tell personal stories of what they did and learned in coming together with others across lines of race, class, and religion to address an amazing range of public issues including affordable housing, toxic landfills in poor neighborhoods, school safety-crossings, and minimum wage. Here are the grassroots voices of community organizing.

Sen, R. (2003). *Stir it up: Lessons in community organizing and advocacy.* San Francisco: Jossey-Bass.

Billed as a "practical primer" on community organizing, this book is for people who are already engaged in organizing and those considering it. The author puts the case for organizing as a tool for changing the status quo pointedly: "Simply put, today's movements for social and economic justice need people who are clear about the problems with the current systems, who rely on solid evidence for their critique, and who are able to reach large numbers of people with both analysis and proposals" (p. xvii). The book offers chapters dealing with the following specific subjects: history of community organizing in the United States since WWII; the importance of recruiting participants from those most affected; how to develop an issue; concepts and methods of direct action; leadership development; research into issues; building alliances and networks; designing effective media strategies; and internal political education and consciousness raising. A series of "Illustrations" exemplify points being explained in the text in the work of actual community organizations. The book includes an integrated series of structured reflection questions and planning worksheets keyed to the content of each chapter. The book is distinguished by strong feminist, multicultural, and third-world orientations.

ORGANIZING AND LITERACY

Bailey, I., & Coleman, U. (2003). *Access and participation in adult literacy schemes.* Dublin: National Adult Literacy Agency.

This study of participation and nonparticipation in adult literacy programs by the National Adult Literacy Agency—the coordinating, training, and advocacy organization for all those involved in adult literacy in Ireland—is notable for locating issues of access and participation squarely within a larger cultural and social context like gender, poverty, and employment. The authors' analysis of factors influencing participation in adult literacy programs and research-based suggestions for increasing same will be valuable as points of comparison and contrast for U.S. communities addressing the perennial concern of recruitment and retention in adult literacy programs.

Doughty, M. (2001). *The voices of Houston reads to lead!: Building an urban literacy coalition through America Reads.*" In L. Morrow, and D. Woo (Eds.), *Tutoring programs for struggling readers* (pp. 31–56). New York: Guilford Press.

In this chapter, Margaret Doughty, the principal architect of the Houston READ Commission, perhaps the most successful urban literacy coalition (to date), describes the process of engaging 29 community organizations representing a half-million Houstonians in the creation of Houston Reads to Lead!, a community-wide family literacy initiative conceived as a response to the national "America Reads Challenge." Through stories, pictures, and cogent explanations, the chapter takes readers inside the creative relational activity of bringing many diverse partners together to address an issue of common concern.

Literacy USA (formerly National Alliance of Urban Literacy Coalitions) at http://www.naulc.org.

Founded in 1995, the mission of Literacy USA is to support the development of literacy coalitions in the United States. As noted on its Web site, Literacy USA is a "coalition of coalitions . . . functioning as a kind of trade association for literacy coalitions," and acts in the following capacities:

- Serves as a forum for a peer-learning group of coalition leaders across the United States.
- Functions as a clearinghouse of information on best practices, successes, and challenges of literacy coalitions.
- Tracks policy developments and participates in shaping policy.
- Serves as a national voice for local coalitions.
- Interests business leaders in not only funding the cause, but assisting with strategic planning, legislation, and marketing, both on the national and local level.
- Disseminates resources and information to the grass roots and gathers information from the front lines.
- Provides technical assistance to emerging coalitions and those in transition or crisis.

According to Literacy USA, the critical functions of literacy coalitions include:

- Coordinating comprehensive communitywide literacy plans.
- Providing a one-stop source of information on literacy learning and volunteer opportunities.
- Facilitating networking and collaboration among literacy service providers.
- Offering professional development and technical assistance to literacy service providers.

- Collecting data and holding literacy service providers to a high standard of accountability.
- Offering policymakers an overview as well as detailed information on a community's literacy activities and needs.
- Speaking with one strong voice to advocate for literacy.
- Attracting resources and disseminating them for the greatest impact.
- Drawing public attention to the cause.

Literacy USA's membership includes nearly 60 urban literacy coalitions across the country. Together, they represent more than 3,500 literacy service providers serving over 2,500,000 learners. Literacy USA has recently opened membership to state and rural coalitions. Their Web site is updated regularly and contains reports on current trends, local initiatives, and challenges facing literacy coalitions.

Quigley, A. (1997). *Rethinking literacy education.* San Francisco: Jossey-Bass.

In this award-winning book, one of North America's guiding lights on the subject of adult literacy puts the subject into perspective both historically and politically. There is something here to inform and trouble all concerned—practitioners, adult learners, experts, policymakers, and everyday citizens. Quigley does an especially insightful job of showing the ebb and flow of adult literacy as a social issue, evoking as he does so a haunting sense that in this field, as in many others, we repeatedly recycle historical patterns of which we are sadly unaware. Among other things, he challenges readers who have a stake in the issue of adult literacy, from whatever perspective, to organize themselves out of political passivity and perpetual victim status.

THEORY AND HISTORY
OF COMMUNITY ORGANIZING

Greider, W. (1992). *Who will tell the people.* New York: Simon & Schuster.

This volume relentlessly outlines the degradation of America democracy by money-driven, single-interest politics. With a seasoned journalist's eye for compelling details and incisive stories, Greider gives us a diagnosis of the state of U.S. democracy that will confirm for many people that they are quite right to be discouraged and dismayed, if not downright cynical, about the current state of politics in America. However, the book is not a prescription for despair. In a chapter entitled "Democratic Promise," Greider highlights the work of the organizations of the Industrial Areas Foundation as the best current example of the exercise of democratic citizenship in the United States.

Hercules, B., & Orenstein, B. (1999). *The Democratic promise: Saul Alinsky & his legacy.* Chicago: Media Process Educational Films.

This hour-long video documents the historical and continuing legacy of Saul Alinsky, the creator (in the United States) of the activity now referred to as "community organizing." The first half of the video focuses on the history of the emergence of Alinsky as the innovator of a new approach to empowering formerly marginalized people to take the initiative in influencing events in their communities. The second half takes viewers inside Alinsky organizations currently at work in Texas and New York City. "The Democratic Promise" is notable for the up-close-and-personal window that it gives into the life of the larger-than-life Alinsky and the real-life community leaders and organizers implementing and expanding his vision today. The historical perspective provided by this documentary makes plain the links between the American labor movement and Alinsky-style community organizing.

Horwitt, S. (1989). *Let them call me rebel: Saul Alinsky—His life and legacy.* New York: Alfred A. Knopf.

This is the definitive biography (to date) of the person generally credited with creating what has come to be called "community organizing" in the United States. It is indispensable reading for anyone who wants to understand the strengths and limitation of U.S. approaches to organizing as they have evolved into the present.

Rooney, J. (1995). *Organizing the South´Bronx.* Albany, NY: SUNY Press.

The theme of this book is "the search for the appropriate engine of reform to reconstitute and restructure urban life into genuine communities" (p. 235). Its special contribution to the literature on community organizing is twofold. First it describes the work of the

Industrial Areas Foundation in New York City as a whole, then narrows its focus to a detailed case study of that effort in one (large) corner of the city, the South Bronx. The political struggles of South Bronx churches to provide opportunities for affordable home ownership to the members of its participating congregations is a parable for those attempting to bring people together across racial lines to address significant public issues.

Warren, M. (2001). *Dry bones rattling: Community building to revitalize American democracy.* Princeton: Princeton University Press.

Warren offers an extensive study of the broad-based community organizations affiliated with the Industrial Areas Foundation. He discusses such organizing as a framework for political renewal with four key characteristics: grounding in local institutions, developing cooperation in local communities, creating "bridging social capital" (see Putnam, *Bowling Alone,* in the next section of this bibliography), and using power effectively. The volume puts a particularly strong focus on broad-based organizing as a way of overcoming the racial polarization of America's cities.

Warren, M., & Wood, R. (2001). *"Faith-based community organizing: The state of the field."* Jericho, NY: Interfaith Funders. [Available at http://comm-org.utoledo.edu/papers.htm]

This survey of church-based (a common synonym for broad-based) community organizing offers a comprehensive overview of the field of community organizing at the outset of the 21st century. It identifies four national and several regional networks comprised of more than 130 organizations in 33 states representing one to three million members and almost 30,000 active leaders as of the year 2000. The report is particularly helpful in bringing the four national networks into one picture, but less helpful in allowing readers to discern the differing strengths and limitations of the networks.

CULTURAL, SOCIAL, AND HISTORICAL CONTEXTS FOR COMMUNITY ORGANIZING

Brown, M., Carnoy, M., Currie, E., Duster, T., Oppenheimer, D., Shultz, M., & Wellman, D. (2003). *White-washing race: The myth of a color-blind society.* Berkeley: University of California Press.

This is the definitive response (to date) to the argument of the "new racial conservatives," that is, those who argue that race is no longer a defining issue in the life chances of citizens of the United States. Drawing on empirical evidence from economics, education, employment, criminal justice, and politics, this interracial and interdisciplinary team of scholars makes it plain that race indeed continues to be a defining matter in America, systematically and adversely affecting the life chances of African Americans relative to every significant quality-of-life indicator. Their integrative explanation of this pattern of racial differences in key life outcomes highlights the notion of collective accumulation over time by Whites paired with a reciprocal process of disaccumulation over time for Blacks, leading to a state of "durable racial inequality." The volume ends with a set of recommendations for changes in social policy in each of the areas analyzed. No stronger empirically grounded argument can be found for the necessity of creating bridging social capital (see Putnam, *Bowling Alone*) as a response to social issues like adult literacy.

Crick, B. (1972). *In defense of politics* (2nd ed.). Chicago: University of Chicago Press.

This classic statement of the power and limits of politics highlights diversity and the struggle for recognition as the social conditions that necessitate politics, and makes plain the role of enlightened self-interest in all forms of relationships. After a compelling explanation of the nature of political rule, Crick proceeds in subsequent chapters to "defend" politics against ideology, democracy, nationalism, technology—and its friends! This book is required reading for anyone who wants to rethink organizing on behalf of adult literacy, or any other social issue, so that it is seen as a challenge to whole communities, rather than the chosen issue of a group of single-issue advocates.

Lummis, D. (1996). *Radical democracy.* Ithaca: Cornell University Press.

This extended reflection on the many meanings and correspondingly varied practices of "democracy" highlights the capacity to "stand for the whole" as the central virtue required for democratic participation. This view stands in direct opposition to the notion of democracy as a big tent covering the relentless pursuit of single-issue politics, arguing in effect that authentically democratic politics demand the creation of multi-interest agendas characterized by mutual respect and

willingness to compromise. This book articulates the deep understanding of democracy now being actualized in the work of broad-
based community organizations. "Standing for the whole" has in fact
become a catchphrase in the public culture of broad-based organizing in the United States and elsewhere.

Putnam, R. (2000). *Bowling alone: The collapse and revival of American
community.* New York: Simon & Schuster.

This is the most important work (to date) on the subject of "social
capital," which Putnam defines as "social networks and the norms
of reciprocity and trustworthiness that arise from them." Social
capital is the glue that allows individuals to get beyond a narrowly
defined version of self-interest and join together on matters of common concern. The author provides massive empirical documenta-
tion of the unraveling of social capital in the United States over the
past 25 years, and locates that unraveling in the social and cultural
events of the last quarter of the 20th century. Of critical importance
for understanding the lessons of broad-based organizing for the promotion of adult literacy within our communities is Putnam's distinction between "bonding" (or exclusive) and "bridging" (or inclusive)
social capital.

Sandel, M. (1996). *Democracy's discontents: America in search of a public philosophy.* Cambridge, MA: Belknap/Harvard University Press.

In this volume, one of America's foremost political philosophers
gives an account of what has happened to U.S. politics as a result
of the cultural triumph of the economic or individualist view of the
person. He notes: "Self-government . . . requires political communities that control their destinies, and citizens who identify sufficiently
with those communities to think and act with a view to the common good" (p. 202). Sandel's clear historical account of how we got
here, like the sociological investigation of social capital (see the Putnam: *Bowling Alone* reference), helps anyone attempting to mobilize
a whole community to address adult literacy as a common concern
in order to understand which cultural forces will support and which
resist such an effort.

Taylor, C. (1995). The politics of recognition. In C. Taylor, *Philosophical
arguments* (pp. 226–256). Cambridge, MA: Harvard University Press.

In this classic essay, Taylor, an eminent philosopher and political activist, explains the development in 20th-century political thought of the notion that, far from being irrelevant in the world of *realpolitik,* recognition is essential to the sense of worth and value of individuals and groups, and integral to healthy politics in pluralist societies. His work complements and develops, in conceptual terms, the pragmatic treatment of recognition in the IAF broad-based organizing tradition (cf. Chambers, 2003).

Wilson, W. J. (1999). *The bridge over the racial divide: Rising inequality and coalition politics.* Berkeley: University of California.

In this brief, readable volume, America's preeminent sociological expert on the realities of race, class, and poverty in urban America, builds on his empirical studies to sketch his vision of a unifying progressive politics. The volume is notable for eschewing the ideological insistences of both left and right, seeking instead acceptable pragmatic ground for groups uniting in the pursuit of common-good issues like housing, education, and jobs, despite differences in race, class, and religion. His suggested vehicle for the pursuit of such progressive politics is the "multiracial political coalition." He highlights the contemporary work of the organizations of Alinsky's Industrial Areas Foundation as our best operative example of such coalitions.

Wolin, S. (1989). Contract and birthright. In S. Wolin, *The presence of the past* (pp. 137–150). Baltimore: Johns Hopkins University Press.

In this classic essay on citizenship, Wolin defines human "political-ness" as our "capacity for developing into beings who know and value what it means to participate in, and be responsible for, the care and improvement of our common and collective life" (p. 139). (Note the nonelectoral and nonpartisan understanding of politics in the definition.) For Wolin, "politics" means adults in a community coming together (i.e., organizing) to deal with matters of common concern. A broad-based community organization can be thought of as an arena or laboratory in which people can learn and practice what is necessary in order to realize their potential as citizen leaders, in order to develop their politicalness. In this essay, Wolin offers a powerful counter not only to overly partisan politics, but also to privatized withdrawal from public engagement.

About the Editors

John Comings is the director of the National Center for the Study of Adult Learning and Literacy (NCSALL) at the Harvard Graduate School of Education. Before coming to Harvard, he spent 12 years as a vice president of World Education. Comings worked on adult education programs in Nepal for 6 years and in Indonesia for 2 years and has helped design and evaluate adult education programs in several countries in Asia, Africa, and the Caribbean. In the United States, he has served as the director of the State Literacy Resource Center in Massachusetts, assisted in the design of instructor training programs, and directed projects that focused on improving the teaching of both math and health in adult education programs. His research and writing have focused on the impact of adult literacy programs on reading ability and life changes such as health and family planning practices, the program factors that lead to that impact, and the issue of persistence in learning in the United States and developing countries.

Barbara Garner, director of publications for NCSALL and a senior program officer at World Education, edits the NCSALL publication *Focus on Basics* and provides consulting services to World Education's literacy efforts in Africa. She has held many different positions in the field of adult basic education, including teacher, staff developer, program administrator, and curriculum writer.

Cristine Smith is deputy director of NCSALL and a senior program officer at World Education. She coordinates NCSALL's dissemination efforts, including the Connecting Practice, Policy, and Research Initiative run by NCSALL. She also directed NCSALL's 5-year study of staff development in adult basic education and literacy. She has worked on staff development issues in the field of adult literacy for 16 years.

About the Contributors

Inez Bailey is director of the National Adult Literacy Agency (NALA), a nonprofit membership organization concerned with national coordination, training, and policy development in adult literacy work in Ireland. In her work as director, which began in 1997, Bailey has been responsible for initiating the development of a quality framework, including an assessment framework for the adult literacy service, devising a major basic education distance learning project on television and radio, and mainstreaming workplace literacy programs for local authority workers. Bailey first joined NALA in 1995 as program manager of a research and development project, funded under the EU EMPLOYMENT initiative. She co-authored the resulting research publication *Access and Participation in Adult Literacy Schemes* in 1998. Prior to that Bailey worked for County Offaly VEC for 2 years in a number of positions, including manager of Birr Outdoor Education Centre, coordinator of Youthreach Edenderry, manager of a Leader-funded education and training initiative, and researcher on a New Opportunities for Women (NOW) project. Bailey is a graduate of NUI Maynooth where she completed first a BA in English, history, and sociology, then an MA in history and a Higher Diploma in adult and community education.

Kathleen M. Bailey has worked at the Monterey Institute of International Studies since 1981 as a professor of applied linguistics. She has also served as the head of the Monterey Institute's TESOL-TFL MA Program and the director of the Intensive English Program. She is currently the faculty advisor to the Language Program Administration Certificate students and the Peace Corps Masters Internationalist candidates. Bailey has worked with language teachers in Japan, Korea, Italy, Spain, Uruguay, Poland, Argentina, Brazil, Trinidad, Czechoslovakia, Singapore, Australia, Hong Kong, and the United States. Her research and teaching interests include language assessment, teacher education and supervision, the teaching of speaking and listening, and research methodology. In 1998 to 1999 she was the president of the International TESOL Association. She currently serves on the Board of Trustees of the International Research Foundation (TIRF). Bailey holds a PhD in Applied Linguistics from the University of California, Los Angeles.

Michael A. Cowan is executive director of the Lindy Boggs National Center for Community Literacy at Loyola University New Orleans, where he holds an appointment as professor. A psychologist, theologian, and community organizer, Cowan maintains a longstanding interest in bridging the racial divide in America. He is a founding leader of three interracial community organizations seeking justice and reconciliation: The Jeremiah Group (the New Orleans Industrial Areas Foundation affiliate); The Literacy Alliance of Greater New Orleans; and Shades of Praise: The New Orleans Interracial Gospel Choir. He also chairs the Human Relations Commission of the City of New Orleans. He has been a teacher and consultant to the peacemaking process in Northern Ireland since 1982. He is co-author of *People in Systems* and *Moving into Adulthood* (with Gerard Egan); *Dangerous Memories; Conversation, Risk & Conversion;* and *Gathered and Sent* (with Bernard Lee); and *Roots for Radicals* (with Edward T. Chambers, national director of the Alinsky-founded Industrial Areas Foundation). He spends his life doing his best to embrace the tension between the university and city streets, and between the Bible and the newspaper.

Mary E. Curtis is a professor of education and founding director of the Center for Special Education at Lesley University in Cambridge, Massachusetts, which is dedicated to understanding and promoting the knowledge and skills needed by educators to improve the teaching of students with disabilities. Curtis is the author of numerous articles on reading diagnosis and remediation, the role of vocabulary in comprehension, and the reading skills of at-risk teens. She is a member of the Adult Literacy Research Working Group, and has provided technical assistance to the Division of Adult Education and Literacy, Office of Vocational and Adult Education, for its Student Achievement in Reading (STAR) Pilot Program.

Before coming to Lesley University in 1999, she directed the Boys Town Reading Center, where she oversaw research and development on *Reading Is FAME®*, a remedial reading curriculum shown to reverse reading failure in older adolescents. Curtis earned her PhD in psychology at the University of Pittsburgh, and she has been an associate professor of education at Harvard University, associate director of the Harvard Reading Laboratory, and a postdoctoral fellow at the Learning Research and Development Center (Pittsburgh, PA).

Brad Edmondson is vice president of ePodunk.com, a Web site that provides in-depth information on 26,000 places in the United States. His previous experience includes 6 years as editor-in-chief of *American Demographics* magazine, 5 years as a newspaper editor, and 2 years as a columnist for the *Wall Street Journal.* His freelance articles have appeared in *The Atlantic Monthly,* the *Washington Post,* and other publications. His articles and speeches concern such topics as the aging of the baby-boom generation, the future of higher education, changes in health and fitness behavior, and how America is being transformed by immigration. He is a graduate of Cornell University and lives in Ithaca, New York. He can be contacted at brade@lightlink.com or at (607) 272–1832.

M. Tara Joyce is coordinator for Adolescent Services and Adult Resources at the Tennessee Center for the Study and Treatment of Dyslexia at Middle Tennessee State University. At the Center, Joyce provides professional development for teachers and other school personnel at the middle and high school levels, and she guides Center services for adolescents. She teaches the Adolescents with Dyslexia and Other Literacy Difficulties graduate course at Middle Tennessee State University as part of the Dyslexic Studies Certificate program. She gives workshops on dyslexia for adult literacy programs in Tennessee. Joyce has worked with students with reading difficulties at the elementary, secondary, and adult literacy levels. Her doctoral research at the Harvard Graduate School of Education was on adult beginning reading. Before moving to Tennessee, she was the trainer and coordinator for an adult literacy program in Boston. Joyce also taught reading education courses at Boston University, Lesley University, and Cambridge College in Massachusetts.

Noreen Lopez is an adult education trainer and consultant who specializes in the areas of adult education technology and public policy. Her previous experiences include serving as director for LiteracyLink, a Public Broadcasting Service (PBS) project based in Alexandria, Virginia; manager of new product development at Contemporary Books; state director of adult education for the Illinois State Board of Education; faculty member in the graduate studies program at Northern Illinois University; and several years as a teacher and program director at the local level in Illinois. Lopez has served on advisory groups for the National Institute for Literacy, National Center for Adult Literacy, the National Education Goals Panel, and the PBS CONNECT project. She has held numerous positions in state and national adult education professional organizations, including recently serving on the founding board of the National Coalition for Literacy as it filed for its new 501c3 status. She obtained her BA from Mundelein College in Chicago and her MEd in urban education from Loyola University in Chicago, and completed post-Masters work in adult and continuing education at Northern Illinois University.

John Oxenham first worked in adult literacy and education in 1964, when the Government of Zambia's Department of Community Development appointed him to organize a national literacy program in 7 of the country's 72 languages. After 4 years in that post, Oxenham worked on literacy and adult education in Indonesia, Turkey, and India. Most recently, he has collaborated on studies of programs that combined literacy with livelihoods and the social, economic, and political dimensions of development. His review of the world's experiences in literacy education and their bearing on achieving the Millennium Development Goals is expected to be published in late 2004. Currently retired, Oxenham still works on education issues, particularly adult education and literacy.

Diane J. Sawyer, an internationally recognized scholar in reading and reading disabilities, is a professor in Elementary and Special Education at Middle Tennessee State University, where she holds the Katherine Davis Murfree Chair of Excellence in Dyslexic Studies. Her work in the cognitive/linguistic bases of reading acquisition has led to research and application of various language parameters to reading acquisition and to the difficulties encountered by dyslexic and learning disabled children. In June 1993, she received a special grant from the Tennessee State Legislature to establish a Center for the Study and Treatment of Dyslexia. Sawyer has been a consultant to many school systems in the United States, to the U.S. Department of Education, and to the Ministries of Education and of Social Affairs abroad. She has written numerous articles and book chapters on reading instruction, reading difficulties, and the language base of reading acquisition and reading difficulty. Sawyer is active in several professional organizations dedicated to educational research and practice and is a frequent presenter at local, state, national, and international conferences. She has served as co-chair of the International Dyslexia Association committee on teacher education in colleges and universities, and chair of the Board of Trustees for Laubach Literacy International.

M Cecil Smith is a professor of educational psychology at Northern Illinois University. His research and teaching interests include adult literacy acquisition, adult development, adolescent development, and research methods. Smith has edited three books on literacy and adult development, and his work has been published in journals such as *Reading Research Quarterly, Journal of Literacy Research, Educational Researcher,* and the *Journal of Adult Development.* He was awarded a postdoctoral fellowship at Educational Testing Service in 1994 and conducted analyses of the *National Adult Literacy Survey.* More recently, he has participated as a member of the research team and a technical advisor to the *Longitudinal Study of Adult Learning,* a NCSALL project at Portland State University. Smith is a consulting editor for *Teaching of Psychology* and an editorial board member for several journals.

Author Index

Note: *Italic* indicates pages on which full bibliographic references appear.

A

Aaron, P. G., 100, *105*
Abramson, S., 102, *111*
Adams, R., 101, *106*
Adkins, M. A., 147, *158*
Alderson, J. C., 138, *158*
Alinsky, S., 246, *262*
Alley, G. R., 96, *107*
Anders, P. L., 59, *65*
Anderson, R. C., 44, 45, 46, 50, 60, 61, *64, 67*
Andrew, M., 169, *191*
Anglin, J. M., 55, *64*
Arendt, H., 246, *262*
Artzer, M., 83, *110*
Ash, G. E., 44, *65*
Asher, J. J., 132, *158*
Ayres, R., 100, *106*

B

Bachman, L., 127, 136, *158*
Bailey, I., 214, *238,* 253
Bailey, K. M., 139, 145, *158*

Baker, D. P., 72, 96, *108*
Baker, K., 100, *105*
Baker, S., 100, *105*
Baldwin, L. E., 46, *65*
Baldwin, R. S., 48, *68*
Balmuth, M., 73, *105*
Bandeira de Mello, V., 175, *191*
Banikowski, A., 96, *109*
Banke, S., 140, *158*
Barker, T. A., 77, *111*
Barone, D., 86, *106*
Bartfai, N., 168, 175, 176, *193*
Baumann, J. F., 44, 50, 51, *64, 65*
Bean, R. M., 56, *67*
Bear, D. R., 85, 86, 87, *106*
Beck, I. L., 46, 48, 49, 52, 56, 57, 60, *65*
Becker, W. C., 62, *65*
Beder, H., 188, *191*
Bellah, R., 249, 250, *262*
Belzer, A., 176, *191*
Bennett, R. E., 53, *66*
Berdan, R., 138, *163*
Berliner, D. C., 167, 168, 169, 172, *191, 192*
Biemiller, A., 46, 53, 62, *65*
Birman, D., 147, *158*

285

Subject Index

Note: *f* indicates figure; *n* indicates fotnote; *t* indicates table.